Imitation and Innovation

Imitation and Innovation

The Transfer of Western Organizational Patterns to Meiji Japan

D. Eleanor Westney

Harvard University Press

Cambridge, Massachusetts, and London, England

1987

Library of Congress Cataloging-in-Publication Data

Westney, D. Eleanor.
  Imitation and innovation.

  Bibliography: p.
  Includes index.
1. Organizational change—Japan—History—Case
studies.   2. Police—Japan—History.   3. Postal service—
Japan—History.   4. Japanese newspapers—History.
5. Japan—History—Meiji period, 1868–1912.   6. Japan—
Civilization—Occidental influences.   I. Title.
HD70.J3W47   1987   338.6'0952   87-273
ISBN 0-674-44437-X (alk. paper)

For my mother, who never faltered in her support,

and my father, who thought the book would never get finished

Acknowledgments

This book has been many years in the making. At its roots lies an earlier, rather brash attempt to test and refine modernization theories by analyzing the variations across Japan's prefectures during the Meiji period on a wide range of standard indicators of modernization: school enrollment ratios, capitalization and number of banks, volume of mail, volume of telegrams, factory employment, and so on. Before I was finished I had begun to realize that most of the indicators of modernization I was using were the outputs of organizations, and that without understanding what was shaping the development of the organizations I could not interpret what was happening to my indicators. Moreover, it was clear that the organizations in question had all been modeled in some fashion on Western organizational forms, and that understanding more clearly how those forms were adopted and adapted in the Meiji social context was more challenging than running regressions on their outputs. A grant from the Social Science Research Council enabled me to spend a year on leave from Yale at Princeton, where the basic ideas for this book began to take shape.

Since then I have benefited from the comments and suggestions of a number of friends and colleagues. At Yale, Rosabeth Kanter, Hugh Patrick, Paul DiMaggio, and Wendell Bell read early versions of the manuscript and gave both encouragement and advice. Colleagues at the Alfred P. Sloan School of Management at MIT have read several drafts, and I especially want to thank Lotte Bailyn, Donald Lessard, Edgar Schein, and John Van Maanen for their comments and suggestions. A workshop on the Tokugawa-Meiji transition organized by Marius Jansen and Gilbert Rozman provided a forum for getting reactions to elements of my basic framework from a number of insightful Japan historians and social scientists:

Marius Jansen and Gilbert Rozman themselves, Albert Craig, Albert Altman, Henry Smith, William Wray, Martin Collcutt, and James White. A later colloquium on the comparative study of control systems, sponsored by the Taniguchi Foundation and organized by Umesao Tadao and Matsubara Masatake, provided some valuable comments from a number of Japanese and international scholars, including Harumi Befu, Fujii Joji, Hamashita Takeshi, Hata Nobu-yuki, Kurt Radke, Suzuki Tadashi, and Yano Toru.

I owe an enormous debt to the many Japanese scholars and re-searchers who have compiled the voluminous histories of the or-ganizations whose development I trace in this book. Few societies provide sociologists with such an embarrassment of riches, from the thirty-volume compendium of materials on the history of the postal-telecommunications system of Japan to the scholarly articles on the transport system of the post in the early Meiji period in one particular prefecture.

Thanks are due to Michael Aronson of Harvard University Press for his patience and encouragement through seemingly endless re-writings. I am grateful to my sister, Jean Westney, for entering two very long chapters into the computer one hot August. Finally, I want to thank my parents for their unfailing love and encourage-ment. They have been waiting for this book for a long time.

Contents

Tables

Figures

Imitation and Innovation

Introduction

To many of the Westerners who came to Asia in the 1860s, arriving in Japan seemed to be stepping back centuries in time, into a world of sword-wielding knights, subservient peasants, tradition-bound merchant guilds, and haughty feudal lords. But within a few years of the Meiji Restoration of 1868, the Japanese adopted a wide range of new institutions and manufacturing and communications technologies from the West in a massive effort to reshape Japan into a nation that would be the equal of the Western powers. Westerners watched with interest and no little amusement as the emulation of Western culture and institutions began to transform the society. The woodblock prints of street scenes from the early Meiji period, presenting a collage of Western and Japanese dress, vehicles, and architecture, could be taken as metaphors for the entire society, which confronted foreigners with the mixture of old and new, native and foreign, exotic and familiar that to this day often symbolizes Japan for the rest of the world. It was perhaps this mixture that made it difficult for most Westerners to evaluate correctly the extent of Japan's transformation, until its magnitude was dramatically demonstrated first by Japan's victory over its ancient mentor, China, in 1895, and even more convincingly by its defeat of a major Western power, imperial Russia, in 1905.

The five and a half decades from the opening of the treaty ports in 1859 to the end of the Meiji period in 1912 span one of the most remarkable social transformations of modern history. Modern scholars have emphasized the far-reaching changes that occurred during the Tokugawa period (1600–1867) in such fields as commerce, internal communications, urbanization, literacy, and production and distribution, but these had been incremental evolutionary changes. Their significance was not apparent to contemporary Westerners, who observed only that Japan had not experienced the industrial and social revolutions through which the major Western nations had passed since the mid-seventeenth century. Particularly in its political structures, Japan seemed to belong to a vanished age: the country was divided into over two hundred domains, each under the rule of a hereditary lord, himself in turn a vassal of the Tokugawa shogun, who possessed the largest and richest domain and commanded the direct allegiance of the other lords. He also had a formal mandate from the Emperor to protect and keep order in the realm, a mandate that some of the domain lords and samurai felt had been violated when foreigners were admitted to Japan in the 1850s.

The beginning of Japan's modern transformation is conventionally seen as the Meiji Restoration of 1868, in which the Tokugawa Shogunate was overthrown and the Emperor restored to at least nominal direct rule of the country. But the Restoration was far from being the immediate transfer of power to a group of committed modernizers. Indeed, initially many Western observers felt that the ousted Tokugawa regime had been more committed to learning from the West than were its victorious opponents, who fought under the slogan of "revere the Emperor and expel the barbarians." In 1867 the shogun had embarked on reforms that foreshadowed those of the 1870s. He hired French advisers to train the army, authorized the planning of a telegraph line, and began a major administrative reorganization. The fear that the shogun's reforms might soon enable him to consolidate his position beyond challenge finally cemented a somewhat uneasy alliance among four great domains of the southwest, an alliance united by agreement on two basic issues: the overthrow of the Tokugawa, and the maintenance of Japan's territorial integrity against the kind of encroachments by the Western powers that had occurred elsewhere in Asia.[1]

The new government took direct control only of those areas formerly ruled by the shogun or by those domains in the north that had resisted the claims of their traditional enemies from the south to speak for the imperial court. Initially it was a restoration in the genuine sense of the term. Although the Emperor's advisers from the court and the four victorious domains recognized the need for maintaining friendly relations with the Western powers and for adopting Western military technology, they were either not prepared or not willing to draw immediately on the West for institutional models in state administration. Instead, for the framework of the new regime they looked back to the height of the imperial court power, the Nara period of the eighth century, and adopted its structures and terminology.[2] This traditionalist phase was short-lived. In 1871 the central government formally assumed direct control of the entire country, and over the next decade it adopted Western-modeled policies aimed at the reshaping of the institutional landscape: the abolition of the old status system, tax reform, conscription, and new organizations in virtually every aspect of social life. By the end of the Meiji period Japan had become an exemplar of successful modernization, a formal ally of Britain, and a growing power in Asia.

The broad institutional changes of the early Meiji period have been widely regarded as a rational response both to the pressures of the international environment and to the inherent demands of industrialization. But rational or not, it was a response that few other societies were able to make, and it poses a major challenge to scholars concerned with social change. Explanation of the Japanese decision to emulate the Western powers in building an industrial society is the more complex in that it was not the work of a single strong enlightened leader, or even of a small cohesive group of committed modernizers. In the broadest sense, the men who played key roles in setting up the new institutions did have a common social background. They came from the seven percent of the population which was samurai, the hereditary administrative class of the Tokugawa period; and men from the four domains that had engineered the Restoration were overrepresented in the new institutions, particularly at the top decision-making levels of the central government. But they cannot be compared to the cohesive modernizing groups that came to power in the Russian or Chinese revolutions—they had no comparable organizational structure or explicit ideology. By the later years of the Meiji period, a fairly small group of "Meiji oligarchs" had emerged to play a dominant role in politics, and they were all men who had been deeply involved in the institutional changes of the early 1870s. But their later cohesion was the result of their working together to fashion the new Japan rather than the cause, and it was a relationship reinforced by the loss of principal allies and friends to age, assassination, and political differences.

The toll was particularly heavy during that first and crucial decade, and yet the loss of apparently key figures during that time did not seem to impede the pace of the transformation. The assassination of the chief advocate of a European-style army, Ōmura Masujiro, by traditionalist samurai in 1869, for example, did not hamper the adoption of the new military organization; an able young associate, Yamagata Aritomo, took his place. The first minister of justice, Etō Shimpei, who fought hard with the bureaucrats of the Finance Ministry for the resources to build a centralized system of courts and judicial police in the early 1870s, resigned from the government in 1873 over foreign policy issues. In 1876 he led a samurai uprising in southwestern Japan and was condemned to death by one of the courts he had been instrumental in creating. The loss of these innovators and others like them neither discredited their programs nor crippled the new institutions they were trying to build.

Much of the literature on the Meiji period has sought to explain this apparently unlimited supply of able men committed to the modernization of their society on Western models. Many scholars have focused on the motivations of the modernizers, addressing the question of why members of Japan's elite would act to sweep away the old order when in other societies, such as China, the old elite was the main opponent of policies of the sort that triumphed in Japan.[3] Other scholars have concentrated on the preconditions of Japan's transformation: the social and economic legacy of the Tokugawa period that provided the Meiji leaders with a comparatively high level of resources to employ in modernization.[4] These analyses, however, leave unanswered the questions of implementation: how, once the commitments to modernization policies were made, they were carried out, and how the resources inherited from the previous regime were actually used.[5] The answers lie in the analysis of the development of the formal organizations through which the transformation policies were implemented, and which themselves came to shape the nature of those policies. And this leads inevitably to the analysis of organizations that were very consciously set up on Western models.

Japan is commonly regarded as a society that industrialized and modernized largely through its own internal resources. And yet in nearly all areas the nation's transformation relied heavily on the deliberate emulation of Western organizations. The navy was modeled on the British; the army first on the French and then on the German; the educational system on a series of models (the French, the American, the German); the communications systems on the British; the police on the French; the banking system on the American; the legal system first on the French and then on the German. Less specifically targeted emulation of Western patterns led to the establishment of factories, political parties, newspapers, chambers of commerce, clubs, stock exchanges, professional societies—the list seems endless. By the end of the Meiji period there were few organizations in the major Western industrial societies that did not have their counterparts in Japan.

This massive transfer of organizational forms from Western societies that differed profoundly from the Japanese environment raises a number of fascinating issues. And yet the interaction between Western organizational models and the Japanese environment, the factors behind the choice of models, and the emergent characteristics of the developing organizations have received surprisingly little systematic study.[6] One reason for this partial neglect may be that emulating the patterns of another society has connotations of a lack of originality and even of intellectual piracy. Copying is less estimable than inventing; imitation is less honorable than innovation. Paradoxically, the very scale of Meiji emulation of Western patterns may have made its systematic study more difficult. The Japanese of the Meiji period, like their descendents today, felt belittled by the Western image of their nation as an assiduous copier of other peoples' innovations, and the response, among Meiji Japanese as well as among contemporary scholars, was to emphasize strongly the care and selectivity of Japanese emulation. In much of the writing on institutional change in the early Meiji period the dominant image is one of Japanese decision-makers clutching a list of desired institutions, engaging in painstaking comparative shopping, and selecting the brand most suited to their tastes and needs. William Foote Whyte's description captures this "rational shopper" image very succinctly: "Japanese imitation was really highly selective. Japanese change agents examined models from various more 'advanced' countries and selected in terms of their judgment of what would best fit into Japan."[7]

While the "rational shopper" provides a defense against the patronizing tone of the "clever little copier," the image raises other problems. It confounds the processes of the 1870s, the decade of the most widespread use of Western organizational models, with the more deliberate patterns of the 1880s, which built on more than a decade of experience of emulation. In the 1870s Japanese organization-builders were far more concerned with using Western-modeled patterns to transform their society than they were with "what would best fit into Japan." By the 1880s the Japanese environment into which the Western models were to fit had already been profoundly reshaped by the institutional emulation of the 1870s. But even more important, the rational shopper image does not do justice to the level of innovation in Japanese emulation. It has the unfortunate effect of emphasizing the selection of the model at the expense of the much more innovative emergent processes by which, after the model was selected, the organizational patterns from various Western societies were adapted over time to the very different environment of Meiji Japan.

Where cross-societal organizational emulation is concerned, the distinctions between copying and inventing, between imitation and innovation, are false dichotomies: the successful imitation of foreign organizational patterns requires innovation. All organizations must draw on the surrounding environment for resources and must respond to the external demand for their products or services. Since the environment in which the organizational model was anchored in its original setting will inevitably differ from one to which it is transplanted, even the most assiduous emulation will result in alterations of the original patterns to adjust them to their new context, and changes in the environment to make it a more favorable setting for the emerging organization. Some of those changes are deliberate, some are unintended, and virtually all will have unforeseen consequences. For some organizations, the original model will continue to provide a blueprint for development; for others, the original model will quickly lose ground to more powerful influences in the immediate environment.

This book examines the processes of cross-societal organizational emulation by tracing through the Meiji period three organizations that were based on Western models: the police, the postal system, and the newspaper. The first two were government subsystems that were built on specific Western models (the French police and the British post). The third was not a single system but a number of separate organizations, most of which took no specific foreign newspaper enterprise as a model but were clearly inspired by the Western concept of the newspaper. Each organization has a distinctive history, and yet in each we can trace general patterns of imitation and emulation that have broader applications. Each of the three analyses asks the same set of questions. Why did the organization-builders select the models they did? What features of the original Western model were observed and emulated? What departures from the patterns of the model can we observe, and what caused them? How were the resources to build these organizational systems mobilized? Did the organizations become more like their Western models over time, or less? What impact did the new organizations have on the social environment, and did that impact in turn affect the development of other organizations?

The analysis of these transfers of organizational patterns from Western societies to Meiji Japan is more than a vehicle for understanding the development of particular institutions, or even for illuminating the more general processes of Japanese social change. All industrializing societies have emulated organizational forms that originated outside their borders, from the earliest modernizers such as Britain to the developing countries of today's Third World. But despite the ubiquity of such emulation, our understanding of the process and our ability to enhance its effectiveness are still painfully inadequate. Interestingly enough, it has been the Japanese case that has in recent years revealed the poverty of our thinking on the subject. In the wake of the success of Japanese firms in competing with American firms, even in industries long regarded as the bastions of American know-how such as automobiles and steel, many U.S. and Japanese management experts have been arguing over whether organizational patterns that are effective in Japan can be transplanted into the American social environment, either by U.S. firms trying to learn from Japanese patterns or by Japanese firms setting up U.S. subsidiaries. Much of this debate remains mired in arguments over the degree of "culture-dependency" of the social technologies embodied in organizational patterns, with very little systematic empirical or theoretical grounding.

The historical importance of the Japanese case has thus been enhanced by a striking contemporary relevance. Meiji Japan undoubtedly differed much more substantially from the Western societies whose patterns it was trying to emulate than do contemporary Western nations from Japan today. If the general processes of cross-societal organizational emulation can be illuminated from the study of Meiji Japan, the case will provide a rare symmetry in the field of social change, for it seems likely that the growing internationalization of Japanese commerce and industry will eventually make Japan an important exporter of organizational patterns as well as of cars and consumer electronics.

1

The Processes of
Cross-Societal Emulation

As a discipline, sociology has its origins in the recognition and analysis of the social dimensions of the technological and economic transformation of society known as the Industrial Revolution. One of the sociologists' earliest and most fundamental insights was that a necessary condition of the industrial transformation was the development of social structures that could coordinate the efforts of many individuals performing specialized tasks. Coordination was necessary in order to utilize the new technologies based on large-scale applications of inanimate power, to mobilize human, financial, and material resources, and to distribute the increasing output of goods and services; the main mode of such coordination was the formal organization.

Understanding the development of organizations in a society—which includes the emulation of foreign models—does not stop at the analysis of the processes of change within the organization. It also entails placing them in a larger social context. In the transfer of organizational forms across societies the historical context, or timing, is a critically important factor, for it determines the range of models that have developed in other societies and are therefore available to organization-builders. But the availability of models is influenced not only by timing but by constraints on selection: that a potential model exists does not mean that it will be observed, or if observed, that it can be chosen. And finally, the organization that emerges once the model is chosen is the product of complex processes of imitation and innovation that are shaped both by the society's own resources and by its access to the resources of other societies. Before the three organizational histories of the police, the post, and the newspaper address these issues in each specific case, this chapter provides an overview of the context of cross-societal emulation in Meiji Japan and the conceptual frameworks that underlie the three analyses.

Western Organizational Models in Meiji Japan

When Japan began in the early 1870s to reach toward the West for the tools to help it meet the Western challenge, it encountered societies that were themselves undergoing the profound social transformation of what Kenneth Boulding has called the "organizational revolution." This "great rise in the number, size, and power of organizations of many diverse kinds"[1] was the underpinning of the great political, economic, and cultural changes of the nineteenth century, and indeed of the twentieth century as well. The organizational revolution was the base for the enormous expansion in the range of activities and the capacity of the state; for the emergence of what Alfred Chandler has defined as "modern business enterprise," containing many distinct operating units and managed by a hierarchy of salaried executives;[2] and for the creation of new patterns of consumption, leisure, and political activity that were increasingly standardized within broad social classes in each society.[3] These changes were effected through the spread both of the generic social technologies of formal organization (the regulation of behavior and task performance by formal, standardized rules, record-keeping and budgeting, standardized training and criteria of recruitment, a hierarchy of control) and of their application in specific configurations of activities, such as the military general staff, the limited liability company, and advertising-based newspapers.

The organizational revolution of the nineteenth century was integrally linked with the development of the great centralizing technologies that emerged in the 1830s and 1840s: the postal system, the telegraph, and the railway. These networks removed many of the constraints on coordination and control that in the past had limited organizational expansion and the physical separation of subunits, and they provided the means of centralizing and integrating activities on an unprecedented scale. For the first time organizations could combine great size, very high levels of centralization and standardization, and high levels of spatial dispersion. Learning how to exploit the full potential of the new technologies took time, however, especially when they were adapted into existing administrative structures that constrained and in some cases resisted the fullest exploitation of their potential. The postal system, the telegraph, and the railway were themselves important innovators in this regard; they were new organizations that required strong central direction of a large number of widely dispersed subunits, the coordination of a considerable range of technical specialties and activities, and the mobilization of financial, material, and human resources on a considerable scale.

When Japan embarked on its modernization program in the 1870s, all of the great powers were engaged in organization-building on a major scale. France was refashioning the state structures of the Second Empire into patterns more appropriate to the Third Republic and trying to match German levels of military organization. Germany was completing the institutions of the unified German Empire. The United States was rebuilding its administrative structures in the wake of the Civil War and constructing new organizations for production and distribution to meet the demands of a rapidly expanding continental nation. Even in Great Britain there was a growing awareness of challenges to national stability at home and preeminence abroad that could only be met through the adoption of new forms of national administration, education, and industrial organization. Japan could therefore obtain more detailed and sophisticated information on Western organizational systems—and on more complex systems—than would have been the case even two or three decades earlier.

We must not understate the very significant variation among Western societies in the speed and sequence of the organizational revolution, or the differences in structure and behavior that resulted in part from that variation and in part from the different social bases on which the new structures were built. At the same time, however, it is essential to emphasize the fundamental *similarity* of the transformation. The functional specialization, the reliance on common techniques of coordination and control, the concept of the salaried office with formally defined responsibilities and powers—in short, the major attributes of Max Weber's ideal type of bureaucracy— were clearly taking hold in all Western societies during the second half of the nineteenth century. Contemporary observers of the essential similarity of these changes took it as evidence of the unidirectionality of historical evolution. Few considered the possibility that the similarity owed much to the common cultural and social background of Western societies, including a common organizational heritage in the Church and in feudalism, and to the crosssocietal emulation of organizational patterns among these closely linked societies. Yet that emulation was considerable, spurred by competition among the nation-states (especially in the military arena) and justified by ideologies that emphasized the unidirectionality and "progress" of historical evolution. The German emulation of the French Credit Mobilier in the 1850s,[4] for example, or the emulation of Bismarck's insurance programs of 1883–1889 by Austria, Switzerland, Denmark, Belgium, and Italy[5] could be justified as the introduction not of "French" or "German" patterns, but of the most "advanced" institutions.

While all societies have emulated organizational models in other societies, Meiji Japan is so remarkable for the apparent voluntarism of its emulation of foreign organizational forms and for the speed and scope of its borrowing that it is sometimes considered to be unique. A more accurate assessment would place it far along a continuum on which all societies occupy a position. Table 1 shows just how far-reaching and rapid the borrowing process was during the Meiji period. It lists the major new organizations of early Meiji and the source of the models on which they were based. (Throughout this book the term "organizational model" is used for the organization or the population of organizations from which another organization emulates certain features, such as its functions, formal structures, internal processes, and strategies for dealing with its environment. The term in this usage is akin more to that of the artist's model than the scientist's; it refers to the actual organization that is being emulated, not to any abstract representation of it.)

Table 1 reveals not only the considerable variety of sources from which Japan drew its organizational models and the wide range of institutional areas in which Western models were used, but also the rapidity of the initial borrowing. In general, the most far-ranging emulation of organizational models took place in the first decade of the Meiji period, before the introduction of systematic budgeting procedures. The lack of a system for projecting and assessing ex-

Table 1. Major cases of organizational emulation
in Meiji Japan

Source	Organization	Year Initiated
Britain	Navy	1869
	Telegraph system	1869
	Postal system	1872
	Postal savings system	1875
France	Army	1869
	Primary school system	1872
	Tokyo Keishi-cho (police)	1874
	Judicial system	1872
	Kempeitai (military police)	1881
United States	Primary school system[a]	1879
	National bank system	1872
	Sapporo Agricultural College	1879
Germany	Army[a]	1878
Belgium	Bank of Japan	1882

[a] Reorganization on a new model.

penditures caused major fiscal problems, but it had real advantages in organizational terms. No careful assessments of costs were required for setting up a new organizational system, and no careful scrutiny of expenses hampered the initiatives of organization-builders. It is no accident that so many government subsystems were established in the early 1870s, when monitoring procedures were at their loosest, and political rather than economic concerns were dominant—a contrast to the ensuing decade. However, once the systems were set up, they had serious difficulty in getting the financial resources to enable them to expand rapidly.

The 1880s was primarily a decade of reorganization and consolidation, in which the organizations so rapidly established in the 1870s were put on a firmer structural basis and extended throughout the country. These reorganizations were both a response to emergent problems and a result of much greater sophistication in gathering and using information about organizational models. The first generation of organization builders had given way—through deaths, resignations, and transfers into other positions—to men who had more experience with Western-style organizations and more detailed knowledge of the Western models on which they were based. These men faced different organizational tasks than did the innovators of the earlier decade. The problems for the new generation no longer had to do with creating new organizations, but with improving and extending existing systems in an increasingly complex environment. In some cases they drew on developments in the Western organizations that had been the original models. In others, beginning with the army's switch from the French to the German model in 1878, the initial models in several areas were supplanted or supplemented by others. Major shifts occurred in primary education, with a switch in 1879 to an American model, and then again in 1886 to a modified German model; banking, with the establishment of the Belgian-modeled central bank; and municipal and prefectural government, with a switch in 1888 to a German model.

Extensive as it is, Table 1 is only a partial representation of organizational emulation in the Meiji period, because it focuses on institutional areas that had specific, identifiable Western models. These were the most obvious cases of emulation, but they were by no means the only ones. There were two types of organizations based on foreign models: one was explicitly based on a specific organization (for example, the army, which used first the French and then the German model, or the national bank system, which used the American model); the other was based on a general Western model of a certain type of organization (such as the newspaper, the incorporated enterprise, or the factory). In Meiji Japan, the second type was inspired primarily by knowledge that in the West special-purpose organizations existed to carry out a certain activity (the newspaper and the factory are major examples), rather than by any knowledge of or exposure to a specific organization, such as the *London Times* or the Lowell Spinning Company.

Not surprisingly, the organizations based on a general model incorporated at the outset fewer "new" organizational features than did those based on a specific foreign model. They were more likely to adopt primarily the organizational goal—the concept of a specialized organization that turned out a certain product or service—and to fill in other patterns from other organizations in the immediate environment. The organization based on a specific model was more likely to adopt from the very beginning its model's control structure, the internal specialization of tasks, and the methods of obtaining required inputs and disposing of or disseminating outputs. In some cases, organizations created on a general model came over time to look to more specific models to guide their growth and reorganization.

The creators of either type of organization needed to acquire information about Western patterns. The organization employing a specific model, however, required considerably more detailed knowledge and first-hand observation of the model. The major advantage of specific models lay in the greater speed with which complex, large-scale organizations with multiple subunits could be set up and expanded. The major disadvantage was that it took a much larger investment of money and people to acquire the organizational information. They were therefore much more frequently used in state organizations and in state-sponsored systems, as is apparent from Table 2, which lists the principal Meiji organizations in each of these two categories.

Most of the organizations with specific models were government-directed. The government was strongly committed to building national-scale, standardized systems as rapidly as possible, and therefore it had powerful incentives for drawing on specific Western models. Moreover, particularly in the early Meiji period, the government was virtually the only organization that possessed the resources for acquiring detailed information on specific models.

Meiji Japan is widely considered to be a classical case of "mod-

Table 2. Types of organizational models in Meiji Japan

Specific		General
Organization	Original model	Organization
Tokyo Keishi-cho	Paris Prefecture of Police	Newspaper
Kempeitai	French *gendarmerie*	Factory
Postal system	British General Post Office	Incorporated enterprise
Army	French army	Railway
Navy	British navy	Tokyo Stock Exchange
Bank of Japan	National Bank of Belgium	

ernization from above"—the "above" being, of course, the government. Some historians have quarreled with what they see as an
overemphasis on the leading role of the state, and indeed in many
sectors of local administration and industry the initiatives of local
leaders and private entrepreneurs were critical to the social and
economic development of the period. But in the wide-ranging introduction of new organizational forms based on Western models
that dominated Meiji organizational development, the government
undeniably played a leading role. It functioned as what Arthur
Stinchcombe has called an "organization-creating organization"; that
is, an organization that mobilizes resources and uses them to establish new organizations. There are three ways in which an organization can play such a role. It can set up organizational subsystems
which remain under its direct control; it can set up organizations
which are initially under its control but which it releases when they
reach a certain stage of development; or it can provide the resources
for the development of organizations which are not incorporated
into its control structures but which from their inception are at least
formally autonomous.

During the forty-five years of the Meiji period the government's
organization-creating activities spanned all three modes. In the earliest years the resulting organizations were not always based on
Western models. Both the Shogunate and the domain governments
had long played an organization-creating role in commerce, and the
new Meiji government followed the same path. In 1868, for example, the government sponsored the establishment of a trading
company and a financial exchange company in each of the six open
ports, with the aim of getting more of Japan's trade into reliable
(and Japanese) hands. The personnel and operating capital of these
companies were supplied by the large merchant houses, but the
initiative came from the government, which exerted considerable
pressure to ensure their participation (using tactics that one source
dubs "virtual extortion")[6] and closely supervised their activities. The
model for these "semi-official, semi-private" enterprises was drawn
from the management of domain monopolies in the Tokugawa period, and it proved less than successful in the new era: the companies
were dissolved in 1873–74.[7]

For the most part, however, the traditional precedents for an
activist state role in setting up organizations were more important

than the older styles of organization-creation. Most of the Meiji government's organization-creating activities centered on the establishment of Western-modeled organizations. The rapid expansion of state subsystems in the early 1870s, summarized in Tables 1 and 2, was the most striking example of the first mode of organization-creation (setting up subsystems which remain under direct control). In addition, the government undertook the establishment and management of over fifty enterprises in a wide range of industries. These fell into three categories: military shipyards and arsenals; enterprises set up by the Hokkaido Development Office to encourage the economic development of what was in effect Japan's northern frontier; and model factories to introduce new technologies (especially in spinning and machinery) or to reduce dependence on expensive imports (for example, Western-style building materials for the construction of new government offices). The military facilities followed long-established Western models and remained under direct government operation throughout the period, but the government management of enterprises in the second and third categories was regarded as a temporary measure to compensate for the low level of technology in early Meiji, and in the 1880s these enterprises were sold off to private firms. Finally, the government provided a variety of resources to encourage the development of independent organizations. In the textile industry, for example, the government in 1879 purchased ten spinning machines from English manufacturers and sold them to private enterprises in eight prefectures around Japan. It also provided loans for the establishment of spinning mills in other areas. To enable private companies to operate more effectively the government actively disseminated information on new organizational structures: for example, it published pamphlets on the incorporated enterprise in 1871 and detailed regulations on the operations of banks in 1872 and 1876.

The organization-building role of the Japanese government had traditional roots, but it was also legitimated by the trends in major Western societies. As F. H. Hinsley has pointed out,

> It was in the last third of the nineteenth century, wherever it has not been a development of even more recent growth, that governments first undertook the comprehensive regulation of society. Although there had been earlier steps in this direction—all such developments are of long gestation and slow growth—government in this sense

existed hardly anywhere in 1870 . . . The more advanced countries all witnessed in the next thirty years an unprecedented increase in the powers and functions of government and a fundamental alteration in the relations between government and society.[8]

Japan embarked on its emulation of Western organizational forms precisely at the time when the social technologies of organizations made large-scale centralized structures possible and when the state's role as an organization-creating (and organization-regulating) organization was expanding in the major Western societies that provided its models.

The Selection of Models

There is enormous variation in the range of choice open to societies when they adopt foreign models. Often a particular model is forced on a society. Under colonialism, for example, the imperial power usually imposes variants of its own organizational systems, regardless of whether those are the most advanced or the most suited to internal conditions. Less formal dominance relationships can also pressure a society into adopting a foreign model: for example, American military advisers in Cambodia in the 1960s tried to replace French military patterns with more familiar American forms. On the other hand, emulation is frequently voluntary, as in Britain's use of German military, social welfare, and higher education systems in the late nineteenth and early twentieth centuries.

In Meiji Japan the emulation charted in Tables 1 and 2 was voluntary and was motivated by three major goals. One was the achievement of a military capability equivalent to that of the Western powers. Even before the Meiji Restoration it had become evident that this meant emulating Western military organization, but in the first few years of the Meiji period Japan's leaders came to recognize that a much broader program of organizational emulation was needed to match Western military strength, given the institutional underpinnings of what William McNeill has called "the industrialization of war."[9] These included a literate and patriotic citizenry shaped by a common educational system; an industrial base; communications and transport networks; and state structures that could extract the necessary resources to build all these. The second aim of Japan's government leaders was achieving the revision of the unequal treaties that had been signed by the Tokugawa Shogunate and reaffirmed by the new Meiji government. These had deprived Japan of jurisdiction over Westerners within its borders and control of its own tariffs. The key conditions of the abolition of extraterritoriality were that Japan institute a legal and police system on Western models and establish a system of state administration of commerce that met with the approval of the foreign powers. Treaty revision remained a major policy concern for the Meiji government from 1868 through repeated renegotiation efforts until the final success in 1894. The third aim came to incorporate and subsume the other two, and extended the range of organizational emulation well beyond the purview of the state: the desire to make Japan into a modern nation that was the equal of the Western powers, one that would be respected internationally as a modern, "civilized" society.[10] Although there was considerable disagreement over the means to achieve these basic goals, the goals themselves were widely shared by the builders of the new organizations in both the public and private sectors. The pressures for change were therefore, at least initially, generated and legitimated by external pressures. These external pressures did not formally restrict Japan's selection of models, but the choice was by no means unconstrained, although the constraints are not always evident either in the public statements of the Meiji organization-builders or in the "rational shopper" image so dominant in the modernization literature.

Japan's "rational shopper" image owes much to the government's eclecticism in its employment of over 2,400 foreigners drawn from twenty-three different nations, representing virtually every country in Western Europe and North America. Oyama Azusa has suggested that the Japanese distrust of foreigners was behind this multinational selection.[11] Such distrust certainly existed, and it was not ill-founded: foreign powers frequently displayed a proprietorial interest in the organizational systems in which their nationals predominated. Perhaps even more important was the jealousy of the great powers of any step that seemed to give one nation a preeminent role in Japan. The Meiji government had to tread carefully in its early years, both to avoid alienating the major powers and to prevent any one nation from gaining so critical a role in the modernizing process that it could use its indispensability as a lever in its trade and diplomacy with Japan.[12]

The many tours Japanese government officials made to survey a number of Western models also fostered the image of careful eclecticism: these tours usually included most Western European nations, and often the United States as well. Yet the final choice of organizational models was dominated by a very few societies: Britain, France, and to a lesser extent the United States in early Meiji, and Germany in the late 1870s and 1880s. Other European countries like Italy and Switzerland produced employees for Japan's government and enjoyable stops on their tours for its officials, but not models for its institutions.[13]

It could be argued that organizational models were chosen on the basis of their international prestige. This was certainly an important factor in many selections: the British navy, for example, was regarded as the finest in the world; the British post office was the model for most other Western countries as well as for Japan; the Paris police was seen as the most effective in Europe. But for almost as many other institutions selected as models, that reasoning does not hold: the French army, for example, was defeated by the Germans before it was officially adopted as the model for the Japanese army, yet it continued to serve as its model until 1878. It was the prestige of the nation as much as that of the specific model which influenced the choice.

But international prestige alone does not explain the dominance of models from certain great powers. One of the most important constraints on the early use of Western organizational models was access to information, which posed greater problems for Japan than for the other major industrializing societies of the nineteenth century. The nation enjoyed neither the contiguity of European countries, which allowed relatively easy passage of information and personnel, nor the waves of immigration that carried information and skills across the oceans to the United States and the British dominions. Japan's geographical separation from the centres of organizational development was reinforced by a formidable language barrier. Over time, Japanese resources for monitoring developments in the West expanded, as more and more Japanese learned European languages and studied abroad, but during the early 1870s, when most of the initial organizational transfers were made, the problems were formidable.

Accessibility of information was closely linked to the scale of a nation's presence in East Asia. It was this factor that made the United States so significant a source of models, particularly in the private sector. The growing presence of American nationals in Asia and the significant number of American missionaries and teachers in Japan in the early Meiji period made it easy to obtain information about the United States. In other words, the specific networks of contacts and information that emerged in the course of Japan's relations with Western nations were critical in the selection of models. The nations which were the most important sources of organizational models were those which were dominant in Japan's immediate environment.

Selection tended to be a cumulative process; that is, the selection of a model from one society increased the likelihood that the same society would serve as a source for further models. Because Western language facility was a rare commodity in Japan during the early decades of its opening to the West, the use of an organizational model in one area produced people whose language skills could be then transferred to other organizations. For example, the French engineers who arrived in Japan in 1866 to build iron mills in Yokohama taught their Japanese co-workers some French; those Japanese were then available to assist the French mining advisers who arrived in 1868. The French military mission to the Shogunate and the French language school established in Yokohama in 1865 also produced a cadre of Japanese who could communicate with French advisers, and this was a major factor in convincing the Meiji government to continue the use of French military advisers even after the French armies were defeated by the German in the Franco-Prussian War.[14] Organizational models tended to be cumulative for still another reason. The selection of one model opened channels of communication with officials in the foreign country and provided networks of personal contact that made it easier to find the right advisers to help build organizations in other fields, related and unrelated. In the 1870s the British and French benefited most from this "contagion effect"; in the 1880s, after the army's 1878 switch to the German model and with the resort to Germany for a model for the constitution, German institutions had a significant effect on a wide range of governmental organizational systems.

Another factor reinforced the effects of "contagion": the contribution that the selection of models could make toward ending the unequal treaties, through transforming Japan into a society that was "civilized" by the standards of the major Western powers. The standards by which these societies measured "civilization" were obviously those of their own societies, and the surest way for Japan to meet those standards was to take their institutions as models. The "major powers" meant primarily Britain and France: where they led, others would follow, and treaty revision was impossible without their assent, particularly the assent of Britain—as the Japanese government found out in the late 1870s. A full-scale attempt by the Japanese government in 1879 to end the unequal treaties was curtly rebuffed by the British and French. The United States and Germany, however, showed themselves much more favorably disposed to renegotiation, although they refused to act unilaterally. Thereafter the Japanese government made a deliberate effort to use the choice of foreign advisers and organizational models as a diplomatic weapon, by drawing on those countries in preference to the hitherto favored British and French.

For people outside the central government access to models was more difficult. Foreign advisers were also important in the private sector, although the records of their activities and the terms of their contracts are much harder to trace than those of the government employees. It is likely that the foreign advisers in the private sector were primarily drawn from among Western residents of the treaty ports rather than hired in their home countries and brought to Japan, as were most employees of the government. The treaty ports thus provided a potential source of informants and direct exposure to Western organizations operating there; they thereby reinforced the influence of models from the great powers who dominated Western contacts with Asia. More distant but still accessible were the foreign concessions in China, particularly in Shanghai, where a variety of Western organizations flourished.

Publications—both translations of Western works and explications of Western patterns by Japanese—were available from very early in the Meiji period. As more and more Japanese attended institutions of higher education where Western languages were part of the core curriculum, they went directly to Western publications for their information. Henry Dyer claimed that by 1900, for example, Japanese engineers were more apt to keep abreast of the British professional journals than their British counterparts.[15] Foreign study was an option open to individuals, as well as to students sponsored by the government. Here too accessibility was an important factor. The government sent its officially sponsored students primarily to Europe, the source of most of its organizational models. Students who went abroad on their own, however, preferred the United States: it was cheaper to get to, and American missionaries in Japan provided the necessary information and contacts for enrolling in American colleges and universities.[16]

Although the specific conditions that shaped Japan's choice of organizational models were unique, the general patterns may well apply to other nations at other times. The pressure on developing nations to emulate the patterns of the nations that are most powerful in their immediate environment is significant today, as it was in the nineteenth century. Information on models is skewed toward those countries with which the developing nation has the closest interactions, and the "contagion" effect still influences the choice of models. And the leading role of the state in obtaining and disseminating information on organizational models remains a common one in developing countries.

In summary, then, while the resort to foreign organizational models in Meiji Japan was voluntary, the selection of models was constrained by a number of considerations which were "rational" by most standards, but which were not based primarily on the considerations of optimal compatibility with the Japanese environment that underlie the "rational shopper" image of Japanese development. Indeed, to contemporary Western observers, the actual processes of Japanese organizational emulation bore little resemblance to that image. Georges Bousquet, a French adviser to the early Meiji government, described his observations of Japanese organizational development as follows:

> In a fierce debate between two men of state, on the subject of estab-
> lishing a House of Common, you will see citations of Stuart Mill,
> Frederick II, and Bismarck, but there is not a word about the special
> condition of Japan and of the advantages or inconveniences that such
> an institution would present. The last thing the Japanese consent to
> study is their own country, their needs, their own aptitudes; it is a
> question, in their opinion, not of knowing themselves, but of trans-
> forming themselves; not of what they are, but of what they want to
> become. Vainly does one try to suggest to them that, to fashion a
> statue from a block of marble, it is necessary at least to find out its
> texture and its dimensions.[17]

The sweeping transformation of Japanese society through the new
institutions adapted from the West, and the impossibility of imag-
ining Meiji society without them, has tempted later observers, both
Western and Japanese, to project a much greater selectivity and
sophistication into the borrowing process than were apparent to
contemporaries. The fit between the new institutions and their social
environment was not the result of the perspicacity of the organization-builders nor of some kind of uncanny compatibility between
the new and the existing social structures, but of the capacity of the
new institutions for transforming the environment. Part of this process involved the redefinition of "tradition" and what "Japanese"
patterns really were, an ideological challenge that absorbed much
of the energies of Japanese intellectuals and government leaders in
the late Meiji period.[18] The selective invocation of elements of the
past, reinterpreted in the light of the needs of the present (particularly organizational needs for control), was an important part of
the organizational development process in Meiji Japan, as it still is
in Japan today.

Imitation and Innovation in Organizational Emulation

In 1950 Armen Alchian identified the close relationship between
imitation and innovation in the development of organizational forms:

> While there certainly are those who consciously innovate, there are
> those who, in their imperfect attempts to imitate others, uncon-
> sciously innovate by unwittingly acquiring some unexpected or un-

sought unique attributes which under the prevailing circumstances prove partly responsible for the success. Others, in turn, will attempt to copy the uniqueness, and the innovation-imitation process continues.[19]

In the transfer of organizational patterns across societies, both conscious innovations and unconscious innovations produce departures from the original model. No matter how much a new organization's founders may want to build an exact copy of a model drawn from another society, they can never replicate it completely in the new setting. This is hardly an astonishing assertion. We would expect that changes would be necessary when social structures are transferred across cultures. But ascribing any and all departures from a model to the influence of culture does little to advance our understanding. By identifying more precisely the range of factors behind these departures, we can grasp more clearly how culture and new organizational patterns interact and how the processes of cross-societal emulation shape the development of organizations.

Departures from a foreign organizational model are a subcategory of innovations, and as Alchian indicated, they can be either unintended or deliberate. Unintended departures occur for two reasons: imperfect information and the influence of alternative implicit models. Deliberate departures have three major causes: selective emulation; adapting the patterns of the model to a different societal scale (that is, a population or geographic area that differs significantly from the society in which the model developed); and adapting the new organization to an environment that lacks some of the organizations that support it in its original setting.

Perfect information about an organizational model is never available to those engaged in creating a new organization, even when they have direct access to informants within the original model. In large-scale, complex organizations both informants and information-seekers see only part of the organization, particularly its operations at its lower levels, and both may interpret what they see inaccurately. Moreover, informants from within the model often present idealized explications of how the organization works, and stress the formal aspects of organizational structure and processes rather than the informal processes. A universal problem in constructing a new organization—or reconstructing an existing one—in emulation of a given model is that few of its members have any first-hand experience of how the original organization works. Those who do are usually in the top echelons of the new organization, and they are likely to concentrate on the subjects of immediate concern to them, particularly the acquisition of resources, the nature of regulatory controls over the organization, and the means of internal coordination and control. There are always some gaps in the information about the model, and it is unlikely that they will all be filled in a manner that duplicates the features of the organizational model.

The second source of unplanned innovation is the workforce of the new organization. The cost of providing first-hand experience of the original model for any but a handful of top-ranking organization members can be prohibitive, and even when some of the recruits have such experience, the overwhelming majority is unfamiliar with the organizational format and its roles. The problems of role socialization in the new organization are therefore considerably greater than in the original model, where experienced members routinely socialize the new recruits, where incoming members have had opportunities to observe the organization before entry, and where there may well be external educational institutions to teach the required skills.

However, recruits to the organization do not enter it without some conception of organizational roles and structure. Many are recruited from existing organizations—particularly the supervisory personnel and the higher-ranking officials. These roles are usually filled by people with some age seniority, who are therefore bound to have spent some time in other organizational or occupational roles. It is to be expected that such people enter the organization with an implicit model of roles and structures based on their past experience. Since they play key roles in the control and communications systems of the new organization, their implicit models can exert considerable pull on that new organization in its adjustment to the new environment, particularly if they share a common organizational background. An example that both illustrates this point and shows how careful planning can reduce its impact is the recruitment policy of Nissan in setting up its plant in the United

States. In order to develop a Japanese-style work system, the company explicitly avoided recruiting people with previous experience in the automobile industry, to minimize the prospect that their employees would bring into their jobs a preconceived idea of how work in an automobile plant should be organized.

Unintended departures because of powerful implicit models constitute one source of innovation that is rooted in culture. A second is selective emulation, in which the builders of the new organization choose not to adopt certain features of the original model because they conflict with valued local patterns. The British model of the postal system was adopted in both India and Japan in the nineteenth century, for example, but in both countries the British practice of having women in charge of the smaller branch offices was seen as inappropriate, and was explicitly rejected. Departures because of implicit models and departures to preserve valued patterns are equally useful for analyzing a society's culture: the first exposes the elements of culture carried by organizational recruits, the second those carried by the organization-builders. An examination of these departures and of how long they survive in the new organization can be a powerful tool for revealing the often-buried core of a society's culture.

There are other reasons for selective emulation. A foreign organizational model may be used to legitimate changes that are desired by the innovators, but which require justification by the appeal to an outside model.[20] In such cases, only the desired features will be drawn from the model. The contemporary automobile industry again provides an example of this kind of selective emulation: the Japanese model has been invoked to legitimate management demands for less restrictive work practices in U.S. auto factories, but other aspects of the Japanese model, such as tying annual increases in management salaries to the rate of increase won by the labor union, are rarely even mentioned, let alone emulated.

Selective emulation can also occur when the organization builders try to avoid some shortcomings that have become evident in the original model. Often they do so on the advice of their informants. The most striking example of this in Meiji Japan occurred in 1878, when the army general staff was made directly responsible to the Emperor, five years before the German army freed its own general staff from the jurisdiction of the war minister and gave its chief direct access to the Emperor. The German army had been pressing for this change throughout the 1860s and 1870s, as the Japanese architect of the 1878 reorganization was well aware; Japan, with fewer entrenched opponents of an autonomous military command, was able to follow the German plan before the Germans themselves.[21]

The need to adapt a foreign model to a significantly different geographic or demographic scale can also be a source of deliberate innovation, especially in national systems. Meiji Japan was singularly fortunate in that few departures of this type were necessary. In population and in area Japan was remarkably close to the major European societies that served as its major sources of models (Table 3). The state structures of the continental European powers could be emulated by the Japanese with relatively few adjustments. National organizational systems adopted from Britain, as we shall see in the analysis of the post, required more adaptation.

The most important factor in deliberate departures from the organizational model is the social context into which the organization is introduced when it is transferred out of the institutional environment in which it developed. An organization operates in what William Evan has called an "organization-set" composed of the other organizations that regularly interact with it to provide needed resources or services, absorb its products, and exert formal control over some aspects of its functioning (this last category includes

Table 3. Population and size of selected countries

Country	Population (000)	Area (sq. km.)
China[a]	430,000	11,418
England[b]	26,072	244
France[b]	36,103	547
Germany[b]	41,059	541
Japan[c]	33,111	372

[a]Source: Gilbert Rozman, *Population and Marketing Settlements in Ch'ing China* (New York: Cambridge University Press, 1982), pp. 12–13. Population data are 1850 estimates.
[b]Source: *European Historical Statistics 1750–1970.* Population data are 1872 census figures.
[c]Source: *Nihon Kindaishi Jiten.* Population data firm, 1872.

government agencies, institutional shareholders, and so on). A manufacturing firm, for example, relies on other firms for its parts and materials, banks for its financing, railways and transport companies to deliver its inputs and take away its products, a postal or telephone system to maintain regular contacts with customers, a network of firms that take delivery of its products, and a set of legal and government structures that regulate aspects of its organization's behavior and structure.

The concept of the organization-set is a useful one in examining societal patterns of organizational development, especially in terms of the cross-societal transfer of organizational forms. One of the key differences between the environment of the organizational model and that of the new organization is that the organization-set in which the original organization functioned is not completely in place in the new setting, and the way in which the new organization responds to this problem has profound implications for its future development.

The new organization can adopt one of four strategies:

1. The organization can turn to another type of structure or organization that does exist within its environment to serve as a functional equivalent. For example, the early Japanese postal system, lacking the railways and the transport companies that provided the infrastructure of the British postal system on which it was modeled, turned to the traditional guilds of runners as carriers for the first postal routes.

2. The organization can be adapted to internalize the performance of a task or set of tasks performed outside the organization in the original setting. For example, given the relatively slow development of the courts of justice, the early Meiji police took over the task of imposing fines and prison sentences on offenders for a wide range of minor offenses that in its model, the French police, were dealt with by judicial officials.

3. The organization can be adapted to do without that particular activity. For example, early Japanese newspapers, in the absence of business firms that were accustomed to advertising through that medium, relied primarily on sales revenues rather than the mix of sales and advertising common in the Western press of the day.

4. The organization can undertake to act as an organization-creating organization and mobilize resources to establish new organizations to perform the required activities. For example, when the early Meiji government began to construct Western-style buildings in the capital in the 1870s, it established a cement factory and a glass factory to provide the building materials that were needed by the new type of construction but had not been manufactured in Japan until then.

The first three strategies have their major impact on the internal workings of the new organization. Each involves some departure from the original model. The first strategy (finding a functional equivalent within the environment) makes the organization adjust to a different type of support organization and therefore to a different relationship with at least one element of its organization-set. The second and third strategies entail a direct change in the activities performed within the organization, and therefore in its internal structures and processes. But adoption of any of these first three strategies is not necessarily a permanent solution. Over time, the organization-set can become more like that of the original model, either because emergent problems lead the organization to turn eventually to the organization-creation strategy, or because those within the organization want to emulate the model more closely, or even because the supporting organizations gradually develop for reasons beyond the direct influence of the focal organization itself. To the extent that information on the organization-set of the original model is available, it can provide a kind of blueprint for entrepreneurship, either for members of the organization or for outsiders. The result is change *toward* the original model over time, in contrast to the factors making for change *away* from the model as the organization adjusts to the new environment in other ways.

Obviously the strategy chosen to cope with the problems of an incomplete organization-set has significance not only for the direction of change in the organization itself but also in the direction and pace of social change in the environment as a whole. The fourth strategy—organization-creation—has the greatest impact on the general pace of organizational development. The actions of organizations in applying available resources to filling in the organization-set for which a foreign model supplies the blueprint constitute an important force for changing the organizational map in many societies.

In general, we would expect that the larger and more varied the organization-set of the original model, the greater will be the demands the new organization places on its social environment, and therefore the greater will be its potential impact on social development. We might also expect that the size and variety of the model's organization-set would affect how quickly and successfully another society can emulate that organization. The pervasive belief among organizational sociologists that the organization-sets (or organizational networks, in a slightly broader meaning) are becoming more complex in modern industrial societies suggests that cross-societal transfers of organizational patterns from more to less developed societies may be increasingly difficult.

If the concept of the organization-set is extended beyond a single organization, society itself can be seen as an interconnected system of interacting organization-sets: the outputs of one organization become the inputs of another. Over time the density of organizations increases, the interactions among them intensify, and changing levels of resources and the emergence of new types of organizations alter the dominance patterns in the system. In turn, the patterns of relationships among organizations are critical in shaping the transfer of resources within that society, including the transfer of information about models and innovations. It may be possible, in these terms, to identify what one might call strategic organizations: that is, organizations which play a leading role in stimulating the development of other organizations, because of the number and variety of the organizations which can use their products or services, or because of the scope of their organization-sets, or both. The term "strategic organization" has obviously been coined in analogy to the popular concept of a strategic industry, one that has important spread effects in the economy. But a strategic industry is not necessarily inhabited by strategic organizations. The textile industry in Meiji Japan, for example, quickly became an important foreign-exchange earner and a major employer, and it is widely seen as a strategic industry in terms of Japan's economic development. But in terms of the development of organizations, the textile factories were not particularly important; their organization-sets were quite simple and their outputs did not directly stimulate the creation of new organizations. In contrast, the Meiji army epitomizes the strategic organization. Its complex organization-set, ranging from a universal school system to provide literate recruits to the industries that supplied its weapons and supplies, stimulated extensive organization-creation by the government in many sectors.

Although none of the three organizations studied here had so wide-ranging an impact on the development of Japan's organizations as the army, each can be portrayed as a strategic organization. The postal system stimulated the development of an array of transport companies and its services were an important element of the organization-sets of a wide range of organizations. The newspaper required the creation of a large and varied organization-set to support its activities, and as the earliest organ of mass communication it supported the growth of organizations that used it as a channel of communication to the public it created. The police system, as one of the keystones of the state's regulatory and control structures, played a more important and yet more ambivalent role: it functioned as a major element of the organization-set of many organizations, and yet it also acted to restrain the expansion of some of them, such as political parties and trade unions.

It will be clear to the reader that the underlying premise of this book is that understanding the development of complex organizations is a major key to understanding social change. In applying the perspectives outlined here to three Meiji organizations, this study aims not only to illuminate the processes of social change within Meiji Japan, but also to develop a deeper understanding of the general processes of cross-societal organizational transfers and the processes of organizational development.

2

The Police

The development of police systems during the nineteenth century has been a subject of considerable controversy. Is the expansion of these state subsystems that enforce a growing body of formal laws and regulations a response to the breakdown of traditional social controls during industrialization and urbanization? Are police organizations more properly viewed as agents of the dominant classes attempting to control the emerging industrial working class? Are they the outward manifestation of the coercion and the violence implicit in the expansion of the modern state? Or are they best seen as one example of the increasing organizational differentiation and specialization occurring in many aspects of social life?[1]

However social historians may define police systems, the Japanese officials of the early Meiji government unhesitatingly viewed them as an essential part of the apparatus of the modern state. This perception was in large part imposed by the Western powers. To achieve the revision of the unequal treaties which denied local authorities jurisdiction over foreign residents, the Japanese had to develop judicial and policing organizations that conformed to Western models. Moreover, the evident utility of police organizations in suppressing opposition and in acting as an administrative and enforcement arm of the central government was a powerful incentive to their rapid consolidation as one of the key organizations in the administrative and control structure of the Meiji state.

Establishing a Western-style police system meant emulating an organization without a specific, focused technology around which to shape organizational roles. Police functions are wide-ranging and diffuse, and their performance involves a variety of material and organizational technologies, no single one of which can be defined as central to the organization. The resulting structures are complex, and they vary considerably across societies. The police system chosen by the Japanese government as its model was the largest and most highly centralized in Europe: that of France. The French police system was the oldest in Europe, dating back to the late seventeenth century.[2] Indeed, in France, as in many societies, police organizations were among the oldest formal organizations. As David Bayley has pointed out in his comparative study of the development of European police systems: "In modern Europe, police agencies antedate most other institutions . . . Police systems exhibit an enormous inertial strength over time; their forms endure even across the divides of war, violent revolution, and shattering economic and social change."[3]

By the early 1870s, however, European police systems, whatever their internal organization and the definition of their role may have owed to tradition, were embedded in an organization-set of courts, local government, and national administration. In Japan, the police system emerged virtually simultaneously with the structures of national administration that were formally charged with its control, and in advance of the structures of judicial administration and local government that elsewhere helped to shape the police systems. This sequence alone was enough to ensure that the Japanese police system would not replicate completely the patterns of the much older French system. Its debt to the French model, especially that of the Tokyo police to the Paris Prefecture of Police, was enormous; however, the fact that the Tokyo police was a more powerful model than the French for the development of Japan's provincial police made for marked departures in the national system from the overall French model.

In its first two decades, the Japanese police system developed significant innovations, which produced an organization whose importance in the state system and salience in the social environment surpassed those of its model. In some respects the Japanese actually anticipated later developments in the Western police, including the introduction of formal police education and the recruitment of police administrators from among graduates of the nation's leading universities. The Japanese also developed a system of spatial dispersion using police boxes in urban areas and one-man residential posts in rural areas that gave the nationally controlled and administered police system a level of penetration unmatched in Europe. Finally, the professionalization of the police, a process urged by police administrators in Europe and North America in the late nineteenth and early twentieth centuries, proceeded more rapidly in Japan than in the more "advanced" nations.

The organizational achievements of the Meiji police have been overshadowed by the negative evaluation of their role as agents of political and social control and of their subsequent role in the militarization of Japanese society in the 1930s and 1940s. Only in the last decade or so, with the recognition of the apparent effectiveness of Japan's urban policing, have Western scholars and police experts begun to incorporate the Japanese experience into comparative studies of the police.[4] Most of the features that have attracted contemporary Western interest, however, were already strongly marked in the police of the Meiji period, and owe much both to the original Western model and to the processes by which that model was adapted to its very different environment in nineteenth-century Japan.

Historical Background

THE TOKUGAWA PERIOD

One of Japan's first social historians, Fukuda Tokuzō, writing in 1900, referred to Tokugawa Japan as "an absolute police state,"[5] a judgment E. H. Norman echoed and elaborated in the 1930s.[6] These writers saw great continuities between the control system of the Tokugawa period and the modern Japanese police system. Yet in fact the police system that was created in the Meiji period owed little to the policing structures and patterns that existed in the Tokugawa period.

One of the main characteristics of policing in the Tokugawa period was the differentiation of jurisdiction by status and by region. In a society composed of estates, such as medieval Europe or Tokugawa Japan, both the codes of conduct and the means of enforcing them differ by social stratum. In Tokugawa Japan, as in medieval Europe, there was one law for the nobility—the samurai in Japan—and one law for the commoners. Samurai and commoners accused of similar crimes confronted different procedures and punishments. Moreover, the samurai had at least the formal right to execute on the spot, without trial, any commoner whose behavior violated the obligations of his or her social position. In reality, because the frequent exercise of this right would clearly have been disruptive, tight controls restricted the interaction of samurai and commoners. Policing was further differentiated geographically: each of the more than two hundred and sixty domains was responsible for its own internal policing. The closest approximation to a national policing organization was the office of the *ōmetsuke,* consisting of five high-ranking samurai (appointed by the shogun) and their subordinates, whose mandate was the surveillance and control of the daimyo and senior Shogunate officials.

Actual policing functions were incorporated into the general administrative structures. Eventually policing roles became specialized and differentiated, but even within the largest jurisdiction, the shogun's, they remained part of the general administration. Subordinate policing officials of lower samurai status (*yoriki* and *doshin*) were assigned as needed to various administrative officials. These men were charged with maintaining order, apprehending wrongdoers, and supervising the punishment of criminals. In urban areas they were also responsible for supervising fire control—no slight task in the wooden cities of the period.

One striking feature of the Tokugawa system was the small number of specialized policing officials. In Edo, the seat of the shogun, which by the end of the seventeenth century was a city of over one million people, there were only 290 *yoriki* and *doshin* attached to the office of the city magistrates.[7] Moreover, although a few policing officials were posted to the administrative offices in the countryside (the *daikan* or the *gundai*), the rural areas were largely self-policed. Village communities dealt with petty violations themselves. Crimes that came to the attention of the samurai officials often resulted in the punishment of innocent neighbors or family members, since the principle of collective responsibility was codified in Tokugawa law. Moreover, Japan had adopted the basic principles of Chinese law: confession was the only basis for punishment and torture was an acceptable means of extracting the necessary confession. Because torture had become an integral part of the criminal justice system, commoners were reluctant to let crimes, even those of which they were the victims, come to the attention of the authorities.[8]

When public order was seriously threatened, the policing officials were reinforced by the much larger samurai guard units, which stood ready to curb disorders and apprehend those responsible for them. William Kelley has described the response of domain officials in the Shōnai plain to a peasant demonstration in 1844 protesting the transfer of jurisdiction over the area to a new daimyo:

> Domain officials responded by surrounding the town with several companies of soldiers, dressed in full battle gear and armed with bows, rifles, and other weapons . . . The troops were kept on the periphery of town during the day and night, and the next morning negotiations . . . resumed. They finally agreed to postpone the transfer pending fresh instructions from Edo, and on the condition that the barricades be dismantled, the troops were withdrawn to Tsuru-gaoka.[9]

Quite often the threat of force alone was enough to bring protests under control, as Kelley's example indicates. The high level of self-policing in the villages undoubtedly owed much to the knowledge of the forces that could be summoned in support of the existing order.

However, to call Tokugawa Japan a police state is to confound tight control with police organization. It quickly became apparent after the fall of the Shogunate that more formalized and systematic policing structures were necessary, especially in urban areas and in the open ports. The search for alternatives began early in the Meiji period.

THE SEARCH FOR ALTERNATIVES

Because specialized policing roles had not developed into differentiated policing structures, the fall of the Tokugawa administrative system meant the end of formal policing. This problem immediately confronted the new government in the areas over which it assumed direct control in 1868: that is, the former domains of the shogun and his supporters. These included the open ports, where the presence of the Westerners had added a new problem of social order, and one of particular importance to the new government in its efforts to establish its legitimacy with the foreign powers. Nationalistic samurai who bitterly resented the presence of foreigners in Japan continued to see attacks on Westerners as a means of provoking the open conflict that would expel the unwanted strangers. These men posed a recurring threat to public order, to Japan's relations with the Western powers, and to the central treasury, which had to pay large indemnities for every Westerner injured or slain. The attentions of these violent patriots were not restricted to Westerners. Their swords cut down several prominent members of the new government who were publicly identified as strong advocates of Western technology and institutions.[10] This violence no doubt provided an added incentive for government leaders to seek new and more effective structures of policing.

The search for such structures was channeled toward Western models by the demands of the foreigners themselves. An essential precondition for ending the extraterritoriality so offensive to the Japanese was the creation of judicial and police systems acceptable to Western residents in Japan, and that meant a Western-style police system. Western influence was decisive; indeed, the first specialized police structure based on a Western model was established in Yokohama, not in Tokyo, although the problems of preserving order were most acute in the capital. The exodus of the daimyo and their retainers when the Shogunate fell left many residences virtually untenanted and prey to looting. Many low-ranking samurai were left behind when their masters departed, and they roamed the streets of the capital, penniless and armed. These problems were compounded by the influx of samurai from the southwestern domains, elated by their recent victory in the civil war and apt to regard Edo as conquered territory. The search for effective policing mechanisms in Tokyo led to no fewer than four successive reorganizations in the first four years of the Meiji period. However, Western models were first used in Yokohama, where the substantial foreign community had a very definite idea of what constituted effective policing and would settle for nothing less.

Until 1868 the responsibility for policing the foreign settlement in Yokohama had rested with a composite troop of English, French, and Japanese nationals under an English commander. When policing jurisdiction reverted to the Japanese government in 1868, the new all-Japanese force naturally emulated the patterns that had become familiar to its members. English-style patrols, drills, ranks, functions, and armaments were employed. When the English consul complained that the force was not fully effective, the governor of the prefecture dispatched three subordinates to study the police systems in the foreign concessions in Hong Kong and Shanghai, which were also based on the English model, and reorganized the Yokohama force on the basis of their findings.[11] The Yokohama force in turn provided the model for another major treaty port, Kobe, and eventually had an influence on the first Western-style police in the national capital.

Until the abolition of the domains in 1871, Tokyo was patrolled by troops of samurai recruited from the various domains. They proved less than satisfactory: there were problems of coordination among the various domain troops, and problems of discipline among samurai who were more conscious of their social status and its traditional prerogatives than of their organizational role obligations. In December of 1871, therefore, Tokyo's first Western-style specialized police force, the *rasotsu*, was established.

The task of recruiting the members of the new force was entrusted to two men from Satsuma: Saigo Takamori, one of the heroes of the Meiji Restoration, and one of his proteges, Kawaji Toshiyoshi. Whether because the Satsuma leaders in the central government perceived the strategic importance of the police (as they had in the case of the new army in which Satsuma was so strongly represented), or because they were simply eager to find employment for some of the samurai who constituted so large and restive a proportion of their region's population, Satsuma men dominated the new force. Two thousand of the three thousand recruits to the *rasotsu* were Satsuma samurai; the rest were samurai from other domains.[12]

One of the first tasks of the new organization was to resocialize the samurai to make them more amenable to the demands of their new roles. In order to create a strong and pervasive organizational identity to replace the personal status of the samurai, the old prerogatives of the samurai and key elements of his life-style were prohibited. The men were not allowed to wear the ubiquitous badge of status, the sword, which at the time was still publicly worn by most samurai. Instead, men on duty carried only a wooden baton. They were forbidden to consume that staple of samurai conviviality, sake: alcohol was prohibited on and off duty except for the five major festival days of the year.[13] The men had to wear uniforms or Western dress at all times, even to the bath. Such strict regulation of private life was made possible by housing all officers and men, married and single alike, in barracks. Any breach of discipline was severely punished by fines, extra duty, detention, or dismissal.

Five months after it was first established, the force was expanded and reorganized. This time the patterns of the Yokohama police were grafted onto the *rasotsu* by the wholesale adoption of the Yokohama police regulations, including those for police patrols, drills, and ranks. The English model, via the treaty ports of China and Yokohama, thus exerted a direct influence on the early Tokyo police.

In the rest of the country there was enormous variation in policing structures. In the countryside, local self-policing continued for the most part to follow the patterns of the Tokugawa period. The prefectures and some of the towns hired some men to maintain order, and in 1869 the government issued a decree standardizing the titles of such policing officials within the territories directly administered by the center. In the rest of Japan, however, there was no uniformity in the numbers and the titles of the officials charged with enforcing regulations and preserving "public morality." In general, the Tokugawa pattern of a low density of policing officials seems to have prevailed: in the new Fukushima prefecture, for example, only seven *hobō* (constables) were appointed in 1869 for the entire prefecture.[14] In the early 1870s, however, with the creation of the Justice Ministry, the central government undertook to explore the possibilities for constructing a nationally standardized police force.

CHOOSING A MODEL

In 1872, less than a year after the establishment of the Tokyo *rasotsu* and only five months after his appointment as Japan's first minister of justice, Etō Shimpei sent eight young staff members to Europe to study legal systems, the courts, penal systems, and especially the police. The group visited France, Belgium, Germany, Russia, Austria, and Italy, and its report is seen as the foundation of Japan's modern police system. Jurisdiction over the police was removed from the Justice Ministry and given to a newly created Home Ministry; a clear formal distinction was made between the judicial and the administrative functions of the police, as in France; and a virtually autonomous police organization on the Paris model was established for Tokyo. The head of the new Tokyo force was a member of the mission and an officer of the *rasotsu,* Kawaji Toshiyoshi, whose role in producing the report and subsequently supervising the creation of the new Tokyo police system earned him the title of "the father of the Japanese police."[15]

On the surface this selection process appears to fit closely the "rational shopper" image, with its careful inspection of a wide range of alternatives and a report by the investigators that became the basis for a studied choice by top decision-makers. In fact, there are two clear indications that the model had been chosen before the Justice Ministry's mission had left Japan: the choice of an interpreter, and the group's itinerary. The only member of the party selected from outside the ministry was Numa Moriichi, a former Shogunate retainer who had worked with the shogun's French military advisers and therefore spoke some French, although it was far from fluent. And of its ten months in Europe, the group spent slightly more than four in Paris, with one month each in Brussels and Berlin. The visits to Austria, Holland, Italy, and Russia seem to have been little more than sightseeing. Most striking of all, England, which had provided the principal model for the police of the treaty ports, was omitted from the itinerary altogether.[16]

The primary purpose of the trip was therefore less a genuine investigation of alternatives than legitimation of a decision already made and a quest for information on the chosen model. The speed with which the report's recommendations were implemented reinforces this inference. The group returned to Japan in September of 1873. Only two months elapsed after the group's return before the Home Ministry was established, and little more than three months before the Tokyo police organization, the Keishi-cho, was set up. But if the French model was not selected primarily on the basis of the observations of the mission, on what basis was it chosen?

A major factor was the range of perceived alternatives. Western police systems in the nineteenth century are conventionally classified into two types: the continental and the Anglo Saxon. The continental type performed a wide range of administrative functions (such as recording population movements, supervising commercial establishments, and enforcing public health regulations) and engaged in wide-ranging political surveillance and control. It was also highly centralized under the national government; many of the police were members of a national police force (the *gendarmerie* in France, the *carabinieri* in Italy). Precisely these features made it a powerful negative model for the English. They developed the so-called Anglo-Saxon type of police, which performed a more limited range of functions and was at least ideally supposed to refrain from overt political involvement or surveillance. Local rather than national government supervision and control was the rule in the Anglo-Saxon model, except for the police of the national capital, which reported directly to the national government.

Japanese leaders in the Meiji period were less likely than their counterparts in Great Britain or the United States to regard the characteristics of the continental model with distaste. For leaders who identified one of the critical problems facing the new regime as the legacy of localism generated by centuries of feudalism, the centralization of the continental model had a powerful appeal. Indeed, it seems to have been the decisive factor in weaning Etō Shimpei from his initial preference for the English model.[17] The perceived urgency of creating a standardized and effective police force throughout Japan in order to end extraterritoriality also caused the government leaders to shy away from the Anglo-Saxon model's reliance on local initiative and local control. Moreover, the multifunctional nature of the continental model was very attractive to leaders in a society that was only beginning to construct a modern administrative system and where a standardized local government structure had not yet been formed even on paper. Finally, the role of the continental police in political surveillance and control made it far more appealing to the Japanese, in an era of widespread antigovernment activism, than did the more circumscribed Anglo-Saxon model.

The initial preference for the multifunctional continental system was reinforced in other ways. Although the Justice Ministry mission visited as many of the continental systems as it could, however briefly, the information available before the mission's departure was heavily biased toward the French model. Japanese historians have found the first published reference to Western police organizations in an 1868 travel journal written by Kurimoto Hōan, the Shogunate's envoy to Paris. He described the Paris police and praised highly both their usefulness and their public image (Kurimoto had lost his way one night in Paris, and a courteous policeman helped him to find his hotel). More systematic information was circulated in the following year, when one of the councillors in the central government asked Fukuzawa Yukichi, Japan's foremost expert on Western "civilization and enlightenment," to prepare a report on Western police systems. Ironically, the councillor who requested the report was Hirosawa Saneomi, who was prompted both by the demands of the foreigners for effective policing and by the threats of anti-government terrorism. He was assassinated by traditionalist samurai in 1871, before the modern police system he advocated was established. The document he commissioned from Fukuzawa traced the evolution of policing structures from Greek and Roman times (it reads rather like a translation of an extremely detailed encyclopedia article—which it may have been). Fukuzawa described in some detail the police systems of France, England, and the United States, the organizational structure of the Paris, London, and New York police forces, their uniforms, salaries, and the number of officers. He emphasized the relatively high quality of the French police and praised the high level of centralization under the French Ministry of the Interior.[18] The French model was thus seen as the principal representative of the continental model. It was also the most prestigious: the international reputation of the French police, especially the Paris police, was probably unequalled. The force was the oldest, the most effectively centralized, and the most effective at preventive policing.

The selection of a model was also influenced by the "contagion effect." France had already been selected as the model for the army, the primary school system, and the courts and the legal system. Police jurisdiction at the time of the mission rested with the same Justice Ministry that had selected France as the model for the legal system, and the ministry naturally tended to favor the same source for such a closely related organization as the police. Channels of information on French systems were already firmly in place. In 1872, for example, the ministry's adviser, Georges Bousquet, gave a series of lectures on the administration of the courts and the legal codes in which he included information on the judicial and administrative police.[19]

The preselection of the model explains in part the speed with which the new organization was set up. However, the proposals of the mission might well have taken longer to implement and been subjected to greater scrutiny had not political events following its return dramatically increased the scope of policing tasks and simultaneously weakened the existing police structures. The mission returned to Japan in September 1873. In the following months a major government crisis erupted, and among the men who resigned as a result were Saigo Takamori, the personal patron of Kawaji Toshiyoshi and cofounder with him of the Tokyo *rasotsu,* and Etō Shimpei, the minister who had dispatched Kawaji's group to Europe.

One might expect that these resignations would spell disaster for Kawaji's report, and indeed had the mission's task been to select a model for the police system, the report might well have followed its patrons into the political wilderness. However, since government leaders had already come to a general agreement on the choice of the model, the crisis instead increased the urgency of establishing effective police forces in the country as a whole, and in the capital city in particular. A substantial number of the Satsuma samurai who made up the bulk of the Tokyo police force followed their hero, Saigo, when he resigned from the government and returned to Satsuma, while disaffection undermined the loyalty of many who remained. This defection significantly reduced the capacity and reliability of the existing policing structure. Moreover, the fact that Saigo and Eto were now in active political opposition exacerbated problems of political control elsewhere in the country. In organizational terms, the political crisis of 1873 meant a sudden and dramatic increase in the demand for the "outputs" of the proposed police system.

Building the New System

When the Police Bureau was transferred from the Justice Ministry to the new Home Ministry in January 1874, principal jurisdiction over the police system went with it. The members of the Justice Ministry's investigative mission to Europe remained behind—with the single and notable exception of Kawaji Toshiyoshi, who became the first superintendent of the new Tokyo police. That the one man in the police system with first-hand experience of the French model was assigned to the Keishi-cho, rather than to the national Police Bureau, reflected the higher priority given to the development of the Tokyo police during the first years of the new system.

Throughout the 1870s the Keishi-cho commanded the lion's share not only of the information resources allocated to the police system, but also of the financial resources. With less than three percent of the country's population, Tokyo in the mid-1870s employed approximately one-quarter of Japan's policemen and absorbed over one-third of the central government's total police budget. The priority given to the Tokyo police continued the emphasis of the Justice Ministry on establishing the Tokyo force as a model and a source of personnel for the rest of the country.

The development of the prefectural police system, not unnaturally, was a slower process. The problems of developing a centralized and effective organization to police the one million inhabitants of the national capital were by no means inconsiderable. The task of developing such an organization for thirty-six million people in the rest of the country was even more formidable. Yet the choice of the French model entailed precisely that: the construction of a highly centralized and standardized police system penetrating the entire country, rather than the pattern of a loosely coordinated network of local police forces which prevailed in England, the United States, and to a certain extent in Germany. Little more than a beginning was made over the decade that followed the central government's assumption of jurisdiction over the entire country; it was not until 1881 that the structures necessary to enforce the jurisdiction of the Police Bureau and to fashion a genuinely national police system were consolidated.

THE KEISHI-CHO, 1874–1881
The information base for the new Tokyo police was primarily the work of Kawaji Toshiyoshi, who supplemented his own first-hand observation of the Paris Prefecture of Police with translations of documents such as police regulations and handbooks. The formal report he submitted to government officials on his return from France focused on two external rather than internal organizational features: financing, and the control structure (the jurisdiction over the police by other administrative agencies). These aspects of the

organization were highly formalized and readily accessible to inquiry. They were also the central concerns of the audience to whom the report was addressed: the government officials who would have the task of fitting the organization into the emerging state structures and mobilizing resources for it.

As in the Paris Prefecture of Police, the burden of the Keishi-cho's financial support fell largely on the central government. Japanese officials were apparently as ready as the French to believe that the policing of the national capital was a matter of national security and could not be entrusted to the vagaries of short-sighted, expense-conscious local administrators. The Keishi-cho (following the example not only of Paris but of all major European capitals) was therefore placed directly under the jurisdiction of the central government rather than the municipal government. Following the Paris pattern, the head of the Keishi-cho was made directly responsible to the head of the government (the *Dajō-daijin*) on matters of political policing and security.

The Keishi-cho also emulated the broad range of functions performed by the Paris police, including the enforcement of public health regulations; licensing and regulation of prostitutes; supervising a wide range of commercial activities such as pawnshops, second-hand shops, theaters, and inns; monitoring the sale of dangerous goods such as gunpowder, swords, and firearms; carrying out regular population counts; the surveillance of dangerous individuals; enforcing the laws regulating the newspapers; and watching over public morals, a broad mandate that included activities as diverse as arresting gamblers and marching men to the barber to enforce the prohibition of traditional hair-styles.

The Tokyo police also adopted the Paris police powers of administering fines and short terms of imprisonment to violators of police regulations covering a number of offenses, such as littering and public drunkenness and disorderly conduct. The slower development of the judicial system in Japan meant that the range of "police offenses" (those for which the police had the authority to administer punishment) was greater than in France, and there was no possibility of appeal to the courts until 1885.[20] Like its Paris counterpart, the Keishi-cho controlled the city's fire department and administered its jails. These tasks and more were formally assigned to the Keishi-cho during the first three years of its existence, often at Kawaji's recommendation. The prefectural government of Tokyo tended to baulk at the rapid extension of police jurisdiction, especially because the Tokyo police followed the Paris pattern of independence from local officials. In his frequent disputes with the prefecture, Kawaji often built his case to the home minister by invoking the Paris model as legitimation for his claims, usually with success.[21] When he lacked a Parisian precedent, as happened with his proposal for an internal passport system, he usually failed.

In the Paris model policing functions were not clearly differentiated from local administration. This lack of differentiation had been a feature of the Tokugawa period, and one of the effects of using the Paris model was to perpetuate and indeed legitimate a continued low level of differentiation. Nor were policing functions clearly differentiated from military functions, at least not in Kawaji's view. His report had made special mention of the military role of the European police:

> Although the normal duty of the police constable is to serve as the police of the judicial districts, unavoidably they must shoulder firearms and act as soldiers. Therefore weapons are kept ready in the Police Bureau in every country. Confronting all circumstances, the police must be ready to restore order through their power. To employ the army needlessly is a disgrace. Therefore in cases of uprisings and violence in the provinces the police must have the power to mobilize a number of men.[22]

Kawaji's conception of the police as the guardians of internal order and security, just as the army and navy were the guardians of external security, was articulated even more clearly in his first set of regulations for the Keishi-cho, as we shall see below. It reinforced the military aspect of police organization and the idealization of the police role in the polity, both of which were to become more prominent over the next three decades.

The Tokyo police organization that emerged in 1874 and was consolidated over the next seven years was therefore a powerful and virtually autonomous organization that, like its model, played a central role in the life of the national capital and had close ties to the central government. The description of the Paris system penned by one historian could apply equally well to the Keishi-cho: "The Prefect of Police ruled a centralized domain that in many respects was a microcosm of the national administrative system—a 'government within a government,' according to one Prefect of Police."[23]

The large administrative role of the Keishi-cho is explicable in part by the slow development of a modern bureaucratic system of municipal administration in Tokyo. In 1880, for example, when the Keishi-cho had a force of 4,400 men, the sum total of prefectural, city, and local officials in Tokyo was 912. It was not until the second decade of the twentieth century that the number of prefectural and municipal officials equaled the number of police. But the very extensiveness of the functions of the Paris model may well have justified, at least to national leaders, the slow pace of development of municipal and local administration in Tokyo.

The use of Paris as a model for the financing and control systems and the range of police functions is clear and documentable; its role as a model for the size of the Keishi-cho is only probable. When Kawaji visited the Paris Prefecture of Police, its force of *agents de police* stood at 6,800. It was probably this standard that enabled him to persuade the government to authorize initially a Keishi-cho force of 6,000. Tokyo prefecture, however, had a population of less than a million at the time, whereas the Department de la Seine had well over two million. A comparably sized police force therefore made Tokyo considerably more heavily policed.

One further aspect of the French model was described in Kawaji's report and emulated by the Keishi-cho: the functional differentiation between the judicial and the administrative police. The report distinguished between the two not in terms of what they did, which Kawaji may well have thought self-explanatory, but in terms of who had jurisdiction over them: the administrative police functions came under the control of the Home Ministry, mediated outside the capital by the prefectural governor (the Japanese equivalent of France's prefects); the judicial police functions were supervised by the Justice Ministry and subject to direction by the court prosecutors.

The appeal of this system is readily understandable in the context of the early Meiji competition among the emerging administrative structures. Kawaji was proposing to move the Police Bureau from the Justice Ministry (whose concerns with the police had been subordinated to the compilation of law codes and the setting up of the court system) to a new Home Ministry in which the police would be a more predominant concern and which would broaden the scope of the police well beyond the role designed for them by the justice officials. Adoption of the French model allowed the Justice Ministry to retain control over the police functions of greatest concern to it (and thereby undercut its opposition to the plan). But the center of police operations moved to the Home Ministry.

The political advantages were, however, accompanied by organizational disadvantages that emerged more clearly over time. Payne has indicated that there were problems within the French system itself: "On the surface, the nineteenth century French police seems complex and unwieldy . . . However, these divisions were sharper in theory than in practice."[24] Such practice, evolved over time to deal with the problems of the formal structures, is much more difficult to emulate than the articulated theory. And even in France, practice often failed to resolve the problems. "This mixed police system, full of overlapping jurisdictions and procedures which blurred many neat theoretical distinctions, nurtured countless occasions for administrative conflict. Built into the system, such conflict often smouldered and occasionally flared openly."[25] That an organizational structure so closely akin to the problematic matrix structure of to-day's large-scale corporations would be difficult to manage is hardly surprising. Why did the Japanese leaders adopt such a complex system? Were the political advantages of satisfying both the old and the new controllers of Japan's police system so great as to outweigh the problems? More likely, the four months of observation in Paris were not sufficient to enable Kawaji to see the problems that lay beyond the "neat theoretical distinctions" of which the French police administrators and legal experts were so proud.

That imperfect information had some impact on the early patterns of the Keishi-cho is hardly surprising. The wonder is that the impact was not greater. Kawaji was the only member of the Keishi-cho to have any first-hand experience of the Paris model. And the Keishi-cho stands out as one of the few new government organizations in the Meiji period to employ virtually no foreigners. The extent to which an organization used foreign advisers depended in large part on its leaders, and Kawaji did not appear to feel comfortable with foreigners. He had none of the experience in the treaty ports or in international negotiations that provided such figures as Itō Hirobumi, Mutsu Munemitsu, and Maejima Hisoka with experience in dealing with foreigners. The only foreign adviser employed by the Keishi-cho was a Frenchman, Gambetgrosse, a resident of Japan who must have recommended himself to Kawaji more for his ability to speak and read Japanese than for his professional expertise: his background was in law, not police practice.[26] His contribution was very likely more in translating and explicating written materials on the French police than in supplying advice. The Keishi-cho continuously monitored European systems, that of Paris in particular, through publications and regulations. An 1877 regulation formalized what was already routine practice: the Records Section was ordered to obtain and translate materials on the European police on a regular basis.[27]

This monitoring led to the further adoption of some Paris patterns, such as the assumption in 1876 of the responsibility for licensing brothels and enforcing regular examinations of prostitutes for venereal disease. But the most dramatic example of close emulation occurred in 1877, when the Keishi-cho took over the formal responsibility for policing the entire country. This move followed an identical measure taken by the French police three years previously. To cope with the inadequate policing systems outside the capital, the Paris prefect of police was entrusted with the direction of all the French police between June 1874 and February 1876.[28] The Tokyo police retained control over the national system for almost twice as long, but the institutional pattern was identical.

Important as it was, the Paris model was far from being the only influence on the emerging structures of the Tokyo police. The legacy of the past (including the *rasotsu*, whose personnel were absorbed into the new organization, and its immediate progenitor, the samurai guard units) and the demands of the rapidly changing environment of early Meiji combined to shape the organization into patterns that differed significantly from those of its model.

Kawaji's 1873 report noted that in France, indeed in Europe generally, police recruits were largely drawn from among men who had completed their military service, and suggested that in Japan a group with comparable discipline and physical and moral training was the samurai. Government leaders obviously agreed: when they authorized the recruitment of 2,000 additional men in 1874, they ordered that preference be given to samurai. In the early 1870s, when samurai were suffering from economic privation and status loss, the police provided an opportunity for honorable employment that was attractive because of its identification with the new government.

The new recruits were not to be Satsuma men, however; the government designated seventeen of Japan's prefectures as recruiting grounds, and assigned a quota of men to each.[29] Kagoshima (formerly Satsuma) was not one of them. This was an obvious attempt to weaken the Satsuma influence in the Tokyo police, which stemmed from the Keishi-cho's absorption of the Satsuma-dominated *rasotsu*. The influx of new recruits may have weakened the Satsuma grip, but it was certainly not broken: the strong Satsuma coloration that the Keishi-cho inherited from the *rasotsu* continued throughout the Meiji period and beyond. In the forty-one years between the founding of the Keishi-cho and 1915, the top position in the Tokyo police hierarchy was occupied by Satsuma men for all but six and a half years. As late as 1893, when the first Tokyo Imperial University graduates entered the force, they were warned by their friends that they were throwing away their careers: only Satsuma men, it was believed, could hope to rise in the Tokyo hierarchy.[30] With such a heavy Satsuma presence in top positions, it is hardly surprising that Satsuma men continued to be favored as recruits. Their predominance in the ranks led to a saying among Keishi-cho constables that in order to survive and prosper in the Tokyo police, one had to learn Satsuma dialect.[31] As late as 1931, distant Kagoshima prefecture (formerly Satsuma province) ranked after neighboring Ibaraki and Chiba as an area of origin of Tokyo policemen.[32]

The domain basis of recruitment to the police was uniquely Japanese; the pattern of systematic bias in recruiting was not. Most urban police forces of the nineteenth and early twentieth centuries recruited heavily from areas or groups outside the population in which they were to function. In Great Britain, for example, London bobbies were largely recruited from the agricultural counties;[33] in France and Germany the police of the national capitals chose men who had completed their term of military service.[34] The rationale given for such selective recruitment varied from society to society. The rural recruit in Britain was said to be healthier, more responsive to discipline, uncorrupted by the degradations of urban life. The former military man on the Continent was seen as disciplined, reliable, and able to command respect. In Japan the samurai in general, and the Satsuma man in particular, was portrayed as the heir to inheritor of the feudal traditions of loyalty, service to the public good, and self-discipline. What the English countryman, the European soldier, and the Satsuma samurai had in common was that they were outsiders to the social environment which they policed. They made better policemen because their outsider status minimized conflicting obligations and enhanced their commitment to the organization.

In Japan the shared origin of men in the low and high ranks strengthened the solidarity and the organizational identity of the Tokyo police. But it also linked the Keishi-cho with one of the two most powerful of the domain cliques that dominated the Meiji government. As the Meiji period unfolded those cliques became increasingly identified with repressive political policies and grew steadily more unpopular. The public image of the Keishi-cho suffered accordingly. Whatever the long-term liabilities of the Satsuma connection, however, it was probably of considerable benefit to the organization in its early years. In a time of keen competition among developing organizational systems, such informal ties linking an organization with the top men in the agencies charged with controlling it and allocating its resources could be of immeasurable advantage.

The Satsuma connection was not the only legacy that the Keishi-cho inherited from the *rasotsu*. The 1874 Keishi-cho regulations carried many of the *rasotsu*'s detailed prescriptions of roles into the new organization. Off-duty behavior was circumscribed almost as narrowly as on-duty requirements, and the total environment of the police barracks inherited from the *rasotsu* made it unlikely that violations of any of the regulations could be long concealed. Equally important in the system of control, and more long-lived, was the diffuse authority and the wide-ranging personal responsibility of the officers for the men under their command. The 1874 Keishi-cho regulations for officers clothed this in traditional Confucian terms: "The officer is parent and older brother; the subordinate is child and younger brother."[35]

As one might expect from the family analogy, officers were held personally responsible for the behavior of subordinates: the immediate superior, for example, was charged with keeping the men under his authority from getting into debt. Any officer directly responsible for misleading a subordinate or setting a bad example was summarily punished. One case from the early records of the Keishi-cho involved the head of one of Tokyo's sixteen major police stations, who was about to depart for his home town for a brief visit. In traditional fashion he marked the occasion by giving a party for his subordinates, complete with sake, geisha, and presumably song. However, the traditional entertainment violated the prohibition of alcohol and the company of women of the pleasure quarters. When the Keishi-cho headquarters heard about the affair, as it inevitably did, the chief was demoted by one full rank.[36] The diffuse obligations of authority were retained from pre-Meiji social structures, but strong negative sanctions were used to redirect those obligations to fit the demands of the new organization. The range of sanctions that backed up the regulations was largely modeled on the Paris pattern (dismissal, demotion, and fines). In actual practice there was a fourth: extra duty. Regulations allowed policemen who were fined for breaches of duty, such as reporting late or damaging their uniforms, to work off the fine in extra duty at a fixed rate. The strict regulation of off-duty life gradually relaxed. In 1879, the regulations of 1874 were modified considerably, the reason given being that young men now entering the force had no experience of the harsh regimen of the lower-ranking samurai, and too many were finding the policeman's lot too arduous to endure for long.

One more feature of the Keishi-cho can be traced to the samurai legacy: the emphasis on public education and improvement. As early as the first set of regulations in 1874, Kawaji proclaimed as one of the central functions of the police the guidance and enlightenment of the Japanese people in the as yet unfamiliar ways of civilization and enlightenment.[37] One way of doing this was through publications: the Keishi-cho put out books and pamphlets, often illustrated,

to educate the public in the new laws and regulations. The police
also assumed the responsibility for disseminating information about
public health regulations.

The less laudable aspects of the samurai legacy were also much
in evidence in Kawaji's early regulations; the text contains four
passages comparing Tokyo's citizenry to children and the police to
their parents—a relationship of unbounded authority as well as
benevolence. A mid-Meiji English-language textbook, entitled *The
Practical Use of Conversation for Police Authorities,* indicates clearly
the kind of deference and compliance the police expected from the
public. (It also suggests how hard it was to learn English from Meiji
texts.) Here is a model conversation between a constable and an
English sailor:

> "What countryman are you?"
> "I am a sailor belonged to the Golden Eagle, the English man-of-
> war."
> "Why do you strike this Jinrikisha-man?"
> "He told me impolitely."
> "What does he told you impolitely?"
> "He insulted me saing loudly 'the Sailor the Sailor' when I am passing
> here."
> "Do you striking him for that?"
> "Yes."
> "But do not strike him for it is forbided."
> "I strike him no more."[38]

Few English sailors would be as submissive as the model dialogue
suggests, although it captures the response deemed appropriate by
the Tokyo policeman. The arrogance of the police toward the citizens of Tokyo became legendary. A popular Meiji nickname for the
Tokyo policeman was *oi-kora*—"hey you," which was the usual way
the policeman stopped a passerby: in Satsuma dialect this was how
a status superior summoned a particularly lowly inferior.

The difference in the recruitment base of the Tokyo Keishi-cho
and the Paris Prefecture of Police was only one of the contrasting
influences on the two organizations. The physical environment was
another. Kawaji does not appear to have anticipated that the great
difference in the size of Tokyo and the French capital would require
adjustments in the control system and the patterns of spatial dis-

persion. The jurisdiction of the Paris police covered 185 square miles containing a population of nearly two and a half million. The prefecture of Tokyo covered 312 square miles and a population of one million. With the expansion of the Keishi-cho jurisdiction to include the seven Izu islands in 1881, and the addition of the Santama region to the west in 1893, the total area stretched to 822 square miles, a territory greater than that covered by the police of any major European capital (London's came closest, with 699 square miles).

Spatial dispersion—the number of organizational subunits and the pattern of their distribution—is a variable that significantly affects the nature of any organization's coordination and control systems, particularly the level of centralization and the nature of role specialization. It is of particular importance to police systems because it determines the visibility of the police (a crucial factor in their capacity for preventive policing), the speed of their response to problems, and their capacity to gather and disseminate information. Given the differences in area, the problem of how to distribute personnel and posts within the Keishi-cho's jurisdiction could not be solved by the simple transposition of Paris patterns.

Initially the Keishi-cho pattern of spatial dispersion was based on the Paris model. Paris in the early 1870s had two levels of police posts below the central headquarters: one district headquarters in each of the city's twenty *arrondissements,* each in turn supervising the activities of three stations. Two tiers of police posts were also initially set up in Tokyo, but the districts were inherited from the *rasotsu* and their configuration differed from that of Paris: six district headquarters were established, each supervising sixteen local stations. Although this gave Tokyo much the same number of base-level police posts as Paris, Tokyo had significantly fewer higher-level headquarters to assume the burden of supervision and control. Moreover, the physical layout of the two cities exacerbated the problems. Tokyo had been built as a castle town, and in accordance with the conventions of military strategy had been laid out to make rapid movement and direct access to the strategic centre of the city difficult. Streets followed indirect and winding lines, with frequent T-intersections to slow down any advancing enemy forces. The difficulties for rapid police deployment can be imagined.

Within three years, however, the Keishi-cho replaced the Paris-

modeled two-tier system with a three-tier hierarchy. The bottom
tier was the police box (*hashutsujo* or *kōban*), a small three-man post
which became the basic unit of Japanese urban policing and remains
so to this day. The police box was in effect a consolidation of the
beat system, a dominant feature of policing in Paris and other European cities. The best had originated with the London police, and
in 1854, when the Paris police reorganized, it took the London
system as the model.[39] Constables were assigned to fixed beats, which
they patrolled for extended assignments, often for several years, to
enable them to become familiar with a given area and its inhabitants.
The Japanese system also adopted the beat, but the police boxes
stationed auxiliary forces much closer to the patrolling officer, and
the police box itself became a neighborhood institution. In a city
where rapid movement was notoriously difficult, the system provided the public with better access to the police (and the police with
readier access to the public).

Moreover, the increased capacity for monitoring and directing
the activities of the base-level constable was important in securing
the standardization of role performance during the rapid expansion
of functions, regulations, and procedures that characterized the Keishi-
cho during its first decade. In the European and English systems,
the constable spent most of the day on his individual beat, subject
to sporadic checks by officers whose duty it was to monitor on-duty
performance.[40] In the Tokyo system, with its much greater dispersion of fixed posts, the base-level constable was rotated at regular
intervals among these positions: patrolling a beat, standing guard
outside the police box, working inside the post on record-keeping
and other paper work, and taking a relief period. The proportion
of the working day spent under the direct observation of one's peers
and immediate superiors was thus considerably greater in the Tokyo
context.

This pattern was potentially compatible with at least two different
strategies of role specialization. One was a high degree of specialization that would limit constables to routine tasks and summon
specialists from the district station as they were needed. The other
was a low degree of specialization that would have the constables
handling a wide variety of police tasks. In Paris, with its much lower
degree of spatial dispersion, the first strategy prevailed; in Tokyo,

the second. Although Tokyo adopted the formal distinction between the administrative and the judicial police, for example, this did not lead to the individual role specialization so marked in Paris, where the uniformed administrative police and the plainclothes investigative judicial police each had its own hierarchy, rank system, and reward structure.[41] Despite the administrative distinctions among the administrative police, the judicial police, the public health police, the public morals police, and so on, in actual fact for most of the Meiji period the same men performed most of these tasks, under the supervision of specialized administrative units in the Keishi-cho central headquarters.

Any organization with a large number of spatially separated subunits faces a problem of coordinating and controlling their activities. Communication is a key factor, and it depends on the available technologies of communication and the organizational patterns of information-processing. The Paris Prefecture of Police had taken shape well before the communications revolution of the nineteenth century. Perhaps for that reason it was relatively slow to utilize the first major new communications technology: the telegraph. Not until 1885 were all the Paris police stations linked to the headquarters by telegraph;[42] before then communications were carried by messengers. The limitations of this method were apparently not critical for an organization with low dispersion across a limited territory. The Keishi-cho, on the other hand, had both a high degree of spatial dispersion and a large jurisdiction. Moreover, it was established almost simultaneously with the introduction of the telegraph into Japan. Within three months of the Keishi-cho's inception in 1874, a telegraph link was constructed between the Home Ministry and headquarters, and within two years the headquarters was in turn linked by telegraph to each of the thirty-three stations in the next organizational tier (nearly a decade in advance of the Paris system).[43]

The pattern of communication made possible by the telegraph was one that reinforced the organizational hierarchy: that is, each station was linked to that immediately above it and to those immediately subordinate to it, but not laterally to other stations on the same level of authority. At the top of the hierarchy stood the Keishi-cho headquarters, located in the heart of Tokyo, a few streets away from the Imperial Palace. From the headquarters came the regulations and instructions governing functions and procedures, and to it flowed a regular stream of reports from the main police stations. In the classic terminology of organizational sociology, these stations, with the substations and police boxes below each, constituted the line of the organization; the administrative divisions of headquarters constituted the staff.

From its inception, the Keishi-cho's line structure differed from that of its model. In Paris two police officials reported directly to the prefect of police: the chief of the administrative police and the chief of the judicial police. In each of the ten police districts there was one commissaire for the administrative police, who reported to the first chief and one for the judicial police who reported to the second. The line was thus administered in two separate chains of command. In the Keishi-cho the line consisted not of two divisions of police personnel but of the police posts: a hierarchy of stations *(shō)*, substations *(bunshō)*, and police boxes. In the 1870s the line was directly supervised by the superintendent of the Keishi-cho himself, Kawaji Toshiyoshi. He met once a month with the chiefs of the police stations in each of the six large police districts (there were five or six stations in each) to hear reports by the chiefs on incidents in their jurisdictions, on police activities and individual police performance, and the general state of the populace within each jurisdiction; he also answered questions on procedure and dealt with requests for additional resources. In 1881 a separate bureau, the Junsa Honbu, was set up to take over the supervision of the stations and substations.

There was an even higher volume of communications between the stations and substations and the police boxes. Constables assigned to duty in the police boxes first reported each day to the station in their district, receiving in the process any new instructions.[44] Moreover, for his relief period during the day the constable returned to the station. This constant flow of personnel was coupled with a high volume of standardized written reports, compiled continuously in the police boxes. A Westerner traveling in Japan in 1878 observed somewhat querulously, "An enormous quantity of superfluous writing is done by all officialdom in Japan, and one usually sees policemen writing. What comes of it I don't know."[45] What came of it was a steady flow of information, monitoring the social environment of the police as well as the performance of police officials, information that was a critically important element of the coordination and control system.

The organization of the Keishi-cho staff departments also departed significantly from the Paris model. It resembled the original in having a number of function-based specialized administrative bureaus, responsible either directly or through a short chain of command to the centrally appointed head of the organization. However, the Keishi-cho did not directly emulate the specific functional divisions. The Paris system had evolved gradually since the late seventeenth century, and as new tasks emerged new functional divisions were added. Raymond Fosdick, the American specialist in police administration, described the Paris system in 1914, as "a series of branches, divisions, and sections centred irregularly about the office of the Prefect,"[46] a characterization that applied equally well to the organization in the 1870s.

The early organization of the Keishi-cho staff departments was more rational: that is, it had more neatly delineated functional divisions and a clearer hierarchy of command. The subsequent reorganizations of the Keishi-cho (and they were frequent) only accentuated the contrast. The difference is not only the inevitable contrast between an organization that had evolved over nearly two centuries and one newly created. The Keishi-cho was organized very much like a Meiji government ministry, and the inference that the government bureaucracy was the operative model for its internal organization is inescapable. The central government, as the provider of the Keishi-cho's financial resources and a major actor in its immediate organizational environment, was a more powerful and more accessible model for the structure of internal divisions than the Paris organization. If the theorists of bureaucracy are correct in ascribing increased efficiency and effectiveness to clear hierarchies of command and functionally differentiated offices, then this was clearly an advantage for the Tokyo police.

The most striking innovations in police organization instituted by the Keishi-cho were in the area of formal police training, where Japan actually moved ahead of the Western societies whose structures it was emulating in other respects. The first training school for police recruits in the West was established in Paris in 1883; in Britain, formal recruit training was not introduced until 1907. In Japan, the first police school was set up in Tokyo in 1880.

The training period in the Tokyo school (the Junsa Kyōshujo) was three months, during which entrants attended classes on law, police regulations, criminal investigation, report writing, drills, salutes, and martial arts. The first class numbered 350, of whom only 150 were new recruits. The other 200 were men already in the force who had indicated a desire to resign, and had been assigned to the school as a disciplinary measure.[47] The purpose of formal police training was twofold: not only to screen and train recruits but also to slow the extremely high rate of turnover by reinforcing organizational identity and commitment. How great an impact it had on turnover is difficult to judge from the surviving data. The school operated for only a year and a half; it was closed in 1881 when the Keishi-cho's budget was greatly reduced. The budget reduction itself was a factor in the school's closing, but equally important was the simultaneous reduction in the authorized manpower of the Tokyo force to a level considerably below its existing strength. The basic personnel problem of the organization changed overnight from a shortage of qualified policemen to a surplus. Under such conditions the school became an unnecessary luxury. Despite the brevity of its existence, however, its influence was considerable. Six other prefectures that still had problems recruiting and keeping competent men followed the Tokyo example and set up their own training schools.[48] Most important, in the mid-1880s the manpower problems of the police system as a whole prompted a return to the formal training school, this time on a nationwide, standardized basis.

The establishment of formal police training is a dramatic example of the strong influence a more powerful organization in the immediate environment can have on a newly emerging organization using a foreign (and therefore distant) model. The inspiration for the Tokyo police school came not from Paris but from the Japanese army. Kawaji's successor and the founder of the school, Oyama Iwao, was an army general who came to the post of superintendent from heading the army's training institute (the Shikan Gakkō). In nearly every society the military has been one of the formative influences on police organization. The military has been a natural— indeed the only—organizational model to which the creators of police organizations could look for ways of controlling and coordinating the activities of large numbers of armed men authorized to use force in the name of the government. The founders of most police organizations have been former army officers, who have brought with them the organizational model of the military: a hierarchical structure with a strong emphasis on the chain of command, adherence to detailed formal regulations, and discipline and obedience. The extent of the impact of the military model on a nation's police system depended on several factors, the most important being the power and prestige of the military in that society. In societies where the military's power and prestige were quite high—such as Germany, Italy, and to a slightly lesser degree France—the military influence was readily apparent in uniforms, in weaponry, in salutes and drills, and in the background of police personnel, most of whom were recruited after the completion of their military service. In societies where its prestige was comparatively low, such as England and the United States, outward signs of military influence were kept to a minimum.

The military self-image of the Keishi-cho was apparent from its inception. Kawaji began his first set of police regulations by drawing an analogy between the role of the army and navy as the guardians of Japan's external security and that of the police as guardians of internal security.[49] Moreover, in the first decade of its existence the Keishi-cho served as a military force in its own right: detachments of police were dispatched from the capital to help subdue the rebellions that flared in Japan throughout the 1870s. In 1876, for example, the Keishi-cho sent 60 men to help suppress the Akizuki rising in Kyushu, over 100 men to put down the Hagi samurai rebellion, and 20 men to Chiba to deal with peasant disturbances.[50] The most extensive operation of this kind was during the Satsuma Rebellion in 1877, when several thousand Tokyo policemen served side-by-side with army troops, and over seven hundred were killed in combat.[51] The military exploits of Kawaji and his police units became an important part of the traditions of the Keishi-cho. Just how important was revealed in 1894, when on the outbreak of the Sino-Japanese War the Keishi-cho petitioned the army command for authorization to send a detachment of police to fight in the front lines—a request the generals refused with indignation.[52]

The fact that Kawaji's three successors were army generals gave additional impetus to emulation of the military model. The appointment of army personnel to top administrative posts in the fledgling police organization, combined with the joint deployment of army and police forces during political unrest, made information on the military model more readily accessible than information on the Paris police. Punctilious salutes, military drills, and the importance of the uniform in the early Keishi-cho all testify to the importance of the military model. The prestige of the uniform is particularly telling. In North America, England, and France the upper ranks of police officials and administrators wore civilian dress; the uniform was confined to the lower ranks and therefore associated with low organizational status. The Keishi-cho, by contrast, was a uniformed organization from the constable right up to the superintendent; it was plainclothes work, so coveted in other systems, that had low prestige. So low was the status of the plainclothes detective that the *keiji junsa* (detective constables) were selected from the regular police without any formal examination, but they had to submit to one to qualify for return to the uniformed force.[53] Against the background of such overt emulation of military forms and traits, it is hardly surprising to find that the military exerted a profound influence in the police training and professionalization that were to increase in importance in the 1880s.

By the early 1880s the basic organizational features of the Keishi-cho had taken shape. Table 4 summarizes those features, identifying the principal elements taken from the Paris model and the major departures from that model. Not surprisingly, the principal sources of alternative patterns were organizations that supplied the Keishi-cho's resources: its personnel (the samurai bureaucracy, the *rasotsu*, and the army) and its finances (the central bureaucracy).

THE PREFECTURAL POLICE, 1874–1881

During the 1870s the influence of the Paris model on the Keishi-cho was much stronger than the impact of the French system of provincial policing on Japan's national system. The Japanese emulated only a part of the complex French system, but in doing so they laid the foundation for a national police that was considerably more powerful and more centralized than the French. Inadequate information was one reason for this partial emulation. If the Keishi-

Table 4. Principal organizational features
of the Keishi-cho

Emulated from Paris	Emulated from other organizations (source)	Innovations
Financing	Control of individual role performance *(rasotsu)*	Upper-level career patterns
Formal-regulatory structure		Spatial dispersion
	Orientation to public education (samurai)	Utilization of new communications technology
Political role of chief		
Functions	Vertical administrative unit differentiation (government bureaucracy)	
Size		
Formal role differentiation	Training and education (army)	
Specialization of administrative divisions	Informal recruitment criteria *(rasotsu)*	
	Weaponry (England via Yokohama)	

cho was handicapped by having only one man with first-hand experience of its model, the prefectural police system was in much worse straits: it had no one. Although the Police Bureau, which had formal jurisdiction over the police of the entire country, had been transferred to the Home Ministry, the members of the mission to Europe had remained in the Justice Ministry.

Even if all the members of the Justice Ministry's mission had in fact been transferred, it would not have been of much use to the fledgling provincial police. Although the mission's mandate had been the investigation of the national police system of each country visited, its members had concentrated their attention on the national capitals. Police officials of each host country were eager to direct their visitors' attention to the showpieces of the system (Paris, Brussels, Berlin, and Vienna). The Japanese were unlikely to resist this emphasis; given the Justice Ministry's decision to concentrate on the development of the Tokyo police, the national capital had the highest priority in the Japanese system as well.

In the early 1870s the government in virtually every country on the mission's itinerary was less than satisfied with the condition of its provincial police. The mixture of local policing officials and national forces and the layers of potentially conflicting jurisdiction over police performance posed problems of coordination and control even in France, where a higher degree of standardization had been achieved by 1873 than in the German or Austrian empires, with their many principalities and semiautonomous local forces.

In France, outside the national capital, there were at least three major categories of policing officials. In urban areas, the civilian police *(agents de police)* were the basic policing force. They were under the principal jurisdiction of the Ministry of the Interior and the direct supervision of the ministry's chief representative in the prefecture, the *préfet*. They also reported to the *maire* of the commune, subject to the general oversight of the *préfet*. In rural areas, the major policing agents were the *gendarmes;* Howard Payne, in his discussion of the French police system, calls the *gendarmerie* "the only really effective rural police."[54] The *gendarmes* were the military police, who were under the direct control of the Ministry of War but subject in their policing duties to the direction of the Ministry of the Interior, the *préfets,* and the *maires.* At the local level the *gendarmes* were reinforced by a number of rural police functionaries—the *gardes-champêtres* were the most numerous—who were appointed by the local municipal authorities and subject to their authority.

It was an extremely complex system, with a control structure that had evolved over more than a century to accommodate and direct a variety of policing agencies. It would undoubtedly have taken the Japanese observers considerably longer than their four months in France to comprehend the competing jurisdictions and duties. Kawaji's report presented a simplified picture of the system: he distinguished between the civilian *agents de police* and the military *gendarmerie* (he used a transliteration of the French terms) and clearly identified the rural policing role of the latter. But the existence of the local functionaries and the complexity of the control structure below the level of the *préfet* are topics he ignored in the official report, if indeed he had any information on them at all.

Even Kawaji's simplification of the system was not destined to serve as a model. Establishing the Japanese equivalent of the *gendarmerie* would be the responsibility of the army, not the Home Ministry, and in the early 1870s the army was too preoccupied with the consolidation of its own organization and the introduction of conscription to do more than discuss—and reject—the possibility of establishing a military police force to perform largely nonmilitary services for the civilian administration.

The Home Ministry, the Japanese equivalent of the French Ministry of the Interior, therefore assumed full responsibility for the development of the police system outside the national capital. It was a formidable task, and the ministry possessed nothing comparable to the organizational base which the Keishi-cho inherited from the *rasotsu* in Tokyo. Under the Justice Ministry, the Police Bureau had been allowed only limited financial resources. The ministry as a whole had been competing for budget allocations with the emerging army and navy, telegraph system, post, transport system, and administrative structures. Moreover, within the Justice Ministry itself financial support was needed not only for the police but also for the court system, the training of legal experts, and the employment of French legal advisers to help frame new legal codes, all of which were seen as crucial in the fight for treaty revision. And within the police system, most of the available resources were allocated to Tokyo. Insofar as prefectural policing was concerned, therefore, the bureau had to concentrate, of necessity, on standardizing terminology and titles—regulations which entailed no expenditure. Indeed, the effort devoted to this seems disproportionate: the offical term for "policeman" was changed five times between 1871 and 1874.[55] Although an elaborate national plan had been drawn up dividing the country into two tiers of police districts, with quotas for stations and manpower, actual organization-building had largely been confined to Tokyo and the treaty ports.

As a result, the Police Bureau in 1874 confronted a diverse array of policing structures. The treaty ports, particularly Yokohama and Kobe, had developed uniformed, disciplined, and fairly large police organizations on a modified English model, with a high level of autonomy.[56] Cities and towns in other areas had recruited their own local police, often from the ranks of former Edo period *yoriki* and *doshin*. Neither their uniforms nor their functions were standardized, and their policing activity was not infrequently a part-time occupation. The prefectural governments recruited full-time policemen with somewhat more standardized titles and functions, along the lines laid down by the Police Bureau of Justice Ministry days, but the variation in scale, distribution, and quality of manpower was considerable.

In developing the framework for ordering and standardizing these varied forces, the Home Ministry adopted from the French system at least part of the upper level of the control structure, that linking the civilian ministries of the center and the prefecture. Formal regulatory power over the police was vested in the Home Ministry, and the preparation of police regulations was the province of its Police Bureau. Direct supervisory control over police administration was entrusted to the prefectural governor (the Japanese counterpart of the French *préfet*). He was given the authority to make all police appointments in the prefecture and to direct police activities in accordance with the ministry's regulations. The French model also served to define the functions of the emerging police system, although it did so indirectly, by way of the Tokyo police. The Regulations for the Administrative Police, which the Home Ministry issued in 1875, were based on Kawaji's 1874 regulations for the Keishi-cho.

The Japanese police system did not, however, incorporate the various local forces that had emerged at the time of the Meiji Restoration into the national policing system, as France had done. One of the first actions of the Police Bureau when it moved to the Home Ministry in 1874 was to order the dismissal of the municipal police forces, on the grounds that they were of low quality and untrustworthy.[57] Two years later the bureau revealed the underlying principle behind this move in its formal declaration that henceforth policing activities were restricted to the officers recruited by the prefectural forces.[58] The elimination of local forces was undoubtedly more feasible in Japan, where their creation was quite recent, than in France. It was also easier because the police system was set up in

Japan *before* the formal structures of municipal administration were consolidated, and hence the local forces had no institutionalized defenders. It was not until 1878 that the governance structures of cities, towns, counties, and villages were established.

The Police Bureau in the Home Ministry retained its jurisdiction over the system for only three years. In January 1877 the bureau and the Keishi-cho were amalgamated, for the same reason the Paris prefect of police had given in 1874, when he assumed the formal direction of the police of all of France: the unstable political situation and the low standards of quality and performance among the provincial forces. The merger was to be the means for extending the more formalized policing system of the capital to the entire country.

The Police Bureau had labored under serious handicaps during its three years (1874–1877) at the helm of the prefectural police. It had a staff of only thirty men, the majority of whom had no direct police experience, even including the first bureau chief, whose background was in prefectural administration. Its task was to provide guidelines and regulations; however, it controlled neither police budgets nor the appointment of key personnel, which were in the hands of the prefectural governors. For enforcement of its early guidelines the Police Bureau therefore depended heavily on the prefectural administrations. This was a more solid basis than one might suppose. The Home Ministry, the real sponsor of police development, appointed the top prefectural officials. The powerful governors were not local notables who held office by virtue of a local power base, but appointees of the central government, usually from outside the region in which they served. Within the prefecture, officials were appointed either by the center or by the governor; many were brought into the prefecture by the governor and came from his domain. Consequently they did not perceive an organization like the police to be an alien intrusion into their territorial preserves. In their struggles to implement the "civilization and enlightenment" policies of the Meiji government during the first decade of the period, they met the most serious resistance from local groups: samurai fighting against the loss of their centuries-old privileges and peasants resisting the intrusions of the new land tax, schools, and conscription. The prefectural officials saw the police as potentially valuable auxiliaries and as the enforcement arm of the

new order, and indeed as an essential protection for themselves
against local violence. Between 1873 and 1876 the number of full-
time prefectural policemen in the country (outside Tokyo itself)
increased by over one-third, from 13,000 to over 17,500.

Clear evidence of the commitment of prefectural officials to improving the police emerged at a one-month-long conference of prefectural and local officials called in Tokyo in June of 1875. Several
of the resolutions presented to the government at the close of the
conference concerned the police. They called for the more rapid
establishment of police systems in the prefectures, a fixed division
of the financial responsibility for the police between the central and
the local treasuries, and clear standards for the recruitment and
deployment of police personnel.[59]

The Police Bureau responded quickly to these demands. Within
a few months it standardized police uniforms and set police ranks
and salaries on a nationally unified basis. Later in that same year the
bureau set out criteria for recruitment[60] and issued standards of
deployment according to population. It did not, however, change
the 1874 general standard for financing, which allocated half the
cost of maintaining the police to the central treasury, and half to
the prefectures. This standard for financing was a marked departure
from the French pattern; according to Philip Stead's study of the
nineteenth-century French police, "English writers have noted with
something like amazement how the central authority in France kept
control of local police forces without contributing very much to
their support."[61] Although other Meiji organizations did follow the
French model of central control and local financing—most notably
in primary education—the police system was deemed too important
to rely solely on the hard-pressed local treasuries.

Of all these regulations, the standardization of uniforms was the
most successful. The rules for deployment were largely disregarded
until well into the 1880s,[62] and the actual contributions from the
hard-pressed central treasury rarely met the target of 50 percent.
Despite its concern with the police system, the national government
in the late 1870s did not manage to cover its half of police expenditures. As a result, both the size and the caliber of most prefectural
forces remained below the Police Bureau standards.

The transfer of jurisdiction over the national police system to the

Keishi-cho in 1877 opened up a path for more effective nation-wide standardization. However, the four years of the unified police system saw few major advances in police development outside Tokyo. The political unrest of 1877 changed the short-run priorities of police officials from organizational standardization to rapid expansion of manpower: the total number of police in Japan went from 23,428 in 1876 to 37,890 in 1877. Most of the 1877 recruits were temporary additions to the force, used to suppress the Satsuma Rebellion and released at the end of the campaign (the number of police fell back to 24,413 in 1878). Moreover, the amalgamation of the Police Bureau and the Keishi-cho shifted the center's focus of activity back to the police of the national capital. With the physical transfer of the Police Bureau into the Keishi-cho headquarters, national police administration was physically detached from the Home Ministry at a time when that ministry was preoccupied with an enormous range of tasks. Its jurisdiction was at its most extended, covering public works, communications, the encouragement of industry and the management of model factories, agricultural improvements, and local government as well as the police. The Home Ministry had few resources to spare for making sure that the Keishi-cho maintained a national perspective. As a result, despite the opportunity provided by the unified structure, there was relatively little follow-up to the 1875 standardization moves.[63]

After the Satsuma Rebellion had been suppressed, the central government turned once again to the need for more effective centralization and standardization of the national police system. But the information resources of the system were apparently seen as inadequate for an effective reorganization. Kawaji's 1872–73 mission to Europe had paid little attention to the provincial police, to specialized areas of police activity, or to the relations between the police and local administration. These lacunae were becoming noticeable in the late 1870s. The rapidly developing institutions of Meiji society were creating a more complex environment for police organization. The system of local government instituted in 1878 had created a new set of institutions below the prefectural level, and some of their functions overlapped with the tasks of the administrative police. Moreover, with the decisive defeat of armed samurai resistance in the Satsuma Rebellion, antagonists of the regime turned to new forms of political opposition, especially political parties and societies, to demand wider political participation and the creation of an elected national assembly. Japan's government leaders therefore wanted to direct the police to new forms of political policing, not only within the capital but throughout the country.

The need for more effective policing was evident even in one of the core institutions of the Meiji state: the army. In August 1878, 260 men of the First Division of the Imperial Guards Artillery in Tokyo rebelled, killed their commander and weekly duty officers, shelled the office of the finance minister, and advanced on the imperial palace. The rebellion was quickly suppressed and the grievances contained (resentment over low pay and the monopolization of rewards and decorations for the Satsuma campaign by the higher-ranking officers), but it raised serious questions about the adequacy of the internal control structures of the military, and led army and government leaders to reconsider the establishment of a military police force.[64]

Deciding that further investigation of Western police systems was needed, the government in 1879 dispatched a second police mission to Europe, again led by Kawaji Toshiyoshi, who was now the head of Japan's entire police system. This second mission showed how much the police administration had matured in the years since Kawaji's first tour in 1872–73. Two interpreters traveled with Kawaji and the five ranking police officers who accompanied him. Four of those officers were assigned a specific area of inquiry: one the study of general police administration and the political police; another the military police and its relations with the civilian police; another the judicial police, and another jails and firefighting. The fifth served as general secretary and organizer for the group.[65] Kawaji himself became fatally ill on the journey and returned to Japan to die, but the younger members of the mission completed their research. They returned in 1880, and their reports formed the basis for major changes in Japan's police system. The following year, 1881, was one of the major turning points in the development of the Japanese police.

The events of 1881 gave a new urgency to the consolidation of an effective national police system. A major political crisis forced yet another leading figure of the Meiji government, Okuma Shigenobu, out of office and into active opposition; the minister of finance, Matsukata Masayoshi, instituted a severe deflationary policy that had far-reaching social and political as well as economic effects; and the government announced its commitment to adopt a constitution and hold elections for a national parliament by the end of the decade. In the minds of some government leaders, this last decision set a timetable for more than the drafting of a constitution. It was a spur to the consolidation of the structures of administration and control, before a popularly elected assembly emerged to claim a role in shaping them. One result of these events was an upsurge of political activity throughout the country, activity that most members of the government saw as a threat to the social order. They demanded aggressive control measures that could only be enforced by the police. Within the Home Ministry itself, the priority given to police development was enhanced by a more parochial stimulus: in 1881 many of the functions of that ministry were transferred to a new Agriculture and Commerce Ministry. This gave police administration a much higher profile within the less diversified Home Ministry.

The cornerstone of the consolidation of the national police system that took place in the 1880s was the creation in 1881 of a new position at the top of each prefectural police administration. The *keibu-chō* was the first prefectural police official to be appointed directly by the central government. The fact that his rank in the national civil service hierarchy was not only higher than that of any previous prefectural police official, but higher than that of most other prefectural bureau chiefs, raised considerably the prestige, influence, and of course the autonomy of the police organization. As head of the prefectural Police Central Headquarters (the Keisatsu Hombu, an upgrading of the former Keisatsu-bu), his duties were to enforce national police regulations and standards, to make appointments to major prefectural police posts, and to report directly to the home minister on matters of political policing.

Many of the *keibu-chō* of that decade were former officers of the Tokyo police. They provided a channel for the transfer of Keishicho patterns to the prefectural police, a role that was reinforced by the institution, in 1882, of annual conferences of the *keibu-chō* in Tokyo. At one stroke, therefore, the creation of this position strengthened the power of the Home Ministry over the prefectural police, provided the mechanism for enforcing standardization, raised the status of the prefectural police within the prefectural administrative hierarchy, and created a national police career ladder. The longest career ladder rose from Tokyo's Keishi-cho: of the six inspector-generals who began their government careers in the police after Kawaji in the Meiji period, one later became a cabinet minister (twice home minister), one became a prefectural governor, and three were elevated to the House of Peers. The opportunities for upward mobility attracted young men of great ability, ambition, and considerable education. The first two Imperial University graduates joined the Tokyo police in 1893, long before university graduates were entering Western police forces. The implications of the rise to power of men whose primary organizational socialization was in an organization so strongly control-oriented as the Japanese police are hard to document unequivocally, but they probably played a role in reinforcing the strong control orientation of the general administrative structures of Meiji Japan.

COMPLETING THE FRENCH-BASED SYSTEM: THE KEMPEITAI

The last element of the French police system to be emulated in Japan was the *gendarmerie,* and the relatively late establishment of the Kempeitai, as the Japanese force was called, meant that its place in the police system differed considerably from that of its model in France. The French *gendarmerie* was established in 1791, before a specialized police force had developed outside the major cities. It moved into that vacuum as the center extended its control over the countryside, and community leaders came to accept and even welcome it as an alternative to building their own police forces. In 1881 the gendarmes constituted 60 percent of the police in France (not including the local *gardes champêtres*).[66] In Japan the regional civilian police system was developed first, and although the establishment of the Kempeitai lagged only seven years behind it, the general police structure was by then in place throughout the country, covering all jurisdictions, rural as well as urban. By 1880 Japan had over 26,000 civilian policemen, whereas France had just under 14,000. Even after the establishment of the Kempeitai in 1881, the civilian police organization was sufficiently well entrenched that it dealt with inadequate policing in the countryside by expanding its own ranks rather than by calling on the Kempeitai. The Kempeitai therefore had to find a rather different niche in the national police system from that occupied by the French *gendarmes*.

The formal range of functions defined for the Kempeitai was taken from the French model, as was the formal control structure governing those functions. The Kempeitai was formally a part of the army and was to serve as a military police, in which role it was responsible to the army minister. It was also to perform general administrative police tasks as needed, in which capacity it was formally under the jurisdiction of the home minister. And it had judicial police powers, in the exercise of which it was subject to the direction of the justice minister. In fact, however, in Japan as in France, serving many masters resulted in greater autonomy than serving one. The Kempeitai had a high degree of autonomy from the civilian administrative structures; it reported to them but accepted only limited controls.

Despite the formal resemblance between the French *gendarmerie* and the Kempeitai, the difference in size between the two indicated a significant difference in their roles. In 1881, 20,533 officers and men of the *gendarmerie* were stationed within France itself, a country with a population of thirty-seven and a half million. The Kempeitai was set up in that year with a force of only 1,600; Japan's population at the time was thirty-six million. This was not simply a consequence of the newness of the force; it remained small throughout its first decade, and at its Meiji peak in 1897 it had just over 5,000 men in Japan proper. As Japan became an imperial power and followed the French example in using the military police to control its colonies, the Kempeitai became a much larger organization. With the acquisition of Taiwan in 1895 and the increasing Japanese presence in Korea, culminating in its annexation in 1910, the Kempeitai grew to well over 10,000 men. Most of them were stationed in Taiwan, Korea, and China, however; throughout the Meiji period there were rarely more than 2,000 in Japan itself.[67]

The small size of the Kempeitai in comparison to the *gendarmerie* does not indicate that it was restricted to serving as the policing arm of the military. The decree setting up the organization gave it the same broad-ranging mandate as that of its French counterpart:

the preservation of national peace and security. The initial force was recruited heavily from the civilian police. Twenty-four of its initial thirty-three officers were from its ranks rather than from the army, an indication that its role was seen at least in part as general policing.[68] In contrast to France, however, where the *gendarmes* exercised their mandate primarily outside the major urban centres, the Kempeitai was predominantly an urban force. The first 1,600 recruits were stationed in Tokyo; three years later another headquarters was established in Osaka. Over the next five years detachments were stationed in each of the six cities that were regional army headquarters, and in 1889 (presumably in preparation for the national elections scheduled for the following year) a detachment was sent to every prefectural capital.

From the time of its establishment the Kempeitai was heavily involved in regular police work; until the turn of the century well over half of the people it arrested were civilians rather than military personnel.[69] Although over half of the civilian arrests were made with at least the formal cooperation of the regular police, the Kempeitai also acted unilaterally. Its principal role was that of an auxiliary urban police force, with a special emphasis on political policing.

The establishment of the Kempeitai marked the high point of the emulation of the French model. The Japanese continued to monitor developments abroad: they translated European publications and regulations, sent police officials on visits to Europe (in 1884 and 1889), and employed German police instructors in the police academy. From 1881, however, the dominant trend changed from emulation of the French system to innovation that extended the capacity of the police beyond that of most of the European systems the Japanese were monitoring so closely.

Surpassing the Model: The Reforms of the Mid-1880s

In 1883 Yamagata Aritomo, the architect of the modern Japanese army, became home minister, a post he continued to occupy until 1890. Not only was Yamagata the longest-tenured home minister of the Meiji period; he also took the keenest interest in the development of the police system. As one of the most dedicated advocates of consolidating the state's administrative and control apparatus before the Diet elections of 1890, he saw the police as key agents of governmental control and social stabilization.

Despite the high priority Yamagata assigned to police development, the size of the police force increased slowly over the decade (see Figure 1). In 1880 Japan's total police force stood at 26,018;

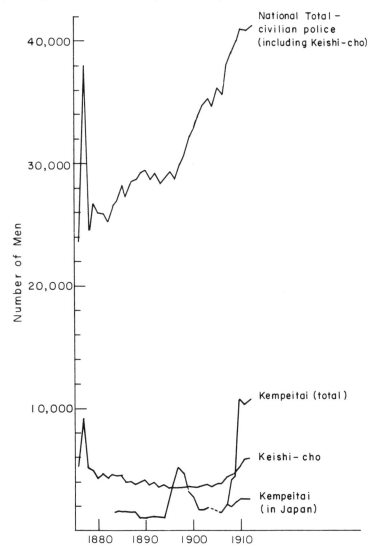

Figure 1. Total number of police personnel in Japan, 1876–1912.

by 1890 it was 29,338.[70] The real expansion of the force came in the following decades and built on the institutional foundations laid by the changes of the 1880s. The mechanisms developed under Yamagata's direction for increasing the standardization of the police system and for deepening its penetration into the society recast the organizational patterns of the police into the basic form they would assume until the end of the Pacific War, and to some extent beyond. These reforms not only departed from the French model that had so powerfully influenced the Japanese system, but in terms of police training and professionalization they anticipated later developments in Western police systems.

POLICE TRAINING

Despite the advances in the standardization of the prefectural police systems under the supervision of the *keibu-chō*, enormous variation still existed in the quality of police personnel and their expertise in police work. As the Japanese prepared in the mid-1800s for another attempt to revise the unequal treaties, the question of the quality of the police and its acceptability to the Western residents of Japan assumed considerable importance.

When Home Minister Yamagata turned his attention to the problem of the quality of police training, the Tokyo school of 1880–81 and its emulators in other prefectures provided an important precedent. They did not, however, provide a model. Nor did the Paris Prefecture of Police, although it had established its first police school in 1883. Yamagata, who throughout the 1870s had presided over the creation of the modern Japanese army, looked for guidance to the organization with which he was most familiar—the military. Following advanced European models, the Japanese army had from its inception relied on formal education and training to create a professional officer corps. The proposals Yamagata submitted to the Council of State in 1884 followed the two-tier model of the army closely: a national academy for officers on the model of the army's Shikan-Gakkō, and prefectural training institutes that would screen recruits and train them and provide retraining for experienced constables, on the model of the army's Kyōshidan.[71]

The national Police Officers Academy was established in Tokyo in 1885, the first institution of its kind in the world. It offered one course of study for officers and another for constables, and each prefecture was assigned a quota of entrants. According to the reminiscences of some of its students, the honor of being selected to attend the academy was keenly felt: being selected implied both a recognition of one's individual abilities and an obligation to transmit the content of the training back to one's fellow officers in the home prefecture.[72] During the twelve-month training period instruction was given in police laws and regulations, police practice, general law (civil and criminal), military-style drill, and—in anticipation of the treaty revisions—the English language. Most of the instructors were high-ranking officers of the Keishi-cho and the Police Bureau. However, the academy followed the army's example in bringing in German instructors: Heinrich Friedrich Wilhelm Hoehn and Emil Robert Kassausky from the Berlin police.

One reason for the choice of German rather than French instructors was the increasing strength of German political and legal models during the 1880s. Yamagata was particularly favorably disposed to German models, which he also used in the local government reforms later in the decade. Indeed, a recommendation of the appointment of a German with police experience to act as an instructor was part of his original proposals for the national police academy. Yamagata was not alone in his preference; the lack of progress in renegotiating the unequal treaties with Britain and France produced a general preference for German advisers throughout the government in the mid-1880s.

The motives behind the employment of the Germans are easier to trace than their exact influence on the Japanese police. The senior officer, Hoehn, undoubtedly became a key figure in the Japanese police, well beyond the confines of the academy. Two volumes of his lectures, covering many aspects of police practice and administration, were collected and published under the auspices of the Police Bureau and were widely used as texts and references in the prefectural police schools. He also served as an adviser to the Police Bureau, a job that sent him on inspection tours throughout the country to observe local police organization and make recommendations. During his four years in Japan he visited twenty-nine of the forty-six prefectures.[73]

The German influence had little impact on the formal structure of the Japanese police system, which was already largely in place by the mid-1880s. The area of Hoehn's own expertise was the more elusive field of police practice. A list of his lecture topics indicates that the most frequent single subject was daily police practice, which included report-writing, communications, duties at each level of the hierarchy, discipline, patrols, and so on. The administration of police stations was the next most frequent topic. The rest of the lectures dealt with specialized police functions: monitoring population movements and keeping population records; public health and sanitation; political policing; the policing of trade, construction, and traffic.[74]

Hoehn provided more detailed and systematic information than had ever been made widely available to the Japanese police; indeed, his instruction was probably more detailed than that collected by either of the police missions led by Kawaji. The contribution of the German model, as reflected in his lectures and probably in his conversations with police officials, was most significant in reinforcing trends that were already apparent in the Japanese police in two areas: a growing emphasis on political policing and the increasing strength of the military model.

In Bismarck's Germany the 1880s were years of political tension and a mounting emphasis on political policing. Hoehn's lectures reflected the German situation. They covered the surveillance of political factions, a summary of political policing practices in Berlin, and warnings against the dangers of the Socialist Party (an organization which had yet to make an appearance in Japan).[75] Hoehn also brought to Japan the military orientation and identification so prevalent in the Prussian police.[76] Like most German police officers he was a former army officer, and his attention to proper attire, deportment, properly crisp salutes, and hair length became legendary among Japanese police of the day.[77] Both in political policing and military deportment, the German model legitimated and reinforced existing tendencies rather than introducing new ones. The Japanese government had begun to look to Germany for mechanisms of political control quite early. For example, the regulations for public meetings of 1880, like Germany's, required the presence of a uniformed policeman at every political gathering. He had the power to stop the meeting if he deemed it prejudicial to public order. As for the influence of the military model on the Japanese police, it antedated Hoehn's arrival by nearly a decade.

The importance of the academy for the Japanese police therefore did not lie in the substitution of an explicitly German model of police organization for the French model, as some police historians have suggested.[78] Its significance was primarily as a channel of information and training through which police practice was standardized throughout Japan. By 1889 ten percent of the police inspectors *(keibu)* in the country were graduates of the academy. Through them its influence reached much further. Graduates were expected, on their return to their prefectures, to transmit their acquired knowledge to fellow officers, and the quota system insured that every prefecture would have a corps of trained graduates. Moreover, some of its graduates became instructors in the prefectural police training institutes, the next step in the institutionalization of formal training in the Japanese police system.

These training institutes were set up in accordance with a Home Ministry directive of 1886, which required the establishment of such an institute in each prefecture and laid out the criteria of admission, the course of study, the duration of training, and the qualifications of the instructors. All recruits, after meeting certain standards of height, health, personal and family background, and literacy, had to undergo from one to two months of training and pass a series of written examinations before they could enter the force. The course of study prescribed seven hours of instruction daily and included lectures on police regulations, criminal law and procedure, martial arts, and deportment. All instructors were to be graduates of the national academy. By 1887 an institute had been set up in every prefecture in Japan. They continued to operate under ministry guidelines, with several extensions of the length of training, until the Pacific War.

The national Police Officers Academy was not so long-lived. It closed down in 1889, after only four cohorts had been graduated. The official reason given for the closing was the shortage of funds, but perhaps more important was the fading of Japanese hopes for rapid revision of the unequal treaties and therefore of the prospect that the Japanese police would soon assume jurisdiction over foreigners within Japan. A national police officer training school was reestablished in 1897, after the treaties had at last been revised in 1894 and two years before the revisions were to come into effect.[79]

The role of police schools in standardizing police organization and operations was extremely important, but perhaps even more significant was that formal training was a major step toward the professionalization of the Japanese police, a process that was to advance rapidly in the coming decade.

SPATIAL DISPERSION

By 1885 just over 3,000 police posts were distributed around Japan, arranged in a descending hierarchy of stations *(shō)*, substations *(bunshō)*, and police boxes, which were an urban phenomenon. In rural areas police units were concentrated in stations and substations in large towns and transportation centers, from which regular patrols were dispatched and subunits sent out as they were needed to deal with specific problems. The standard for dispersion set by the Police Bureau was one post for every 30,000 households.[80]

During the mid-1880s police officials from the center undertook extensive inspection tours throughout Japan (the head of the Police Bureau, Kiyoura Keigo, and the German police instructor, Heinrich Hoehn, were especially influential and active). They unanimously criticized the negligible police presence in the rural areas and deplored the length of time police took to reach the scene of any incident outside the cities. The system of concentrating posts in the towns restricted the police to a reactive role in the countryside, rather than the preventive and administrative roles they were increasingly assuming in urban areas.

The Police Bureau therefore adopted in 1886 a radically different strategy, which not only greatly increased the number of police posts but also made police jurisdictions more congruent with the emerging units of local administration. The new system increased the number of police posts in the country as a whole from 3,068 in 1885 to 11,357 by 1890, a jump of 270 percent (Figure 2). The first step in the expansion was to establish a police station in each county *(gun)*. The second was to create a new type of base-level police post under the jurisdiction of the station: the one-man residential post (the *chūzaisho*). The question of where to locate these posts was largely resolved by the Home Ministry's plan for merging natural

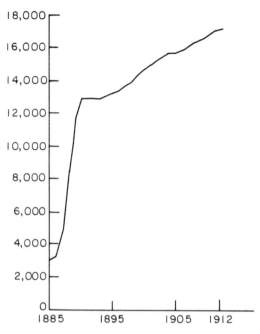

Figure 2. Total number of police posts in Japan, 1885–1912.

villages into larger administrative units; when put into effect between 1888 and 1890, it reduced the official number of villages in
Japan from 58,413 to 13,778. The administrative village centers
provided convenient locations for the new police posts; indeed, the
police became the chief administrative agents enforcing the amal-
gamations and settling the many disputes that arose in the process.

The reasons for devising the new system are easier to trace than
any sources for it. It had no direct counterpart in France or Germany,
where the dispersion patterns of the rural police more closely resembled the earlier Japanese system.[81] It may well have been a deliberate extension to the countryside of the dispersion pattern
developed in Tokyo in the late 1870s. Whatever its origins, the new
system had obvious advantages. Even remote rural areas now had
a policeman in relatively close proximity to the scene of any crime
or disturbance. Moreover, that policeman had developed first-hand
knowledge of the area and the people under his jurisdiction. Kiyoura
Keigo, the head of the Police Bureau who is credited with devising

the new system, aspired to a system in which "there would be no place into which the eyes of the police would not see, and no place where their ears would not hear."[82] A related advantage was that the greater contact with individual policemen lessened somewhat the popular fear of the police, a fear that had stemmed from the arbitrary exercise of policing power in the Edo period and the use of torture to obtain the confessions that were the only legally recognized grounds for conviction in the early Meiji criminal justice system.[83] (Indeed, torture was not prohibited until 1876.) Under the new dispersion system, the policeman became one of the village notables, along with the mayor and the schoolmaster;[84] he was regarded with respect and some awe as the direct representative of the state in the village.

The rapid change to the new system had high initial organizational costs. Many policemen, a great many of whom were urban-bred samurai who despised the countryside and peasants alike, left the force rather than take up a lonely residence in a rural post. Resignations were particularly numerous among constables with ten years or more of seniority.[85] This was the more serious because with the new dispersion policy there was a greater need for the services of these experienced men. But the resignations, however painful in the short run, may well have had long-run advantages for the system. The new replacements were graduates of the prefectural police training institutes, which had been established in the same year as the new system. The reforms of the 1880s meant that, with remarkable speed, the close relationships observed in the Keishi-cho among the patterns of spatial dispersion, the level of role specialization, and the development of formal training and professionalization also came to characterize the prefectural police.

POLICE PROFESSIONALIZATION

The growing professionalization of the police in the twentieth century is a theme of much of the literature on Western police systems. Many of the patterns that later emerged in European and North American police forces were anticipated in the Japanese police of the late nineteenth and early twentieth centuries. Had Western police organizations given to developments in Japan a fraction of the attention that their Japanese counterparts devoted to Western patterns, they might have gained valuable insights into the processes and possible consequences of police professionalization.

The concept of the profession refers to a type of occupation that demands specialized formal training, invokes ideals of public service, and envisages a concept of the professional role that extends well beyond the formal work setting. These ideals and self-images are reinforced through the activities of a professional association, which defines the ideology of the profession and helps to disseminate the developing body of specialized knowledge on which the profession is based. In the sociology of occupations, professionalization is widely seen as an occupational strategy to achieve the status, income, and autonomy of the prototypical professional such as the doctor or the lawyer.[86] Professionalization and the bureaucratization of large formal organizations have been widely regarded as antithetical.[87] Yet in the Japanese police, professionalization was an organizational rather than an occupational strategy. Officials at the top of the police hierarchy turned to a professionalization strategy in order to cope with organizational problems of restricted financial resources, high rates of turnover among personnel, and the maintenance of control over individual role performance in a system where the *average* police post numbered just over two men and the mode was one.[88]

The principal reason advanced for the tension between professionalization and bureaucracy in general is that employees who aspire to professional status seek more autonomy. Their rejection of bureaucratic controls is based on the claim that internalized controls produced by professional training and socialization will produce uniformly high standards of role performance. In formal organizations where a high level of individual autonomy is needed because of the nature of the tasks performed or because of spatial dispersion, the control exerted through a hierarchy of authority may not in fact be incompatible with the internalized controls of professionalization. The classic case of such "organizational professionalism," where professionalization is an organizational control strategy, is of course the modern military.

Modern military professionalization has developed in a close relationship with a highly bureaucratic organization. Military officers and men are trained both in obedience to a hierarchy of authority (the chain of command) and in the exercise of a considerable degree of autonomy, in a context in which these two seemingly contradictory demands are in fact compatible. In the combat situation to which military training is oriented, the high-ranking military commanders make strategic decisions at a considerable distance from the volatile situation of the front line. The lower-ranking officers in the field must, on the basis of trained professional judgment, assess their situation and transmit accurate information to serve as the basis for the strategic decisions. They must also decide how best to carry out their orders and transmit updated information on which to base reassessments of strategy. In this context the field officers and top commanders must share a professional expertise that is thoroughly ingrained in both.

The officer in charge of a police station and the individual policeman in his post are in situations organizationally analogous to the front lines—not perhaps in terms of physical danger, but in terms of physical distance from the organization's decision-making center, the complexity of the tasks, and the need for immediate responses to unpredictable events. All these factors make coordination and control highly problematic. One police historian has called this "one of the paramount issues of police administration."[89] The high level of spatial dispersion in the Japanese system exacerbated the problem because it made direct supervision of the base-level constable an unrealistic mode of control. The similarity between the control problems of the police and those of the army, coupled with the large number of military men in key positions at the top of the police hierarchy, made the army the natural model for professionalization and organizational control in the Japanese police.

The police faced two additional problems for which professionalization offered a solution: high turnover rates, and the low level of financial resources. Although hard data on turnover rates are spotty, the figures that are available clearly indicate that the smooth curves of the aggregate changes in the size of the police force conceal very high departure rates. In 1902 the national departure rate was 16 percent, and the combination of replacement recruits and the additional recruits necessary to keep ahead of population growth meant that 20 percent of the 1902 police force was composed of new members. Turnover rates were even higher in predominantly rural prefectures.[90] Whether these rates were high by international standards is not clear, since few Western police systems of the day published their turnover ratios, perhaps because comparable turn-over rates caused less concern in the West, where mobility into and out of jobs was a more established phenomenon.

Whatever their significance in comparative terms, the Japanese turnover rates caused great concern among police administrators.[91] Given the combination of very low salaries and the heavy demands of the job, especially in the one-man rural posts where the twenty-four-hour duty was unrelieved, the high turnover rates are far from surprising. At the turn of the century, the modal salary for constables was ten to eleven yen a month, at a time when government surveys put the expenditures of a three-person household headed by a rick-shaw-puller at thirteen yen a month, and those of a similar household headed by a foundry worker at seventeen yen a month.[92] The constable did enjoy some advantages over the day laborer: additional allowances for housing, uniforms, and shoes amounted to from one to four yen a month, depending on the region. The police also offered a career ladder, with increases of pay with increases of rank. Moreover, after 1882 a national pension scheme on the French model was introduced: constables with five years of service received a one-time severance payment, and those with ten years were eligible for a small pension.[93] Finally, once-yearly merit bonuses were allo-cated on the basis of an elaborate system of categories based on rank and merit. Evidently, for a large number of constables these addi-tional inducements were insufficient.

Reducing turnover by substantial increases in salaries and bonuses was a strategy that was forestalled by the reluctance of the national Diet and the prefectural assemblies to provide the substantial budget increases that would have been necessary. Elected officials resented the heavy involvement of the police in the repressive measures taken against the political parties in the 1880s and 1890s (discussed in more detail below) too strongly to cooperate in increasing alloca-tions of public money for the police. One strategy open to police administrators was to direct available financial resources to the lower ranks rather than to the more expensive upper ranks, and in fact an increasing proportion of the salary budget went to constables. How-ever, instead of using it to increase salaries, the Home Ministry used it to expand the number of constables in order to keep up with population increase and expanding urbanization.[94] In consequence, the ratio of constables to officers rose steadily between 1886 and 1909, further exacerbating the coordination and control problems, reducing the intensity of supervision, and demanding higher levels of voluntary compliance with performance standards from base-level personnel.[95]

From its inception the Japanese police exhibited at least one of the manifestations of professionalization. Strong public service ideals were clearly enunciated in the earliest Keishi-cho regulations, and they were subsequently incorporated into the regulations issued by the national Police Bureau. They sounded a theme that was to echo through the police literature of the Meiji period and beyond: the role of the police centered on the preservation of the nation and the protection of the people. To reinforce these ideals within the police and to the public, individual exemplars of the policeman's selfless commitment to public service were exalted as symbols of the police ethic, from Kawaji himself to a young constable from Aichi prefecture who died of cholera while enforcing public health regulations and aiding suffering victims during the epidemic of 1886. In Tokyo a special cemetery was established for policemen who died in the line of duty or whose dedication to the police earned them special recognition.

The principal mechanisms for inculcating the public service ethic were the police training schools. By the mid-1880s Japan could boast formal police training on a scale not approached in the West until well into the twentieth century. This fundamental aspect of professionalization was supplemented by others, less crucial but still significant. The annual conference as a mechanism for disseminating information was institutionalized in the early 1880s, with national conferences in Tokyo and lower-level conferences in each prefecture.

The high value placed on specialized knowledge and the developing sense of professional identity can be seen in the emergence of a professional literature. In the 1880s the Police Bureau collected and published the lectures given at the national academy. Kiyoura Keigo (the head of the Police Bureau from 1884 to 1891) compiled two volumes on police procedure and translated three books on the Prussian police, both of which enjoyed fairly wide circulation among police officers.⁹⁶ Perhaps even more significant were the journals which emerged in the 1890s: a one-hundred-page monthly from a major commercial press, and the long-lived *Keisatsu no Me* (The Eyes of the Police), founded in 1892. These journals carried news of police cases, features on police organization in Japan and in Europe, stories on the major figures of the police hierarchy, and features on police procedure and changes in regulations. The audience was not restricted to the police community, but subscribers were overwhelmingly policemen and former policemen.⁹⁷

The process of professionalization culminated in the formation of a national Police Association (Keisatsu Kyōkai). Japan's top police officials proposed it as early as 1894, but the Sino-Japanese War delayed its inception. It was formally established in 1900 by the inspector-general of the Keishi-cho, the head of the Police Bureau, and the home minister; its membership included all police officers and men down to the newest constable. The association's avowed aims were to encourage the advancement of knowledge and expertise in Japan's police system and to act as a welfare organization for its membership. The monthly dues levied on every policeman were used for lecture series, conferences, and martial arts tournaments; for a monthly magazine (the editor of which was hired from the commercial journal *Keisatsu no Me*); and for welfare payments to the families of men killed or injured in the line of duty.⁹⁸

The extent of the association's commitment both to professionalization and to the organization was most clearly demonstrated by its support for police officers' education. The second national officers' academy was closed on the outbreak of the Russo-Japanese War in 1904, and the national Diet adamantly refused to restore its funding when the war ended. Therefore the Police Association undertook to establish a national academy at its own expense. By raising its dues and charging a small subscription fee for its magazine, it raised the funds to open the third national Police Officers Academy in Tokyo in 1909.⁹⁹ It offered a six-month course for officers selected from each prefecture. The curriculum, the staff, and the regulations were the responsibility of the association officials—who were, of course, the country's top-ranking police officials. The association continued to bear the expense of the school until the national treasury finally assumed the obligation in 1918. To my knowledge maintaining a national education facility through the dues paid by the membership of a police association is without parallel outside Japan.

The consequences of professionalization are not easily assessed. Certainly Westerners were impressed with the caliber of the Japanese police force, although in a fashion typical of Western observers of Japanese organizational phenomena they ascribed its superiority to the samurai legacy rather than to the organizational mechanisms of socialization and training. Augusta Campbell Davidson, writing in 1904, provides a typical example: "Most policemen are, I believe, samurai; hence the position of 'the force' in Japan is different from what it is with us, as its members are understood to be gentlemen by birth."[100] By the early twentieth century, of course, few members of the force were of samurai origin. The Japanese police were, however, disciplined, reliable, and apparently, by the late nineteenth century, virtually incorruptible. These were precisely the benefits of professionalization that the police reformers of twentieth century Western societies envisioned.[101]

Although its success as a control strategy seems indisputable, police professionalization was not without its costs to the society, if not to the organization itself. The public service ideal was defined by the police, not by the public, and it was defined in collective rather than individual terms. The autobiography of one Japanese police official contains a revealing anecdote which dates from 1920 but which undoubtedly depicts a situation that prevailed one, two, and even three decades earlier. Two young constables, new graduates from the police training institute, reported for their first day of duty in a Tokyo police station. Their new chief gave them a short talk welcoming them to the ranks and enjoining them to dedicate themselves to work for the people of the ward. On leaving his office, one young constable turned to the other and said, "As a police officer of Japan, I am a central government official, and I intend to work hard to serve the nation. Isn't it strange that he should tell us to work hard for the people of Nihonbashi ward? There may well be a contradiction between the interests of the people of the ward and those of the nation."[102]

Insulation from the local political and social environment was undoubtedly one of the consequences desired by the architects of Japanese police professionalization. Faced with the possibility that one day the political parties might (as in most Western countries) control the Cabinet and therefore the appointments to the top administrative posts in the police and in the prefectural governments, the leaders of the Meiji government at the turn of the century were striving to maximize the professional autonomy of the civil service. The professionalization of the police served much the same function for the chief agents of political and social control, the police.

An unanticipated consequence of this insulation from the local environment, however, was the tendency for the police to overreact to challenges to their authority. Their professional training and their role as guardians of the state and the Emperor made them extremely conscious of their own dignity. In 1897, for example, in the course of a protest over the high price of rice in Nagano prefecture, a mob advanced on the local police station, in what was a traditional pattern of protest. In this case the police reacted strongly, charging the mob with drawn swords and inflicting several serious injuries. The police chief was forced to resign in consequence. This was by no means an isolated case. The most famous such incident was the Hibiya Park riot in the wake of the Portsmouth Treaty ending the Russo-Japanese War.[103] Police overreaction and violence were widely blamed for the transformation of a peaceful protest into six days of rioting that left over two thousand citizens and nearly five hundred policemen and firemen injured. The combination of a strong sense of professional authority, demanding work, and low pay led to a situation in which the police met challenges from the environment with something akin to rage.

SUMMARY

The development of the police system of the Meiji period was strongly influenced by two types of extra-organizational pressures. One was the ongoing effort at treaty reform, which required the Japanese government to convince the Western powers that its police and judicial systems were capable of providing Westerners in Japan with protection and justice on their own standards. In anticipation of each round of negotiations in the 1880s—1882, 1886, 1888—the police system was reorganized in order to enhance the level of standardization throughout the country and improve the quality of the force through training and education. The second source of external pressure came from the government's determination to maintain internal order in the face of threats to its dominance. Both forces pushed the police toward greater standardization, control, and penetration of society.

By the end of the Meiji period Japan's police system exhibited an evident kinship to the European police, especially to its French model. The dual structure of judicial and administrative policing; the *gendarmerie,* or military police, whose primary role was as an auxiliary civil police force; the wide range of functions; the mode of financing; and a powerful and centrally administered police organization for the national capital—all these features were derived from France. The speed with which the Japanese government was able to construct the national police system owes much to the fact that it had a "blueprint" in hand, in the form of the French system itself and of the French-modeled Tokyo police.

However, the Japanese system exhibited a number of notable departures from the French patterns and those of other European police systems. One was the absence of locally controlled, traditional police like the *gardes champêtres.* The Japanese national system was constructed before local forces—which were beginning to emerge in the early Meiji period—could be assembled and consolidated, and before local governments could develop a vested interest in maintaining an autonomous local force. The corollary of this was that the Japanese system had a much higher degree of standardization and centralization than its French counterpart. Even the role of the Kempeitai—the Japanese *gendarmerie*—was much more circumscribed in Japan, giving the centralized national civilian police the overwhelmingly dominant position in the policing system. The extent of the professionalization of the Japanese police was discussed at length above, and the details need not be repeated here, but it bears emphasizing. The nature and level of "organizational professionalism"—the attributes of professionalization being guided and shaped by the organizations in which the individuals work—made it a key control strategy in the Japanese police, as it was in the army in both Japan and the European countries from which it drew its military models.

By the late 1890s the Japanese police exhibited several features of "Japanese-style management," as that has come to be defined during the last two decades: the emphasis on generalists rather than specialists; a reliance on formal intra-organizational training to provide needed skills and to inculcate loyalty toward the organization and a strong personal sense of duty; the standardized, rational structure of bureaus and sections. Two important influences clearly shaped these patterns in the Japanese police: the samurai bureaucracy and the army. The army had much greater salience as an organizational model for the Japanese police than for the European police, although both systems shared a reverence for the outward trappings and the deportment of the military. It was to the army that the Japanese police owed the organizational mechanisms of professionalization as a control strategy.

Although the Japanese police system continued to monitor assiduously the developments in European police systems, the West showed virtually no interest in the very remarkable achievements of the Japanese in this area. The attention the Japanese police finally attracted was the very critical treatment of the 1930s, when the Japanese system was compared with the police states of continental fascism.[104] Western disinterest in "things Japanese" was not the only cause of this neglect. The Japanese themselves regarded the key departures from the Western model—police education, professionalization, dispersion—not as innovations that might be of interest to Western societies or as reasons for national pride, but as ways to compensate for the more backward conditions of Japan. This attitude is exemplified by the following comment from a leading Japanese police administrator in 1910:

> In 1881 an Imperial edict was issued to the effect that the constitutional form of government would be adopted in 1890, and it became necessary to improve the system of police education in such a way as to make it compare with the system of Western nations by providing all forms of instruction or training which were deemed indispensable for a constitutional country. With this in view, a police training school was established.[105]

One last factor hampered Japanese recognition of the scale of the organizational achievement of the police system: a widespread ambivalence (outside of the government) about the role of the police in society. The police had a major impact on the social environment of Meiji Japan, and many contemporaries felt that the effectiveness of the police system was a negative rather than a positive influence on social development.

Impact on the Social Environment

David Bayley, pointing out the difficulties of comparing the effectiveness of police systems in different societies, has suggested that "the simplest and most precise measure of capacity is numbers of police personnel."[106] By that standard the capacity of Japan's policing system by the end of the Meiji period was far from impressive. In Tokyo, which had by far the greatest density of police of any area in Japan, the ratio was considerably lower than that prevailing in the major European capitals (Table 5). Nor are countrywide comparisons in Japan's favor. Table 6 compares the national ratios of police to population in France and Japan in 1891 and 1911. Such a comparison is of course complicated by the fact that the French system included local policing agents, the traditional *gardes champêtres,* who had no counterpart in the more centralized Japanese system. But as Table 6 shows, even if one compares only the centrally supported forces in the two countries, Japan is considerably below the French level, and because of its much more rapid rate of population increase the "capacity" of the police by Bayley's measure appears to be declining over these two decades.

To judge the influence of the police on the social environment solely from these data would, however, be extremely misleading.

Table 5. Population to police ratio in major capitals, 1913

City	Population per policeman
Tokyo	525
London	352
Paris	336
Berlin	324
Rome	207

Source: European data from Fosdick, *European Police Systems,* p. 130; Tokyo data from *Nihon Teikoku Tōkei Nenkan* 1914.

Table 6. Population and police: France and Japan, 1891 and 1911

	1891		1911	
	France	Japan	France	Japan
Total population (000)	38,133	40,719	39,192	72,554
Number of police (centrally controlled only)	36,559	28,670	39,238	40,863
Number of police including local forces	73,029	—	70,435	—
Population to police ratio (centrally controlled only)	1,043	1,420	999	1,776
Population to police ratio including local forces	522	—	556	—

The high level of dispersion of the police meant that, as one long-time resident of Meiji Japan put it, "You cannot travel far in Japan, certainly not in a Japanese city, without coming across the ubiquitous policeman."[107] The impression of ubiquity was reinforced by the range of police tasks. Not only the petty criminal but also the average citizen had frequent encounters with the local constable. By the early twentieth century Japanese police were charged, among their many duties, with preventing minors from smoking, compiling house-to-house checks of population, and inspecting houses twice a year to ensure that spring and fall cleaning was being done adequately (this last from 1904 on). Although it is impossible to measure the frequency of contact between the police and the public, the police touched the lives of the average citizen in Japan at least as much as they did in European countries.

The police also provided a ladder of social mobility, particularly after the late 1880s shift to the dispersion system and the recruitment through formal examinations. The dispersion system caused a great exodus of samurai from the ranks and opened up opportunities for non-samurai to enter; the examinations removed the biases that had previously made recruitment dependent on the vagaries of the station chiefs. Ambitious young men could, with three years' experience and a certificate of diligence from their superior officer, sit for competitive examinations for admission to the higher ranks.[108]

A more complex issue is the effect of the police on the patterns of organizational development in Meiji Japan. The role of the Meiji police was varied and complex. They were at one and the same time agents of change and guardians of tradition; they facilitated the expansion of certain organizations and restricted the growth of others, such as political parties and newspapers. The ultimate evaluation of their impact on the society depends very much on the weight and value assigned to these apparently contradictory roles.

During the first two decades of the Meiji period, the police served as perhaps the most important agent enforcing the jurisdiction of the new regime against the violent protests and rebellions that challenged its policies for creating a new Japan. The Japanese historian Oikata Sumio sees the early role of the police as crucial not only because they subdued much of the actual disorder, but also because they provided an organization which could coopt many of the samurai into a state-supporting rather than a state-opposing role.[109] The police themselves were a force for social change. In their enforcement of public health regulations, their supervision of the standardization of weights and measures in retail trade, their jurisdiction over public morals, they acted to standardize certain aspects of social behavior throughout the country. In the spread of new communications technologies, the police system played a key role: in many areas, for example, the first telegraph line (and later, the first telephone line) was constructed to link the local police station with the prefectural headquarters. And their capacity for collecting and passing along information enhanced the control capacity of the state. This capacity had several aspects: the monitoring of population movements exemplified by the regular population counts; the supervision of commercial practices; the surveillance of suspect individuals (between 1887 and 1899 the police kept between 57,269 and 84,737 people under surveillance);[110] and their carefully cultivated role as a source of information for the public. As one example of this latter role, from 1884 on the Tokyo police sought to attract attention to the notice-boards outside each police post by putting out the daily weather report.[111] And in the Sino-Japanese and Russo-Japanese wars, they posted the latest news from the battlefield on the notice-boards.

The apparent contradiction between its role as an agent of social and technological change and its role as guardian of tradition was evident even in the police uniform. Although policemen wore a Western-style uniform, during the Meiji period they carried no firearms on regular duty.[112] At first they were armed with a wooden baton, but after 1882 they were given sabres—not the old samurai swords, but European-style weapons. However, the association with the old emblem of the samurai class was strong, and it was reinforced by efforts to coopt certain elements of the samurai code—or more accurately, of an idealized version of the samurai code—for purposes of organizational control, once the actual political threat from the samurai had passed. Traditionalism also found expression in the growing cultivation of the traditional Japanese martial arts from the 1880s. Another, and perhaps more important, aspect of this traditionalism was the codification of basically Confucian tenets about the social order in the principal documents of police education. Kawaji's 1874 code, in which he used the Confucian family metaphor for the state, for the relationship between the police and the citizenry, and for the relationships within the police organization between superior and subordinate, remained a classic, which policemen read and often memorized throughout the Meiji period.[113]

The police system's role as the government's agent for containing change, however, is the one that has attracted the greatest attention from social and political historians. The government's policies for building a modern Japan had many consequences that were neither anticipated nor welcomed by the leaders of the Meiji government, such as the increasing diversity of political opinion and the adoption of unofficial Western organizational models of political parties, party newspapers, and trade unions. From the beginning, the principal agency to which the authorities resorted in their efforts to isolate and repress undesired changes was the police force, and it is likely that having the use of a highly centralized, very effective control organization reinforced the control orientation of the Meiji government. From the early regulations forbidding the old-fashioned Japanese hairstyle to the violent repression of the socialist movement in late Meiji, the police were expected to act as a dam against the inflow of pernicious innovations even as they acted as a conduit for the desirable.

The aspect of the role that has remained the most visible to later generations was in the political sphere, in the use of the police to constrain the development of organized opposition to the government and its policies. The targets of such police activities varied over the period—the People's Rights Movement of the late 1870s and early 1880s, the political parties of the next decade, the labor movement and the socialists and anarchists from the beginning of the twentieth century—but the fundamental role and many of the strategies remained constant.

The political aspects of this role were the most visible and the most widely resented. The regulations for public meetings promulgated in 1880, for example, required organizers of all public meetings to obtain police permission at least two days in advance. If permission to hold the meeting was granted, uniformed policemen attended, usually stationing themselves on or near the platform so that they could enforce the prohibitions on attendance by women, students, teachers, civil servants, and members of the armed forces and terminate the proceedings if they were deemed injurious to public order. The police also kept political party leaders under surveillance and often harassed their followers. The use of the police to suppress unwelcome and unanticipated political developments is perhaps best illustrated by the nation's first two national Diet elections.

In the first election in 1890 the police played a neutral and, in the estimation of at least one Western historian, an invaluable role: "The police and the courts played a vital and salutary role in the management of the election. Faced with the welter of corruption, petty trickery, and minor violence that attended the campaign, one wonders what sort of stained monster the infant Japanese parliament would have been, but for the careful midwifery it received from the law and its guardians."[114] The success of the antigovernment parties in that election took officials by surprise, however, and the resulting conflict between the Cabinet and the Diet led the government to dissolve the assembly and call a second election for 1892. This time the police role was very different. The home minister and the prefectural governors directed the police to harass the opposition leaders, intimidate the voters, and break up political meetings to assure the election of progovernment candidates. In the resulting violence twenty-five people were killed and nearly four hundred injured.[115] The effort to influence the outcome was unsuccessful; its principal impact was to deepen the hostility of the Diet members to the police system. Until well into the twentieth century, Diet antagonism to any demands for increased police expenditures was a major constraint on the system's development.

The tactics of harassment, surveillance, and even violence met with more success against the labor movement, and Japanese police and government officials found legitimation and even models for such tactics in Germany, France, and even England.[116] The zeal of the police in their campaign against labor organizations was undoubtedly reinforced by the system of "contract police" devised by the Keishi-cho in 1874. The contract police originated with the *rasotsu:* an individual or an organization could, for a fee, obtain extra police protection for specific purposes, such as guarding a special shipment or keeping an eye on an empty house while its owners were away. The Keishi-cho's contract police system was more formal: it allowed individuals or organizations to petition to have a policeman stationed at an additional post. If the petition was approved by the Keishi-cho or the prefectural police officials the petitioner paid a set levy to cover the costs of maintaining the policeman. The constable himself was recruited and trained through the regular police channels and subject to all official regulations and to the regular chain of command. This system provided a way for the financially hard-pressed police to expand their manpower, but it had obvious costs to the public image of the police. The places most able and most likely to resort to the expense of the contract police were banks, and mines and factories with a restive labor force. Of the thirty-eight contract policemen in Hyogo prefecture in 1901, for example (out of a total force of 1,643), five were financed by Mitsubishi companies, four by foreign firms in Kobe, four by textile factories, two by mine-owners, and the rest by assorted manufacturing and financial firms.[117] Contract policemen were only a small fraction of the total force, and steps were taken to prevent those who paid for extra police services from having any direct influence over the individual constable. However, the public linkage between the police system and the wealthy, the property owners, and the employers was added to the very obvious links between the police and the power-holders of the political system, and very likely reinforced both the police role in suppressing the labor movement and public suspicion of the impartiality of the police system.

The police played the role of gatekeeper of change for the press as well. The early support of the Meiji leaders for a vigorous press quickly evaporated when individual newspapers showed more enthusiasm for political commentary than for enlightening the masses. Laws were promulgated to restrain the press as early as 1869. The responsibility for their enforcement passed from the Education Ministry to the Home Ministry in 1875, and was straightway confided to the police. A separate Publications Bureau in the Home Ministry took over the supervision of book publishing in 1876, while the police continued to monitor newspapers, periodicals, and pamphlets. Until 1900 the police had the power to prohibit the publication of material which they deemed prejudicial to public order, and to impose fines and prison sentences on the individuals responsible. After 1900 the power to prohibit publication passed to the courts, and the police were thereby relieved of a highly visible and much resented role, although they do not seem to have welcomed the change.[118]

To describe the police as agents of the government is not inaccurate: their tasks, resources, and powers were defined by the governmental structures outside the police system itself. Yet the passivity implied by such language is misleading. Police officials were closely involved in the decisions the government made about the role of the police. Hard data on Meiji government decision-making is not easily obtained, but there are indications of the centrality of police officials. For example, in the aftermath of the 1890 Diet election, Agriculture and Commerce Minister Mutsu Munemitsu proposed the formation of a special Cabinet Political Affairs Committee to plan Cabinet strategy for dealing with the political parties. He suggested that he be chairman of the committee (not surprisingly), and that the membership include key officials from the Home and Justice Ministries, the inspector-general of the Keishi-cho, and the chief and vice-chief of the Police Bureau. The Home Ministry rejected the proposal on the grounds that its own role was too small,[119] but the proposal itself indicates the importance of top-ranking police officials in planning political strategy. In addition, the career ladders of the police and the civilian administration in the Home Ministry were so closely linked that key members of the formal-regulatory structures of the police were not infrequently former members of the force. Personal networks of this sort enhanced police participation in decision-making.

How successful were the police in containing the unwanted aspects of the new industrial society emerging in Meiji Japan? Their success was greatest in the suppression of formal organizations and associations, both in politics and the labor movement. Police harassment made participation in such organizations costly and even dangerous, and forced their leaders to direct much of their time, energy, and resources into anticipating and circumventing police actions. The damping down of political party activity in the mid-1880s, the suppression of organized labor associations, and the virtual elimination of the socialists in the early twentieth century—these were the obvious successes of the police in its role as an "organization-constraining organization." Even when the organizations continued to exist, the police managed to inflict very high costs on them: suspicion of colleagues as potential police informers, the "paranoia" engendered by surveillance, and the careful planning necessary to avoid police action.

Not surprisingly, the police were less successful in controlling more spontaneous manifestations of class antagonism and political discontent. In 1909, for example, when the major trolley companies of Tokyo announced a fare increase, a mob of over two thousand marched through the streets, breaking trolley windows and smashing fare-boxes. One hundred and ten trolleys were damaged before the police could bring the violence under control.[120] Urban unrest and labor discontent, deprived of organized outlets, smouldered throughout the latter part of Meiji. The police could repress its manifestations, though sometimes with considerable difficulty—the army had to be called in to help suppress the Sado rice riots of 1890, the Portsmouth Treaty riots of 1905, the Ashio copper strike and labor unrest at the Besshi copper mine, both in 1907, and antigovernment riots in Tokyo in 1913.[121] The police could not, however, root out the underlying causes. The high level of centralization and professionalization of the police kept the organization itself largely isolated from many of the social and political changes of the Meiji period, but the social environment could not be controlled with the same degree of success as the internal organizational dynamics of the police system. The very insulation of the police—which preserved its internal controls—may well have slowed its own adaptation to the changing environment, with consequences that had high costs for Japanese social and organizational development.

3

The Postal System

The postal system has always seemed to be one of the more mundane and unchallenging state organizations. And yet the rapid, reliable, low-cost communications provided by the modern postal system and the telegraph were both a necessary condition of the nineteenth-century organizational revolution and an integral part of it. Both systems involved operations that had to be standardized across many scattered subunits and therefore required a high level of central coordination and control. Creating a network of post offices and telegraph offices throughout a country, instantly recognizable and providing identical services in every region, constituted an institution-building feat of no small importance.

The two systems—the post and the telegraph—were complementary rather than competitive. The telegraph was best suited to urgent, short messages; the post, which was both slower and cheaper, to detailed and less immediate communications. The telegraph used the radically new physical technology of electronic transmission, whereas the postal system was based on a more labor-intensive—and management-intensive—set of social technologies routinizing the collection, sorting, and delivery of written communications. The organization of the postal system proved to be more versatile than the one developed for telegraphy. Once its organizational network was in place, the postal system could be adapted to serve a number of additional functions, even forwarding messages for the telegraph system.

In the development of the modern postal system, Great Britain was the acknowledged leader. The key innovations of the modern post—postage stamps, a unified system of postal rates regardless of distance, the concept of the postal service as providing a necessary service and not just a mode of taxation—were developed by the

British General Post Office in the 1840s. It became a model that was quickly emulated by the United States and the other countries of Europe. The British also led the way in using the infrastructure of the post to offer a range of additional services (money orders beginning in 1792, postal savings in 1861, and life insurance in 1864), and to collect various license fees as an agent of the Inland Revenue (dog licenses, gun licenses, brewers' licenses, and so on, from 1869). It is hardly surprising that when the Japanese turned to the task of building a national postal system, the British post office provided the model.

Conditions in Japan at the time of the introduction of the modern postal system in 1870, however, differed dramatically from those prevailing in Great Britain in 1840, when Sir Rowland Hill's reforms established the basic format of the modern post. The new system in Britain reformed an existing government-operated postal system that was already handling over eighty million pieces of mail annually[1] and making a profit of well over one million pounds. Moreover, the demand base was strong and growing: in 1840, Great Britain had the world's most highly urbanized population (48 percent urban), and a highly diversified economy with only 22 percent of the labor force still in primary industry.[2] Finally, the supporting infrastructure of transportation was solidly in place—the roads, ships, and railways—and so were the private transport companies to whom the post office subcontracted the long-distance movement of mail. Of these, the railways were critical for providing the cheap, rapid delivery of a large volume of mail on the heavily used inter-city routes.[3]

By contrast, when Japan introduced the Western-style post in 1870, its population was still over 80 percent rural and engaged in primary industry. Even more important, the country had no railway lines to provide cheap bulk transport. It took two decades after the introduction of a Western-style postal system for Japan to build as many kilometers of railway line as Britain had possessed in 1840 (over 2,000 kilometers). Moreover, Japan's physical terrain—with its many islands, mountains, and unpredictable rivers—posed formidable transport problems undreamed of by the British General Post Office.

Nevertheless the development of the Japanese postal service was extremely rapid. Although it was many years before it approached the British post office in the volume of mail handled,[4] within its first decade it had established a national network of offices and delivery routes that offered much the same extensive array of services as its British model, including money orders and postal savings. In 1877 Japan was accepted into the Universal Postal Union, the international organization that regulated the transmission of mail among sovereign states. By 1880 Westerners in Japan had sufficient confidence in the new service to close the last of their own postal agencies and entrust the delivery of their mail entirely to the Japanese post offices. By the end of the Meiji period, the Japanese postal service ranked with the best in the world, and to Western observers it bore a laudable resemblance to its widely admired model. A 1912 review of foreign postal systems written by a retired British postal official commented: "The Japanese Post Office is, as may be imagined, splendidly organized . . . She is always eager to adopt the newest ways of transacting business."[5]

In reaching this level of development, the Japanese postal system found the British model an invaluable guide, but not one that was—or indeed could be—followed slavishly. In the early years postal officials took an extremely active role in experimenting with alternative modes of transport, including the traditional runners and the more modern rickshaw; vigorously encouraging the development of private transport companies; and cultivating a popular demand for postal services. The focus of their efforts in the middle and later years of the period shifted to adjusting the system to an increasingly complex political and social environment. The task was complicated by the fact that while the social technologies of the British postal service could be emulated fairly closely, the higher-level administrative structures into which they had to fit, as part of the state apparatus, were not modeled on the British system. The processes by which the postal service was introduced and by which it adapted to the rapidly changing Meiji environment, the patterns in which the British model was followed, modified, or even abandoned altogether, and the impact of the postal service on its social environment are the basic themes of this chapter.

There is an interesting contemporary twist to the story of the development of the Japanese postal service. Despite the undeniable achievements of the Meiji post, no one in that era would have suspected that nearly a century after the British post office provided the model for Japan, the currents of organizational emulation would be reversed. Yet in 1976 a British committee visited Japan to examine the structure and the technology of the Ministry of Posts and Tele-communications, and on their return recommended the division of the British post office into two systems on the Japanese model. The legislation that effected this separation in Britain provided a re-markable case of reciprocity in the long-term pattern of organiza-tional emulation.[6]

Historical Background

THE TOKUGAWA POST

Just as the royal posts were the earliest systems for sending written communication in Western Europe, so in Japan the requirements of the polity led to the creation of a network of official posts at the beginning of the seventeenth century. The territories directly ad-ministered by the Shogunate included not only the extensive heart-land of Japan, encompassing the three great cities of Tokyo, Osaka, and Kyoto, but also diverse holdings scattered from the port of Nagasaki in the south to the rich mines of northern Japan. The *sankin-kōtai* system, by which the daimyo spent alternate years in Edo away from their domains, also required regular communications to maintain administrative control in the domains.

The development of transport and communications in Japan was far from easy. Great as is the country's beauty—with steep moun-tains plunging in places almost directly into the sea, and its rapid and unpredictable rivers—Japan's geography placed serious con-straints on land transport. The climate, with its annual rainy season, added to the difficulties. The steepness of the roads, their vulnera-bility to erosion, and the frequent flooding at fords and bridges made large wheeled vehicles impracticable. Fortunately, the prox-imity of most of Japan's castle towns and urban centres to the sea made water transport a practical alternative for the shipping of bulk commodities such as rice. The coast-hugging ships of the day, how-ever, were built for volume, not speed. Horses and humans were faster if the load was relatively light, and they were the carriers on which the communications system of the period rested.

The system the Tokugawa Shogunate devised in the early 1600s and formalized over the next four decades became the basic infrastructure for the remainder of the Edo period. Five great roads were built radiating out from Edo, covering the central area of Japan where the shogun's territories were concentrated. At frequent intervals along these roads the Shogunate ordered the establishment of post stations to provide those using the roads with food, shelter, and most important, relays of horses and men. Fixed levies of men and horses were assigned to the villages in the vicinity of the stations as part of their tax burden. For example, on the Tokaido, the heavily traveled road between Edo and Kyoto, villages had to maintain one hundred men and one hundred horses for use on the road. The post station officials who had to enforce the levies and coordinate the system at the local level were local notables, usually major landowners or tradesmen engaged in maintaining the inn. In one of the Tokaido post stations, for example, by 1803 the designated functionaries (*yakunin*) included three officials of the local guilds (*tonya-yaku*), two village officials, two clerks, two hostlers, two men in charge of the human transport workers, two minor officials, and six runners.[7]

People traveling on official Shogunate business had first claim on the facilities of the post stations, and either used them free of charge or paid a very small set fee, depending on the official's status. Other travelers or shippers were allowed to use the services and the carriers of the post stations, but had to pay fixed charges set by the Shogunate. As the road system of the country expanded, the rest of the domains adopted a similar pattern of post stations maintained by corvée labor. The resulting network of roads and post towns provided the basic framework for land transport and long-distance communication.

Transport and communications systems grew more complex as the volume of traffic increased. Although the two were closely related and employed the same basic infrastructure of the post towns, the movement of goods became increasingly differentiated from the movement of written communications in its labor force. Written communications could travel at much greater speeds than bulkier goods or even than the average traveler. Runners, working in pairs in case of accident, carried letters and documents in relays from one post station to the next. Official Shogunate communications moved by day and night shifts and covered the more than three hundred miles between Edo and Kyoto in sixty hours. Even in relays such speed was physically demanding, and from the beginning required a specialized labor force. Local taxes supported the six to twelve runners maintained at each station.[8]

The Tokugawa peace brought not only a need for a communications system to promote political integration, but also a demand for commercial communications, especially among the three major urban centers of Edo, Osaka, and Kyoto. Large merchant houses with branches in Osaka or Kyoto, and traders buying or selling commodities outside their physical base of operations, needed a rapid and reliable means of communication and were prepared to pay for it. The predictable result was the emergence of privately operated messengers' services. These varied from very small-scale operations which carried messages within one city (often developing an exclusive relationship with a single merchant house) to large-scale enterprises that operated messengers' services among the three cities and maintained branches in the major post towns. An official tally from 1777 in Kyoto, for example, listed ninety-one establishments specializing in transmitting written communications.[9]

Some of the larger enterprises established their own branch offices to manage their relays along the most heavily traveled roads, but most subcontracted that part of the business to local operators who ran the services in the post towns. As the commercialization of the economy widened, these local entrepreneurs grew in number and in the scope of their own subcontracting operations, developing in some areas extensive regional services that began to rival those of the large urban establishments.[10] The commercial carriers came to handle a considerable volume of correspondence, and dispatches of relays grew more regular. Even the Shogunate and the daimyo came to entrust much of the expanding volume of routine official correspondence to designated commercial operators. Such subcontracting was easier and cheaper than the frequent dispatch of special official carriers.

The communications system of the Tokugawa period was therefore fairly extensive, although its expense limited it to commercial and administrative rather than private use. Hiroshige's famous woodblock prints of the post stations on the Tokaido, Japan's busiest road, have preserved for us a vivid picture of the bustling life of the Tokugawa period post towns, with their inns, the long lines of the daimyo processions, the heavily laden post horses. The scenes have the appeal of the exotic, and the near-naked runners with their letter-boxes suspended on long poles over their shoulders seem far removed from the uniformed postmen who populate the prints of the early Meiji period. But important continuities linked the traditional system of communication with the early establishment of the modern post. The Tokugawa legacy included not only the basic network of roads, but also an organizational infrastructure that could be adapted to the introduction of the modern post in Japan, as a rather different traditional system had been used in England several decades earlier.

CHOOSING THE MODEL

It is hardly surprising that the Tokugawa communications system struck Western observers of the 1860s as a "very primitive post."[11] In fact, however, two of the characteristics which drew Western scorn—the absence of direct central government management and the local corvee—made a transfer to the Meiji government extremely easy. The operations were largely untouched by the fall of the Shogunate, and passed easily under the jurisdiction of the new government. The new Meiji administration established an office to take over the tasks of regulating the post stations and enforcing local maintenance of post facilities. Its function was very much like that of the Shogunate's Magistrate of Roads (*dōchū bugyō*), and its principal innovation was in changing the names and titles of the post stations and their officials.

No urgent demands for change developed on the domestic scene. The existing system filled the requirements of the central government and of the commercial community. The internal drive for innovation in communications centered instead on the introduction of the telegraph, which promised a radically new and rapid mode of communication. The strongest pressure for the development of a new postal system in the first three or four years of Meiji came not from any collapse of the existing system, or a sudden increase in the demands placed on the system, but from the foreign community.

Among the institutions the Westerners brought to the treaty ports was the post office. In 1860 the British established postal agencies in Nagasaki and Yokohama; these handled all international mail until five years later, when the French and the Americans each opened a post office for mail to and from their respective countries. Each agency used the stamps of the country operating it, and together they met the needs of the Western community for international correspondence. By the late 1860s, however, as more foreigners moved beyond the boundaries of the ports and as the interactions between Western and Japanese businesses and individuals increased, Western residents started to complain about the absence of a postal service to deliver mail outside the ports.[12]

Given the Japanese sensitivity to Western criticism and to the exercise of foreign sovereignty on Japanese soil, the establishment of a modern postal system was probably inevitable in the long run. Moreover, the pending revision of Japan's tax system would shortly have removed the corvee basis of the post stations. Most government officials, however, had more urgent concerns, and showed little interest in changing the structure of the posts before circumstances forced change on them. The early development of a Western-style post was precipitated largely by the energies and conviction of one young man in the Tax Bureau. As a result of his efforts, a government-operated postal system was one of the earliest modern institutions to which the new Meiji government made a formal commitment.

Maejima Hisoka, the "father of the Japanese post,"[13] did not come from one of the four domains that dominated the early Meiji government. He was a samurai from Takata domain in what is now Niigata prefecture, and a former office-holder in the Shogunate. Perhaps this outsider status intensified his eagerness to promote the new postal system, in order to win a secure place for himself in the new administration.

Maejima was eighteen when Perry arrived in Japan in 1853, and like many young Japanese he had responded to the challenge by turning to Western studies. He had a base on which to build: at the age of twelve, even before Perry's arrival, he had been sent briefly to Edo to study "Dutch medicine." During the mid-1850s he pursued studies in Western military techniques in Edo and in maritime navigation, mathematics, and English in Nagasaki. His extensive

knowledge of things Western won him an official position with the
Shogunate in the mid-1860s, first as a teacher and then as an administrative official.[14] When the shogun resigned, Maejima was among
the officials who followed him to his much reduced domain in
Shizuoka. As Maejima later related, he considered a career in private
business, but he could not accept the idea of using his talents for
his own gain rather than the nation's.[15] In Shizuoka he found a
position under Shibusawa Eiichi, who was to become a leading
figure in the early Meiji government and later one of the great
entrepreneurs of the period. This connection subsequently served
him well. When Shibusawa was invited to join the Finance Ministry
of the new central government, he soon obtained a position in the
tax office for his promising young subordinate. After a year Maejima
was promoted to head the ministry's Bureau of Posts.

Maejima had a keen interest in communications even before his
appointment. He had probably traveled more extensively within
Japan than any other member of the Meiji government: in 1854 he
had journeyed around Kyushu and Shikoku, and in 1858 he went
north to Hokkaido. His inability to communicate with his family
on these trips was a source of considerable anxiety. The shortcomings
of the Tokugawa communications system had even more painful
consequences for him in the mid-1860s. In 1865 Maejima took up
a post in Satsuma's school of Western studies. Later that year his
brother died, and he had to take a leave of absence to return to
Edo, where family matters required his continued presence. He
thereupon wrote a letter of resignation to the domain, which he
took to the Satsuma residence in Edo with the request that it be
forwarded to Satsuma in the domain's correspondence. It never
arrived, and the Satsuma authorities were very angry with Maejima
for his desertion. The resulting ill will from a domain that was a
powerful force in the Bakumatsu and early Meiji periods apparently
worried Maejima considerably and reinforced his sense of the high
costs of an inadequate communications system.[16]

One of Maejima's earliest tasks as supervisor of posts was a review
of the estimates presented by the commercial messengers guilds
(*hikyaku-tonya*) for the cost of the relay service for governmental
communications among the cities of Osaka, Kyoto, and Tokyo.
Maejima regarded these as outrageously high, and after some pre-

liminary investigation on his own he submitted to the Finance Ministry a petition for the establishment of a "new-style post" based on Western models. The petition made the case for the new system not only on the moral high ground of its advantages for the unification of administration and for the encouragement of commerce, two of the major concerns of the new government, but also on the argument that it would generate significant revenues for the government. This double appeal won the approval of both the Civil Affairs Ministry and the Finance Ministry, and the Bureau of Posts received permission to begin the new post among the three major cities at the end of 1870, a mere six months after Maejima's proposal was approved.

The timetable for these plans proved to be too optimistic. The domains still maintained jurisdiction over part of the route of the new post, and their officials were less than cooperative in putting up post boxes and instructing the local operators in the use of stamps, fees, and so on. In the course of a series of meetings with the local appointees of the new system in November 1870 to explain the workings of the new service, bureau officials discovered that the level of comprehension of the written regulations among the putative operators of the new system was appallingly low, and that the shift to the new system required greater preparation than they had anticipated. They therefore postponed its opening for three months while they held meetings for the operators and issued more detailed written instructions. These efforts apparently sufficed: on April 20, 1871, the first post of the new system left Tokyo, arriving in Osaka on schedule seventy-five hours later.[17]

The new system of 1870 was based on a general concept of a modern post derived from the foreign postal agencies of the treaty ports and unsystematic information on Western postal systems, rather than on any specific country's postal system. It combined some standard features of Western systems with several aspects of the old Tokugawa post. The Western-modeled innovations were the use of postage stamps, unrestricted public access to the service, official post offices and mail boxes, a fixed schedule for the postal routes, and the direct government operation of the system through the Bureau of Posts. All these features constituted a radical departure from the patterns of the past. On the other hand, postal rates were calculated by distance; the post offices were limited to the old post stations along the main roads; and local delivery was subcontracted to the local messengers' services that had operated under the old system. Finally, the new system was neither a national system (it served only the major Tokyo-Kyoto-Osaka route), nor was it a monopoly. Although it carried all government communications, it competed for private correspondence with the continued operations of the commercial messengers' services of the three major cities. These were quick to lower their rates and emulate some of the features of the new system (such as daily scheduled departures) to remain competitive. Partly because of this competition, the new government service had a precarious beginning.

The system had been set up along the lines proposed by Maejima Hisoka in his petition, but Maejima himself did not preside over its implementation. Shortly after his proposal had been accepted, his financial expertise and knowledge of English won him a role in the Ministry of Finance's mission to England to negotiate a railway loan. During his year-long stay in Britain, however, he lost no opportunity to investigate the British postal system. Beginning with his voyage on a mail-carrying steamship, where he spent much time questioning the people who handled the mail, he voraciously collected information on the postal service. Once in England, he took whatever time he could snatch from his official duties to talk with postal administrators and gather documentary materials on regulations and operations. He even opened a postal savings account, in order to experience first-hand the workings of the system.[18] Sir Rowland Hill, widely lauded in England as the "father of the modern post," became his hero and his model. He went so far as to obtain a large photograph of Sir Rowland, to which he looked for inspiration.[19] In 1871 Maejima returned to Japan, convinced that his country could and should emulate the British system and armed with detailed information on its organization and functions.

He was appalled to discover that although the new service had indeed been established on the main Tokyo-Kyoto-Osaka route, no further expansion was planned. One of his first acts on his return was to pay a visit to the new head of the Bureau of Posts. He learned that his successor believed that any further extension of the posts was best left in the hands of private commercial operators. Maejima immediately submitted a petition to the Council of State asking to be reinstated as head of the bureau. The granting of his petition marked, whether the government officials realized it or not, the ascendancy of the British model in the Japanese postal system.

The emulation of the British postal service was therefore not the product of a systematic search for models, or even the result of a deliberate choice by the central government, as had been the case for the army and the police. It seems to have been almost fortuitous, the result of Maejima's visit to England on a totally unrelated matter. Maejima's initiative in collecting information on the postal system was his alone, prompted by a mixture of motives that included an intelligent realization of the importance of that particular institution to political, social, and economic development; strong patriotic commitment to Japan's emergence as an equal of the Western nations; and personal ambition. It was a mixture that was far from unique among the young men of early Meiji Japan.

Independently, but virtually simultaneously, the government opted for the British model in the introduction of the telegraph. In that case as well, the British influence was not the product of a deliberate selection process. Instead, the British technicians who were hired to introduce the complex new technology of the telegraph—to supervise the construction of Japan's first telegraph lines between Tokyo and Yokohama in 1869 and to train the first Japanese employees— were asked to write the regulations for the daily operation of the new system. They naturally reproduced as closely as possible the basic organizational structure of the British telegraphs.[20] Even the hiring of British technicians had a strong element of the fortuitous. The Japanese official responsible for building the first line between Tokyo and Yokohama, Terajima Munenori, had turned for advice to an acquaintance, the British chief of the Lighthouse Department in Yokohama, Henry Brunton. Brunton in turn naturally asked his associates in Britain to recommend qualified engineers for the task.

The almost casual emulation of a specific model in the postal service and the telegraph system can be explained by two factors. First, neither the post nor the telegraph performed tasks that had traditionally been the direct prerogative of the state—unlike the military and the systems of administration and control, where the choice of models received much more care and deliberation. Second, in both communications systems, the emulation of the British model began very early, within the first four years of the new regime, while the organization-building energies of the central government were concentrated elsewhere. Had the new systems proven ineffective, a more systematic search for new models would undoubtedly have been undertaken, as it was in education and in banking. Both were successful, however, and the original models triumphed.

Insofar as anyone in the government had given any thought to a foreign model for the postal system, the favored one was that of the United States. Evidence for this is a January 1871 proclamation listing the sites and objects of approved foreign study for Japanese students abroad, which identified the United States as the site for postal communications.[21] From the vantage point of the casual observer, the emulation of the British system rather than that of the United States may seem of little consequence. However, the selection of the British model entailed a wider range of functions (including postal savings), a higher degree of professionalism and bureaucratization in postal administration, and, eventually, a closer linkage between the post and the telegraph than the U.S. model. The following section elaborates on the legacy of the British model, and the adaptations that were necessary in order to fit it into the very different environment of Meiji Japan.

Building the National Postal System

EMULATING THE MODEL

The police system and the postal service had at least one thing in common: during their early years only one man in the organization possessed direct, first-hand experience of the organization on which the new system was based. Maejima Hisoka had, however, several advantages over his counterpart in the police. He was fluent in the language of the Western model and was therefore able to pursue his inquiries into its workings more easily; he had spent a longer period observing its operations; and the organizational system in question was less complex, focused as it was on a fairly limited range of routinized operations and procedures.

Maejima returned to Japan in 1871 determined to institute as quickly as possible two central elements of the British post, which by that time had become common to all the Western systems: a government monopoly of the delivery of written communications, and a unified postal system with fixed rates independent of distance. The two were closely related. As Maejima noted, the volume of mail produced by the monopoly was a necessary condition of the economic feasibility of the unified rates. Convincing the central government that Japan was ready for such a system, however, was not easy. It was nearly a year before Maejima's arguments won him the chance to establish a monopoly on Japan's busiest communications route, between Tokyo and Yokohama, as the first step in constructing the national monopoly. More than a decade passed before national fixed rates independent of distance were finally approved in 1883.

The opposition to the new system was considerable, both from government officials who feared that it would be too complex and too costly at that stage of Japan's development, and from the commercial messengers' services, whose very existence seemed to be at stake. Maejima's own account of his confrontation with the representative of the commercial associations is worth quoting in full, because it summarizes very neatly the arguments he used to triumph over both centers of opposition:

> In Meiji 5/4 (May 1872) I called in the head of the Tokyo *hikyaku tonya* [messengers' associations], Sazaki Sōzuke. He was a good man, energetic and knowledgeable. When he saw me his aspect was one of extreme indignation. He said that for over two hundred and fifty years the communications of our country had been excellent. He protested that although one would expect the government to prize this, on the contrary, its attempt to seize this business for itself was the acme of wickedness, and he pressed unwaveringly for the abolition of the new postal system.
>
> Thereupon, remaining composed, I in turn inquired of him, "If the government were really to accept your advice, and place communications completely into the hands of your people, how much would you charge to deliver a letter to a certain village (in central Japan) that required travel by both land and water routes?" He replied that since it would be necessary to dispatch a special runner, the cost would be one ryō. Then I asked, "What about Kagoshima, or Muroran (in Hokkaido)?" He replied that since that would be difficult even for a special messenger it would take some tens of ryō. There-

upon, advancing one step further, I wound up by asking him, "What if it were Pusan in Korea, across the narrow strait, or Shanghai in China?" He was gripped by mute amazement and was unable to reply. Finally, when I asked, "And what about England or America, what of Russia and France?" he seemed dazed and discouraged, and admitted that he did not know how to find such routes. Since he seemed greatly embarrassed, I explained that communications were of the utmost importance in international trade and in the life of a society, and that throughout the world, an enlightened country had to construct a system for communications within the country and abroad. Gradually I made him understand that the house-based operations of his association, with their message delivery limited to one region or one country, could not accomplish this great purpose.[22]

To ease the transition both for the central government and for the commercial sector, however, Maejima drew on the British experience for a compromise. The Bureau of Posts encouraged the messengers' associations to reorganize themselves as transport companies and arranged to subcontract mail routes to them as the system was extended.

Subcontracting had been a crucial part of the British postal system since the early eighteenth century. The famous mail-coaches, which were the principal carriers of the mail before the advent of the railways, were privately owned and operated. The private carriers contracted with the post office to carry mail, which was the chief, although not the only, source of their revenue. By 1870 the railways had supplanted the mail-coaches, but in the course of his discussions with British postal authorities, Maejima, aware that Japan had yet to construct its first railway, undoubtedly inquired about the methods of prerailway days. Certainly the marked similarity between the earlier British system and the one he introduced on his return to Japan suggests strongly that he did so.[23] The system he instituted required that as of June 1873 all mail had to bear postage stamps and be processed through a post office, but that the long-distance transportation and delivery of mail beyond the central inter-city route would be handled by private transport companies. The subcontracting system proved extraordinarily useful for Japan's postal service in its early years, and eased the transition for hundreds of entrepreneurs from the communications traffic of Tokugawa times.

One more feature of the British system eased the transition. It furnished the means of coping with the potentially exhorbitant cost of establishing the extensive network of post offices and carriers necessary to bring the postal system within reach of the entire populace. The British post office operated through a basic network of specialized post offices, managed by postal system employees who were part of the civil service. This network was supplemented by a large number of rural and urban subunits operated by private citizens who subcontracted with the post office to collect and deliver mail and who combined this activity with other income-producing occupations. The postal authorities supervised them closely and ensured their compliance with all postal regulations with the threat of a termination of their contracts.

The functions of the two types of postal facilities—the post offices and the substations—were virtually identical. The key distinction between them was the degree of their integration into the postal organization and their level of specialization. The reason for having these two categories was of course economic: the substations were located in the home or place of business of the postmaster or postmistress, thereby allowing the post office to expand the scope of the new system at a rapid pace with a low level of direct investment from the central treasury.

The system proved very successful in Japan. A spate of centrally financed construction in the early 1870s provided the key postal stations: 71 of them were built between 1870 and 1875. Thereafter, the Postal Bureau continued building at a modified but fairly even pace: 47 in the next decade (from 1876 to 1885), 58 from 1886 to 1895, and 65 from 1906 to 1912.[24] Despite the relatively low level of centrally financed construction, however, the number of postal stations rose steadily through the spread of British-style substations. Table 7 shows the distribution of postal stations across Maejima's formal five-category hierarchy of stations. The crucial distinction was that the Postal Bureau financed the first and second rank stations, whereas the costs of construction and maintenance for those of the third rank and below fell on the individual subcontractor. By 1882, the year before the adoption of the unified fixed rate, Japan had just over 5,500 postal stations, 1,500 more than England had possessed at the time of its introduction of the modern single-rate post.

Table 7. Post offices in Japan by rank, 1875, 1879, 1882

Year	Total number of postal stations	Rank				
		1	2	3	4	5
1875	3,815[a]	10	69	51	337	3,201
1879	4,584[a]	16	66	68	492	3,708
1882	5,585[a]	25	90	283	1,090	3,775

[a]Includes some unranked post offices.

The English-style system separated personnel into three categories: the civil servants who were part of the central government bureaucracy; the so-called "established" full-time employees of the post offices; and the "unestablished," putatively part-time subcontractors of the substations. The great advantage of this system to the government was that the salaries in the third group were not governed either by regular civil service categories or by the postal system's own regulations for its full-time personnel. The combination of the three-tier personnel system with the two-tier system of post offices permitted the postal system to expand rapidly at a fairly low cost.

Maejima also brought back from England an expanded concept of the functions performed by the postal system. Two in particular extended the range of postal services well beyond those imagined in the earliest days of the "new-style post": the issue of money orders and the system of postal savings. Maejima proposed the establishment of both soon after his return, but skeptical officials of the Finance Ministry raised three objections. They doubted that the demand for these services existed in Japan as yet; they questioned the reliability of postal employees in handling money; and they felt that both money transfers and savings facilities were more properly the business of banks than of the post office.[25] Maejima's persistence and his invocation of the British model apparently overcame their objections. Perhaps, in addition, the very sluggish response to the National Bank Act of 1872, which attempted to create a modern banking system, made them more amenable to considering an alternative service. Preparations for issuing money orders began in

1873, and the groundwork for the postal savings system in 1874. Both went into operation in 1875.

The system of issuing of money orders was modeled completely on the English system. Maejima, according to his own account, simply translated, condensed, and simplified the British regulations he had brought back with him.[26] The Finance Ministry agreed to provide the initial start-up capital. The original plan was that each post office would get funds to cash money orders from branches of the Tokyo Kawase-gaisha, one of the largest of the exchange companies set up under government sponsorship in 1869. Unfortunately, the company was experiencing serious management and financial difficulties even as the plans were being drawn up, and it collapsed before the money order system actually began operations. In its place, the government decided to use prefectural tax offices to supply funds as needed.[27]

Funds were required in rather larger amounts than had been anticipated. The banking system was in its infancy: in 1875 there were only four banks (without branches) in the entire country, and the money order system was the only channel available for the safe transport and movement of funds. As a result, the system in its early years had to cope with a demand for money orders of much larger amounts than was the case in England, where banks took care of large transfers of funds and money orders were used chiefly for small sums. A year after the 1876 expansion of the national bank system, the Finance Ministry attempted to transfer much of this business to the banks by setting a ceiling of thirty yen on money orders.

The establishment of the postal savings system was an even more daring innovation. Britain had introduced the system in 1861, and it was the first nation in the world to do so. Between that time and Maejima's visit to England, only New Zealand (in 1867) and Belgium (in 1870) had followed its lead. Japan was the fourth nation in the world to introduce postal savings, preceding France (1882), Austria (1883), Switzerland (1884), and the United States (1910). It did so without any tradition of institutional savings: although frugality and saving had been widely praised virtues during the Tokugawa period, the only mode of saving had been the time-honoured method of hoarding. Maejima's determination to introduce postal savings into Japan illustrates the observation of Georges

Bousquet, quoted in Chapter 1, that the Japanese leaders of early Meiji were driven by the vision of what they wanted their society to be, undeterred by what it actually was.

The procedures of the British system for postal savings were adopted in their entirety, and the demands on the resources of the local post office turned out to be much less severe than the Finance Ministry officials had at first feared. The British authorities had no more faith in the accounting abilities and reliability of their post-office staff than did their Japanese counterparts. In England all trans-actions and records were handled by the central London office. When a deposit was made at any post office, the money, deposit slip, and passbook were all forwarded by mail to London, where the transaction was recorded and the official entry made in the passbook. All withdrawals were handled in the same way.[28] The adoption of this centralized system minimized the tasks of the local office and allowed the rapid extension of the service. By 1878 postal savings facilities existed at 595 postal stations throughout Japan, and at nearly ten times as many by 1884 (5,307). The difference between the geographic scale of England and Japan called for one modification. Centralizing all transactions in Tokyo took too much time, and in 1883 fifty-one regional offices were designated as centers for processing postal savings transactions.

One interesting byproduct of the centralization of financial trans-actions was that postmen on major routes carried cash, and this made them a potential prey to robbers. The Postal Bureau therefore issued guns to the employees who carried money on major routes, a practice which continued until 1887.[29] This was something of an anomaly, since during these years even the police did not carry guns on regular duty.

Both money orders and postal savings were first introduced in a few post offices in Tokyo and the principal cities, and then extended to other offices as the system built up a reservoir of experienced personnel. Postal savings, for example, did not reach Yamaguchi prefecture in the southwest until 1878.[30] Of the two services, postal savings eventually involved more post offices despite its slower start. The high degree of centralization of its operations made it easier for local stations to adopt.

The new postal system emulated the British model closely not only in the functions it performed, but also in those it did not perform. Chief among these was the parcel post. Great Britain was one of the last countries in the West to add the conveyance of small packages to the functions of the postal service, and at the time of Maejima's visit it had not yet developed a parcel post. It took the 1880 establishment of an International Parcel Post, set up by the countries that had already developed domestic systems, to overcome British resistance to its introduction. The railway companies were the main obstacle: they feared that the revenues from subcontracting delivery through the post offices would be much lower than the fees they could command directly.

The British parcel post began in 1883. Japan's adoption of the system took even longer, and examination of the delay shows how organizational development was affected by the increasing complexity of the organizational environment after the first surge of organization creation in the 1870s. In 1885 the Agriculture and Commerce Ministry urged the establishment of a parcel post, but it was not until 1892 that it was formally approved and initiated. It was first delayed by a major administrative reorganization of the whole postal system, which was integrated into a new Ministry of Communications set up in 1885. Then the top postal officials further delayed it because they were reluctant to cut into the business of the private shipping companies, which exerted considerable pressure against the initiative.[31] Finally, once the Cabinet had approved the system, it was delayed by the difficulty of getting any legislation through the Diet, which was dissolved in 1891 before the measure could come to a vote. In 1892 the parcel post was finally brought into operation, but with a complex system of rates based on distance and weight that yielded seventy categories of charges. The distance charge was not eliminated until 1902.

One of the services offered by the British postal system was not introduced until after the Meiji period. Personal life insurance and contributory pension plans were perhaps the least successful of the various services offered by the British post office in the nineteenth century, both in terms of the numbers of subscribers and the operating profits they produced. Maejima had proposed the emulation of the British system in 1875, but since money orders and postal savings had only just been launched, Finance Ministry officials objected to adding still another complex set of financial transactions to the infant postal system. By the end of the nineteenth century, however, the British post office insurance system was expanding rapidly, and it was being emulated in several European countries. In 1897 the Ministry of Communications, encouraged by a general interest within the government in developing social welfare programs to check growing social unrest, began the first of a series of investigations of the postal insurance system. In 1900 the draft of the revised Postal Savings Law included the establishment of a postal insurance system, but the loud and immediate outcry from the commercial life insurance sector brought that plan to a sudden halt.[32] The plan resurfaced in 1910, only to be caught in one of the recurring intra-bureaucracy rivalries of late Meiji: the Ministry of Agriculture and Commerce was developing on its own scheme for a national system of life insurance and workers' insurance subcontracted to the private sector.[33] Working out the compromises necessary to appease the various commercial and bureaucratic interests took another six years, but finally, in 1916, postal life insurance was instituted throughout Japan.

DEPARTURES FROM THE MODEL

Inputs. Although the analogy between the two island nations of Great Britain and Japan was a favorite of many Meiji statesmen, the very real differences between the two in the level of technological and organizational development demanded some fundamental departures from British patterns in the postal system. The gap was particularly marked in two critically important inputs for the postal system: the transport of mail and the local postmasters.

By the 1870s the backbone of the British postal system was the railroad. Railway carriages fitted with sorting facilities and staffed by postal employees processed mail as it was picked up en route, and elaborate mechanical devices allowed bags of mail to be picked up and deposited along the line without stopping the train. Maejima supervised the adoption of the "traveling post office"—he used a transliteration of the English term—as early as possible. Mail carriages were used on Japan's first railway line, between Tokyo and Yokohama, in the very year it opened (1872). It was nearly two more decades, however, before Japan developed railway lines in sufficient number to carry much of the burden of mail transport.

The means of transportation that was most useful to the Japanese postal system during its first decade was one that had served the British system well in its earlier years: the horse-drawn carriage. The carriage was introduced in Japan in 1869[34] and was used on mail routes wherever the roads permitted. Unfortunately, well-surfaced roads were not numerous in Japan. On land routes where the terrain or the road surface did not permit the use of carriages, the post relied on the traditional relays of runners, now uniformed and keeping to fixed schedules. Few long-distance routes during the early years of the post could be covered without them. Even the main trunk route between Tokyo and Kyoto used a mix of the new and the traditional: horse-drawn mail carriages covered about two-thirds of the route, while the remaining one-third required the services of runners—with one short ferry passage. As much as possible, however, the new system used water routes, and so many of Japan's major cities were on or near the coast that for many years the sea proved an easier highway than the roads.

Another new transport technology of the early Meiji period was quickly adapted to mail delivery: the man-drawn cart developed in China and known to Westerners as the rickshaw. The first rickshaw appeared in Japan in 1870, and it changed the face of urban transport. Within a year of its introduction, there were 25,000 rickshaws in Tokyo alone.[35] The adaptation of these carts for use in the postal system increased the weight of mail that could be transported by one man, although of course it could not increase the speed of delivery. The Postal Bureau experimented briefly with its use on the long-distance mail routes in the early 1870s, but it soon abandoned the attempt because of the frequency of breakdowns and accidents (a heavy mail-cart could not stop or manoeuver as easily as a single runner). The carts were very useful on the shorter routes, however, and continued to make local deliveries well into the 1890s.[36]

The problems of staffing the post offices were even more serious than the difficulties of transport. In England, there were three categories of personnel: the civil servants who were employed by the British General Post Office; the "established" employees, who worked in the directly administered post offices, and the "unestablished" subcontractors. Maejima introduced much the same basic framework into the new Japanese post. However, it was obscured somewhat by a more elaborate formal hierarchy of classification, with five categories of post offices and multiple rankings of the "unestablished" personnel. One reason for obscuring the differentiation was the early difficulty in attracting subcontractors into the lower tier of postal stations. In England the would-be postmaster or postmistress applied to the Post Office for a position that was advertised locally. The applicants were usually tradespeople who felt that their business would improve with the addition of postal facilities, or shopkeepers' wives who wanted to supplement their husbands' incomes. In Japan in the early 1870s, however, the postal service was too unfamiliar to attract a large number of volunteers, and therefore the first cohort of local postal officials had to be actively recruited. This recruitment gave the postal authorities both a major problem and an important opportunity: by carefully selecting the kind of person they targeted as postal station operators, they could shape public perceptions of the status and importance of the system itself.

Maejima was much concerned with the impact of the initial hiring on the status and reliability of the new system and he laid down detailed guidelines to direct the selection process. Officials of the postal department of each prefectural government were to seek out local notables—former village headmen, landowners, local merchants of good reputation—who would confer local recognition and prestige on the new system and actively promote its utilization in the community.[37] The guidelines were apparently followed with considerable success. In one of the prefectures for which detailed records have survived (now part of Chiba and Ibaraki prefectures), sixteen of the twenty-seven local postal station officials for whom background information is available were village headmen, six were in transport or related occupations (one kept an inn), and the rest were either local landowners or prominent figures in local industry.[38] Such men could easily afford to convert part of their premises to a postal station or to construct a new building. They could even hire someone else to manage the operations.

One of the main attractions of working for the new postal system was the prestige conferred by a "government position" in early Meiji. Maejima very effectively played to this feeling when he developed the terminology for the new system. Local postal officials were given the title of *jun-kanri* (quasi-official), at a time when the term *kanri* had a mystique that it was slow to lose. During the earliest years, the postal system was permitted to call its branch stations *yūbin yakusho*—*yūbin* being the term adopted for the post, and *yakusho* a word of older lineage meaning "government office"—regardless of their degree of actual integration into the postal organization. At the end of 1874, however, that term was restricted to major post offices by a central government increasingly protective of its official dignity. However, the postal system continued to use other symbolic rewards of status and identification with the state. In 1882, for instance, on one of the Emperor's grand tours of the provinces, three men in a village were allowed to pay their formal respects to him, and one of those was the postmaster.[39]

The manipulation of status rewards in the recruitment process led to a further departure from the British model: the exclusion of women from the ranks of postal employees. In Britain the local shopkeeper who took on the postal business as a profitable sideline was not infrequently a woman. In Japan, however, where the symbolic linkage of the post to the state was one of the most important inducements to lure local notables into the postal system, women were not considered worthy of the honor of being "officials." To allow women to operate a postal station would have been to lower the perceived status of the system.

Regulatory Structures. A second area of departure involved the system's regulatory structures. The Japanese administrative structures into which the postal system was introduced were not designed on the British model, and therefore the British patterns of integrating the postal system into the state administration were necessarily replaced by the emerging Japanese system of government departments. Initial adaptations of the British model proved inadequate, and led to a continuing series of structural adjustments. Tedious though the description of these adjustments may seem to the reader, it illustrates the main source of problems with Japan's adoption of models from a number of countries: the administration of systems with incompatible regulatory structures. Within each organization, the patterns of the model could be emulated and adapted, but when it came to integrating the organization into the state regulatory structures, some major problems emerged. In the case of the postal system, those problems took decades to solve, and took a serious toll on the expansion of the post.

In Great Britain the General Post Office was headed by the post-master-general, who in the nineteenth century was usually (though not always) a member of the Cabinet and who was ultimately responsible to Parliament. In Japan, the central administrative agency charged with the development of the postal system for its first fifteen years had neither the status nor the degree of formal autonomy enjoyed by the British post office. When Maejima left for England, the agency charged with the functions of the post was only a bureau within a government ministry, and so it remained on his return. During its early years the Postal Bureau was moved to a succession of ministries, its migrations reflecting the administrative confusion over its principal role. It began life in 1868 as part of the Finance Office, then moved in the following year to the Civil Affairs Department (the predecessor of the Home Ministry), then moved back to the Ministry of Finance in 1871, then to the newly established Home Ministry in 1874, and then to the Agriculture and Commerce Ministry in 1881, before finding a permanent home in the new Ministry of Communications in 1885. The moves between the finance agencies and the agencies of domestic administration illustrated a certain ambivalence about its role, sometimes giving priority to its revenue-producing aspect, and at other times emphasizing its service-providing function. Throughout its peregrinations, however, the Postal Bureau retained its staff and its formal functions, and the frequency of the moves undoubtedly enhanced its de facto autonomy.

How its subordinate status affected the development of the postal system is a matter for speculation. One demonstrable consequence throughout the 1870s and the early 1880s was that able administrators rose through the ranks of the bureau into higher positions in the supervising ministry that were unrelated to the postal service or to communications policy. In nineteenth-century Britain, by contrast, the post office offered virtually a lifetime career. Maejima himself, for example, was promoted to a higher office in the Home Ministry in 1876, although by his own request he held concurrently his position as head of the Postal Bureau. His new responsibilities involved him in a range of complex administrative tasks of a different sort altogether, from supervising the recruitment of 10,000 auxiliary police during the Satsuma Rebellion to reforming the land tax.

The postal system's lack of a strong voice at the higher levels of decision-making may well have been a factor in the strong emphasis on its revenue-producing role. The dual role of the postal system—as a source of revenue and as a public service—can cause conflicts over how to use the revenues it generates. In Meiji Japan, where the unequal treaties restricted the government's ability to generate revenues through tariffs, the temptation to use the postal system as a revenue-generator must have been particularly strong. As early as 1878, the postal service was making an operating profit of 6 percent on revenues of nearly one million yen.[40] Like most government systems, the post office ran into difficulties during the Matsukata Deflation of the early 1880s. Although its revenues continued to rise, the rate of growth slowed, and expenditures outstripped revenues as the Bureau of Posts increased the number of postal routes and the number of employees. As a result, in 1885 the postal system, like most government systems in that year, was forced to cut back on its expenditures. Elimination of postal routes and a general reduction of employees cut its 1885 expenditures by 23 percent over the previous year and restored the system to profitability by 1886. For the rest of the Meiji period, the post made a significant contribution to Japan's general revenues: from 1895 on, it was contributing about 2 percent of total general revenues to the treasury, and by 1905 it was making almost twice what it cost to run (see Table 8). In Britain, in contrast, the profitability of the postal system

Table 8. Postal system net revenues as percentages of total revenues: Great Britain and Japan

Year	Great Britain	Japan
1850	39	—
1879–80	37	7
1889–90	35	23
1899–1900	28	31
1909–10	26	45

was never expected to reach the levels attained in Japan. Indeed, its operating profits fell steadily between 1880 and 1910, from 37 percent to 26 percent.

A postal system that makes very large contributions to the treasury may be doing so at the cost of improving the welfare of its employees or extending its services. This was clearly true of the Meiji post. It achieved its impressive profitability by keeping its labor and administrative costs low and by limiting the expansion of the system (not until 1893 did Japan regain the length of postal routes it had enjoyed in 1884, and the mileage of postal routes grew very little thereafter). A stronger advocate for the postal system at the center may well have had some influence in increasing the level of reinvestment of revenues in the system itself.

Examination of the relationship between the post and the telegraph brings out another contrast between the Japanese system and its British model. In Britain, the development of the telegraph by a number of private companies had led to excessive competition on the main communications routes and very uneven coverage in many other areas. As a result of increasing public dissatisfaction in the late 1860s, the British government studied the nationalized systems of Belgium, France, and Switzerland (another example of the endemic cross-societal organizational learning occurring during the nineteenth century) and in 1870 nationalized the telegraph system.[41] The British post office took over the telegraphs, incorporating their offices and personnel into its own organizational structures.

In Japan the postal service and the telegraph developed simultaneously, but independently. The technologies and the mode of organization initially seemed so different as to require not only separate bureaus, but even the supervision of separate ministries. The telegraph, because of the demands of engineering and constructing the transmission lines, developed under the aegis of the Ministry of Public Works. From its beginnings the Japanese telegraph was a governmental subsystem. State ownership was not due to a failure of private entrepreneurship: as early as 1868 individual businessmen had petitioned for permission to build a telegraph line. The government decided, however, that the military and administrative importance of the new technology justified the expense of direct state operation and control.

The postal system and the telegraph therefore developed independently for a decade and a half, with separate networks of local offices, separate administrative structures, and separate regulatory structures. In 1885, however, when the Council of State gave way to the new Cabinet system, the Ministry of Public Works was abolished and the new Ministry of Communications took over both the Postal Bureau and the Telegraph Bureau, along with the bureaus that supervised maritime shipping and lighthouses. The ministry's jurisdiction expanded in subsequent years: the telephone was added in 1891, electricity in the same year, railroads in 1892, all water transport in 1893, the generation of hydroelectricity in 1909.

The change had major consequences for the administrative organization of the post. The ministry created separate bureaus to supervise postal savings and money orders, previously controlled by the Postal Bureau. It also decided to merge, over a period of five years, the telegraph offices (280 in 1885) with the post offices, combining the facilities of the two services. This resulted in the rapid expansion of the accessibility of the telegraph. Not only were telegraph lines installed in a greater number of postal stations, which were then called postal-telegraph offices,[42] but post offices without direct access to a telegraph line accepted telegrams, sending them by mail to the nearest line. The great increase in the number of telegrams after 1890, when the combination of the services was effected, was due at least in part to easier access. A more complex issue was the level of integration to be achieved by the two services at the administrative level. It was an issue that remained unresolved through most of the Meiji period: the postal and telegraph bureaus were merged in 1887,[43] separated in 1889, merged in 1893, separated in 1907, and merged in 1908.[44]

Coordination and Control of Subunits. Instability in the top administrative structures coincided with a decade of changes in the internal coordination and control of the subunits of the postal system. Here too the Japanese postal authorities found it necessary to depart from the British model, and their search for satisfactory structures produced experimentation and frequent changes. In Britain the supervision of the postal stations was highly centralized. The substations as well as the major post offices were directly monitored by inspectors dispatched from the London head office. So high a level of centralization was scarcely feasible in Japan in the Meiji period, given the much greater distances and the less developed transportation system.

Several government subsystems—the police, the schools, the army—drew their own "maps" of administrative districts early in their development, and then abandoned them in favor of the prefecture. The postal system, conversely, began by using the prefecture as the unit of administration and moved to the development of specialized districts. In 1871 a postal section was set up in each prefecture's tax department, with the responsibility for recruiting personnel, setting up postal stations, and supervising the operations of the postal service. However, these very small units lacked both the autonomy from the tax department and the resources to be effective. In 1883, therefore, the country was divided into fifty-two postal districts, each with a specialized administrative office to take over the tasks of supervision and regulation. From that point on, the postal service maintained its own national control structure, independent of the prefectural governments. The move to the more centralized system was made without explicit reference to the centralization of the British model, but it is suggestive that the postal system was one of the very few civilian government subsystems of the Meiji period to maintain a control structure divorced from the prefectural administration.

The lack of any organizational model for the new control system made it difficult for the officials to decide on the appropriate number of supervising agencies and the optimal degree of specialization. The recurrent reorganizations through the rest of the period testify to the problems and to the trial-and-error approach to their solution. The fifty-two specialized administrative units established in 1882 were reduced to fifteen within three years, and abolished in 1889. Instead, in each prefecture one postal-telegraph office was designated a first-rank office, and combined supervisory functions within the prefecture with its normal operations. Their number in turn was reduced by more than half in 1893, in a drive to reduce salary expenditures. Specialized administrative offices were restored in 1910, with thirteen *Teishin kanrikyoku* (postal-telegraph administrative offices).

The main reason for the frequent changes in administrative structure was the importance and complexity of the supervision and control of the third-rank post offices, as they were called after 1885, on which the Japanese system relied so heavily. These were the stations owned and operated by part-time employees. In 1887 only one percent of all the postal stations in Japan were staffed by full-time civil servants attached to the postal system; by the end of the Meiji period they were still only four percent. The effectiveness of the postal system depended heavily on the third-rank stations, which experienced considerable turnover and required constant supervision.

The system's reliance on these stations had been fostered by the effectiveness of the recruitment of local postal station subcontractors through the 1870s and into the 1880s. Local notables, attracted by the status of a semi-official position and often motivated by ideals of public service to their local communities, had proved to be reliable and able managers. The severe deflationary policies instituted in the early 1880s, however, had an impact throughout the economy. By 1884 rice prices had fallen to half their 1880 level, and although the local notables who were the principal postal agents suffered less than the small farmers, they too were hard hit. Many local postal officials submitted their resignations, pleading economic hardship.[45] Others were shed by the system in the drive to reduce expenditures in the mid-1880s. The number of post offices fell by 28 percent from their high in 1883 to their low point in 1889 (Figure 3).

The reestablishment of the local stations and the continued expansion of the postal service network after the economy recovered required decisive action from the center, but in the welter of administrative changes in postal administration in the late 1880s and the 1890s such action was not forthcoming. The volume of mail continued to grow and the revenues to rise, but as we saw above, the postal system had no strong advocate at the center urging the expansion of services. Maejima had left the government in the political crisis of 1881, and although he returned briefly as vice-minister of communications from 1888 to 1891, his energies then were largely devoted to establishing a government monopoly of the telephone, reforming the press law, and setting up—at long last—a parcel post. Without strong individual leadership and a clear institutional policy, the number of postal stations stagnated for nearly

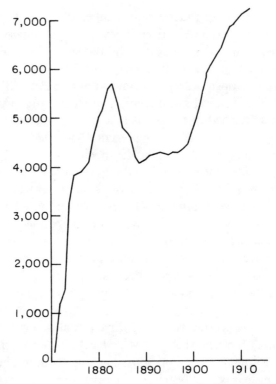

Figure 3. Total number of postal stations in Japan, 1871–1912.

a decade and a half. Not until the turn of the century, when the organizational structures of the ministry stabilized and the Diet came to exercise a stronger popular influence on government policy, did the expansion of the postal service resume.

In the interim the Postal Bureau increased substantially the number of outlets (usually shops) which were allowed to purchase stamps at a slight discount and resell them at their face value. There were 2,918 such outlets in 1880, jumping to 18,853 by 1882; and 26,013 in 1886. The number hovered around 26,000 until 1891, and then rose steadily. By 1912 there were 58,212. The number of mailboxes increased in proportion, so that people who bought stamps could easily mail their letters. This proved a much cheaper way of increasing access to the postal system than increasing the number of post offices, but the stamp outlets did not offer the range of services or the visibility of the formal system.

The merging of the postal and telegraph administration in the Ministry of Communications had at least one positive effect: the development of formal training for postal service officials. The complex and unfamiliar technology of the telegraph made a formal training program necessary from its beginning in 1869. The program continued and expanded over the subsequent decade and a half and training in administration was introduced to supplement the technical instruction. In 1887 the Ministry of Communications undertook to turn the program into the Tokyo Telegraph School, with a two-year course of study. In the following year, with the accelerating integration of the postal and telegraph systems at all levels, a one-year course in postal administration was added to the curriculum, the first such course to be offered in any modern postal system. In 1890 the name of the school was changed, appropriately, to the Tokyo Post and Telegraph School. It offered two two-year courses: one on the administration of the postal-telegraph system, and one on technical and engineering aspects.[46] Formal training had obviously gone well beyond the instruction of technicians to encompass the training of future administrators for the communications system.

The schooling for middle-level administrators, however, did little to solve the problems of standardizing the performance of the many base-level postal stations and their employees. That required different tactics. The central administration used the standard bureaucratic technique of issuing detailed regulations covering all aspects of operations. The postal authorities also revived the conferences that began with the first postal route in 1870, when officials explained the operations of the system to assembled groups of local postmasters and answered their questions. Instructional meetings of this sort were institutionalized in 1875. In addition the central administration issued standardized account books and record-keeping forms in increasing number as the tasks of the post offices grew in complexity. Regulations issued in 1890 list sixteen different record books that were to be sent out to all post offices, and an additional nineteen for the first- and second-rank post offices.[47] Ironically, because of the delay in introducing the parcel post, the central office had to send these materials to each post office via the commercial transport companies.

Control was only one problem of the postal substations. From the turn of the century on, complaints about the insecurity, the demanding work, and the low level of rewards in the third-rank post offices came with increasing shrillness from local postal workers and even from the press. The postal system had been built on cheap part-time labor; in 1905, the pay of employees of the third-rank stations averaged just over nine yen a month.[48] Similar problems in England had led in the 1890s to the formation of a labor union within the postal system and even to postal strikes, as the Japanese authorities were well aware.[49] In an effort to head off any development in that direction, and to slow the high rate of turnover at the local levels, the government in 1909 established the Communications Official Workers' Welfare Association, modeled on the mutual aid associations of the national railways, which in their turn had drawn on a German model. Its chief function was to administer what was in effect a contributory insurance program, whereby the employees paid part of their monthly salaries into a treasury-managed fund, and received payments in case of accident, sickness, retirement, or death. The program was open to all postal employees, with a continuing distinction between the employees of the central bureau and the first and second-rank post offices and those of the third rank. The first group paid in 3.6 percent of their monthly salary, and the government contributed an amount equal to 2.4 percent; employees of the third rank paid 6 percent of their salaries and received no government contribution. The government did not choose to cut into the immense profitability of its postal system to raise living standards for its employees, and it does not take much cynicism to see the Welfare Association as a means of defusing employee dissatisfaction at very low cost.

Building a market. Unlike the British system, with its long and gradual development, the Japanese postal system had to work aggressively to create a niche for itself in its environment. The Japanese post was established not in response to popular demand, but through the initiatives of government officials who were convinced that the post was a necessary part of the apparatus of the modern state. One of the earliest tasks of the postal system was therefore to create a general awareness of the services it offered and to encourage people to use them. These endeavors received little guidance from the British post office, which prided itself loftily on the fact that it never advertised.[50]

One way of increasing public awareness of the service was simply to attract attention. The new service took a number of steps to make itself stand out in the early Meiji environment. The first uniforms of the postmen—an adaptation of traditional Japanese dress, with the crest of the postal service printed in bold red characters on the back—were part of this effort. These were shortly replaced by uniforms modeled on those of the French army. The post offices themselves mounted large flags outside their doors, displaying the two characters for *yūbin* (post), and put similar but smaller flags on mailcarts and carriages. For the next twenty years the service searched for a striking graphic symbol for the post. Such trademarks had been widely used in commerce well before the Meiji Restoration, and the Japanese appreciated their ability to capture public notice. In the late 1870s the Postal Bureau designed a symbol consisting of the rising sun transected by a single horizontal bar. The logo that replaced it in 1887 is the symbol of the postal-telecommunications system in Japan to this day: a "T" surmounted by a parallel line. It was a striking and effective symbol, lavishly displayed on postal flags, bags, lanterns, and postboxes, and even incorporated onto the ever more elaborate sleeve insignia of the postal uniforms.

Another way to promote the new service was the recruitment of local notables who would act as its patrons and promoters. To further that goal prefectural officials traveled to every part of each prefecture in 1871 and 1872 to explain the system to local leaders.[51] Several commentators have noted the irony of using the traditional structures of communication in the local communities to spread the knowledge of the new communications system.[52] Yet the rapid acceptance of the new post is testimony to the effectiveness of the old information networks. In the urban areas, however, Maejima ignored the British postal service's contempt for advertising and placed advertisements in the newspapers that were emerging in Tokyo, Osaka, and the major prefectural centers. His motives may have been somewhat mixed, because Maejima himself was a major force behind a Tokyo daily whose very name was an advertisement for the new post: *Yūbin Hōchi Shimbun*. The paper aimed to publish news from all over Japan that would be gathered and dispatched through the mails by volunteer local correspondents (local postmasters were pressured to perform this role).

Getting people to use the new service was more than a matter of letting them know the service existed. The system had to be accessible. To that end, Maejima introduced in 1873 the preprinted, prestamped postcard. This kind of postcard had originated in Austria in 1869 and was adopted in Britain in 1870, the year of Maejima's visit. It had many advantages for a public that did not have much experience of the mails. It was much cheaper than a letter, and since the message area and the place for the address were clearly indicated, it was easy to use. The postcard became extremely popular in Japan; by 1887 it constituted the largest category of mail processed by the Japanese postal system. Japan was quite unusual in this respect: the ratio of postcards to letters was four times higher than in the European country where the postcard was most popular (Belgium), and nearly twenty-five times higher than in Britain.[53] Japanese postal historians have explained this popularity by a lack of concern with privacy and the large number of short, formalized greetings required by courtesy in Japan.[54] Its cheapness and simplicity surely contributed in equal measure. Whatever the reason, the use of postcards certainly promoted the rapid growth of the volume of mail.

Even when the post was solidly established, postal officials lost no opportunity to raise public awareness. In both the Sino-Japanese and Russo-Japanese wars, the postal service followed a precedent set by the Germans in the Franco-Prussian War and established a military post. Mail from family and friends was delivered to soldiers even in the battle zones, and officers and men could send a certain number of letters postage-free each month (in 1894, the quota was three for officers and one for enlisted men; in 1895 this was raised to four and two respectively). During the Sino-Japanese War, over five million letters were mailed from the battle zone, and over seven million were delivered to the front.[55] Presumably at least some of the soldiers were using the mails for the first time in their lives— and postal officials could hope that familiarity would lead to future use.

The success of the various measures to encourage the use of the post can be judged both by the speed with which it became a net revenue producer for the government and by the steadily growing volume of mail (Figure 4).

The popularization of the less immediately visible services of the postal system was more difficult. The case of postal savings illustrates

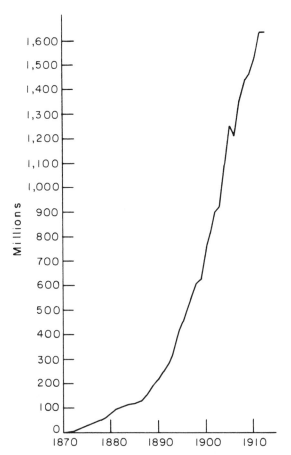

Figure 4. Total domestic mail items in Japan, 1871–1912.

both the problems involved and the ingenuity of the people in the Postal Bureau in developing a niche for the organization in Japanese society. Even before receiving official authorization for the system, Maejima set up a pilot project for employees of the Postal Bureau and the Tokyo post offices.[56] The experiment (begun in March 1874) provided both operating experience and word-of-mouth publicity. When the authorities finally gave their approval, Maejima sent out formal announcements in his own name, apparently for display in public places, extolling the personal benefits of saving and the advantages of a savings system guaranteed by the Home Ministry.

The response was slow. In the first two months of operation in Tokyo the postal savings system attracted only 917 depositors. Maejima resorted to an accelerated public relations campaign: he sent out pamphlets to government offices, commercial establishments, and post offices, emphasizing the security of the system and the personal advantages for savers, as well as the potential contribution to Japan's economic growth.[57] He also urged the employees of the Postal Bureau to spread the word among their friends. The government was persuaded to pay government pensions through the post office from 1875 on, and it encouraged individuals receiving those payments to save a portion in a postal savings account. In 1875 only 158 people received such pensions (primarily retired military officers), but the number gradually increased. The large proportion of government employees among the early postal depositors may well have resulted from the greater effectiveness of Maejima's publicity efforts in the close networks of the government offices.

At any rate the campaign was effective enough to increase steadily the number of postal depositors, even in the face of the decision taken by the new Ministry of Communications to reduce the number of post offices offering the service by 30 percent between 1885 and 1889. The availability of the system remained somewhat limited until 1898; thereafter the greater number of outlets and the resumption of efforts to publicize the system led to a steady expansion in the number of postal depositors (Figure 5).

One interesting departure from the British model concerned restrictions on the public's access to the postal savings system, despite the eagerness of the Postal Bureau officials to expand its use. When the proposed regulations were laid before the Council of State for approval, Justice Ministry officials objected that the unrestricted availability of the system threatened the authority of the household head. They demanded that members of a household be required to obtain the household head's approval for setting up a savings account.[58] This demonstrates the Justice Ministry's strong commitment to legal supports for an authoritarian family structure, even in 1874, when enthusiasm for "civilization and enlightenment" was at its peak. Putting this modification together with the rejection of the British practice of recruiting women as postmistresses, one can see

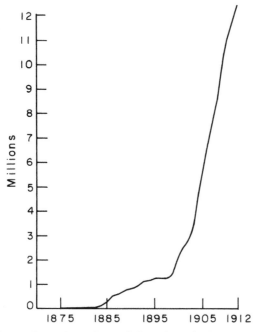

Figure 5. Total number of postal depositors in Japan, 1875–1912.

that even in so apparently neutral an area as the postal service the authorities were determined not to follow foreign models in anything touching the power structure of the household.

SUMMARY

The British postal system provided the model for the range of functions, the division of labor, and the arrangement of tasks in the Japanese post. Maejima Hisoka's extensive observations in Britain and the written materials he brought back from his 1870 visit formed the framework for the early consolidation of the postal system. On the other hand, the very great difference between the two societies necessitated departures from the model. Alternatives to the British methods of transporting the mail and recruiting postmasters had to be found quickly, and the Japanese had to make much more strenuous efforts to create a demand for the services of the post. Moreover, the differences in the formal-regulatory structures of the two countries induced other changes, such as formal training for administrators, unimagined in the original model. And the greater difficulties of communication within Japan, even with the post and the telegraph systems in place, made for repeated changes in the structures of controlling and monitoring the postal subunits.

Table 9 summarizes the principal areas of emulation and innovation. The debt of the Japanese postal service to the British, at least at the level of daily operations, escapes such schematic presentation. It is unlikely, however, that the Japanese communications system would have expanded so rapidly and had so wide a scope without it.

The magnitude of the Japanese accomplishment in building the postal system can be better appreciated through a comparison with the experience of Imperial China. The first proposal for a Western-style national post was presented to the Chinese imperial government in 1861; formal consideration was given to the concept then, and again in 1876, 1885, and 1892.[59] Three and a half decades had passed after the first proposal, however, before a national system was finally established. Interestingly, the Japanese model seems to

Table 9. Principal organizational features of the Japanese postal system

Emulated from the British post office	Emulated from other organizations (source)	Innovations
Formal monopoly and unified rates	Formal-regulatory structures (government bureaucracy)	Inputs of transport technology
Range of functions		Intermediate tier of control units
Division of labor	Formal training (telegraph)	
Differentiation of subunits		Activities to establish organizational niche
Subcontracting		Reverse franking, free post
Two-tiered employment system		

have played at least a minor role in its 1896 adoption: one historian of the Chinese post, Ying-wen Cheng, sees Japan's victory in the Sino-Japanese War as hastening the establishment of the postal system by demonstrating the effectiveness of that nation's adoption of Western-style organizations.[60]

The longer the government considered the idea but did not act, the harder it became to act: private local and regional companies moved into the mail business, and resisted strongly any efforts by the government to encroach on their preserve.[61] One barrier to the earlier adoption of a modern postal system was that China's official post had a long history and enjoyed high esteem, at least among Chinese officials. Any consideration of its replacement—as opposed to its reform—was therefore very difficult. As Cheng has put it, "Most Chinese officials believed that the I-chan (the official courier service) was by far the best postal system that ever existed, if the regulations were only conscientiously obeyed."[62] Although such attitudes did not prevail in early Meiji Japan, they were by no means absent; Maejima's successor in the Postal Bureau and the officials of the messengers' guilds were clearly convinced of the high quality of the traditional post.

More important than attitudes to the traditional post were its organizational structures. While on the surface the imperial Chinese official post and the Tokugawa official post looked very similar—post stations maintained by tax levies for the transmission of official communications—the organizational structure was quite different. The Tokugawa system was locally maintained, and its administration at the local level was separate from the official bureaucracy. In Ch'ing China the post was closely integrated with the civil service, with the result that "any reform of the Ch'ing Official Post would have amounted to a general civil service reform involving 1,030 districts, with nearly two thousand horse stations and tens of thousands of foot courier stations, not counting those in Mongolia and the border regions."[63] Indeed, one of the objections to a Western-style post— and apparently a decisive one—was that when the Ming government had tried to reduce its expenditures by cutting back on the courier service in 1629, the dismissed couriers had taken up arms against the government and contributed to the fall of the dynasty. The moral was clear.

To its detriment, the initial push for the postal service in China came from the overworked British head of the Maritime Customs, Sir Robert Hart. Not only was he a foreigner, and therefore without complete acceptance by China's decision-makers, but he lacked the time and the personal incentives to push aggressively even for a change he supported. His own job was already as much as he could handle; indeed, when in the 1880s the official climate appeared to be more receptive to the idea of the new post, he resisted its immediate introduction on the grounds that as his office would likely be responsible for its operation, he wanted to wait until he had more time and resources to give to its creation.[64] When the authorities finally asked him (in 1892) to put forward a formal plan for a new post, he proposed that the postal superintendents should be Europeans for the first few years—a strategy that would mean more than 300 Westerners on the Chinese government payrolls. The proposal was not accepted.[65]

As the experience of the Chinese with Sir Robert Hart suggests, the Japanese were more effective than the Britons themselves at transferring the British postal system to a new setting. The experience of India provides an even more convincing demonstration. In 1854 an Imperial Department of Posts was created in India to unify the various postal services that had developed under British rule. The post had hitherto been the responsibility of the British administrator in each province, each having different sets of rates calibrated by distance and weight.

Despite its longer history, the Indian postal service (under British management, of course) was slower than the Japanese to introduce money orders (1880 in India, compared to 1874 in Japan), and the postal savings system (1882 in India, 1875 in Japan). And in India the British departed from their own model in ways that hampered considerably the development of the system. One example was the attempt to hold down costs by renting buildings rather than constructing new post offices and by locating post offices (when it became necessary to build them) in cheap sites. Geoffrey Clarke, a former administrator in the Indian postal service, noted that "The chief object of the authorities in the early days of the Imperial Post Office seems to have been economy. As a building in a back street naturally costs less than one in a main street, many of the city offices are hidden away in the most inaccessible places."[66] Clarke also tells of postal facilities in major cities that were located on the second story of a rented building, accessible only by a single, perpetually crowded staircase.[67]

A second departure from the original British patterns was born of the colonial officials' mistrust of the quality of native postal employees. They instituted a system of fines for improper handling of mail. To quote Clarke again,

> It seems hardly credible that in 1854 one of the longest chapters of the Manual was devoted to an elaborate system of fining, under which different offices claimed fines from one another for bad work brought to light by them. The official who detected the finable offense was allowed to keep the amount of the fine subject to a deduction of ten per cent, which was remitted to the Postmaster-General's office . . . Naturally there was great energy expended in detecting offenses for which fines were imposed, and the result was an enormous amount of correspondence and bitter recrimination between offices. This vicious practice continued for many years and was not finally put a stop to until 1880.[68]

The tendency to burden an organization with checks against the inadequacy or venality of the natives is undoubtedly a fairly general characteristic of the transfer of organizational patterns across societies under imperial tutelage. So is an unwillingness to expend resources in setting up organizational systems whose aims are at least in part public service, rather than control. The Japanese did much better on their own.

Impact on the Social Environment

The volume of mail in a country is one of the most commonly used indicators of integration and modernization. Generations of social scientists have echoed Maejima's assertions that a national postal system is a central element in the consolidation of national administration and control, of the growth of commerce and industry, and of the expanding social networks of communication essential to modernization.

One Japanese historian of the postal system has observed that the new post was less a response to a new age in Japan than a means of creating it.[69] For Japan, the post was the earliest developing and the most extensive of the new transport and communications technologies of the nineteenth century. The basic network of over 76,000 kilometers of postal routes set up within the first decade was the key element of the communications system that made possible the increased centralization and integration of the 1880s.

The Japanese government consciously used the postal service as a tool of social and political integration, especially during its first decade, through the manipulation of postal rates. The growth of the press was fostered by cheap rates for newspapers and magazines, as in Britain. In addition, petitions addressed to government officials could pass through the postal system postage-free from 1872. This was a reversal of the pattern in Britain, where the direction of the free post was from the center to the provinces: members of parliament could send mail to their constituents free of charge. In 1873 manuscripts and drafts for newspaper articles joined the list of materials that could use the mails without charge, and in 1876 it extended to all correspondence between private citizens and the Home Ministry's Bureau for the Encouragement of Industry, and seeds and samples for commercial development. The free post was abolished in 1882, as part of the effort to reduce expenditures and raise revenues. Its abolition can also be taken as an indicator of the fading of the traditional relationship between the ruler and the ruled in favor of the more bureaucratized, centralized Western concept of the state.

The mail service itself was of course the single most important element of the postal system's role in increasing social integration and centralization. But other aspects of the postal service also contributed, particularly in the standardization of measures of weights and time. In the early 1870s postal stations throughout the country received Western-style scales for calculating postal charges. Even more important, in 1874 the Postal Bureau purchased and dispatched its first order of 1,000 clocks (some, at least, made by Seth Thomas of Connecticut) to postal stations throughout Japan. They came with detailed instructions on how to mount, wind, and maintain them; on how to interpret the Roman numerals on the face; and even on how to tell time ("When the big hand is on one . . .").[70] The route schedules required a standardized system of keeping time never before needed in most areas of the country.

One of the first tasks of postal officials was calculating the distance of the postal routes and mapping postal stations and delivery areas. In mid-1872 the Postal Bureau completed its first postal map of the entire country; this was reproduced and sent out to all postal stations. Officials had to standardize place names and the characters used for such names—not an easy task even in urban areas. In Osaka, for example, the post office had to issue a series of public notices announcing the characters as well as the boundaries for the different areas *(chō)* of the city.[71]

In its early years the Postal Bureau's role as an organization-creating organization had a significant impact on the development of commercial transport in Japan, especially land transport. In 1870 the bureau issued instructions for the formation of transport companies that explained the nature and organization of a company and provided detailed guidance on how to develop commercial company operations. Through the 1870s, moreover, the postal system was a major source of business for transport companies that followed its guidelines, through the subcontracting of mail transport. One historian has called these early companies "half official, half private."[72] Another scholar has compared them to the specially privileged *tonya* (merchant houses) active in Shogunate business during the Tokugawa period.[73] However traditional in origin, they provided the organizational base for the development of land transport. The Postal Bureau also encouraged them to merge to form regional and eventually national transport companies. The postal system also played a role, although a less influential one, in the development of shipping. Sea routes were important for domestic as well as foreign mail, and government mail contracts were a significant factor in the growth of Japan's first modern steamship companies.

The postal system's impact on organizational development extended to economic development, not only indirectly as a medium of commercial communication, but directly through the emulation of the British system of postal savings. The post offices provided facilities for personal saving on a scale unapproached by the banking system until after World War II. Moreover, through public notices in the post offices and periodic public relations campaigns, the postal system actively encouraged the spread of institutionalized personal saving. Although postal savings grew much more slowly in Japan than in Britain, reflecting the unfamiliarity with institutionalized saving, by the end of the Meiji era Japan had surpassed the absolute number of postal accounts in Britain.[74] Most of the accounts were small; in 1912 the average was only about sixteen yen. However, the total volume of saving was considerable. In 1912 the deposits by the end of the year amounted to nearly two hundred million yen. The investment capital this provided and the enhancement of the individual propensity to save were both extremely important contributions to Japan's economic development.

The chronicle of the Meiji postal system is not one of unmitigated success; in comparative perspective the achievements of the Japanese post, while still impressive, shine less brightly. Figure 6 shows the mail volume per capita in Japan and six Western countries in 1872 and 1912. Although Japan is by no means out of place in the distribution, it ranks considerably below the rest. Many factors explain the difference: Japan's later start, its lower level of urbanization, and the high proportion of its labor force still in agriculture. Several organizational factors also help account for the fact that Japan in 1912 had a lower per capita mail volume than Great Britain did in

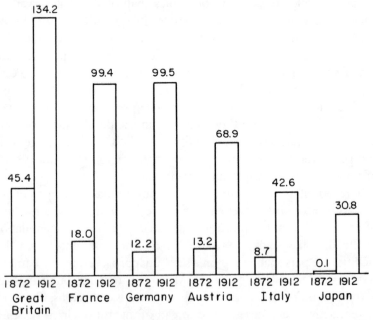

Figure 6. Per capita mail items in selected countries, 1872 and 1912.

1872. Most important was the number of postal stations, which determines the level of access to the system. Great Britain had more postal stations in 1854 (9,973) than Japan did in 1912 when the Japanese population was almost twice that of mid-nineteenth century Britain. Japan had fewer postal stations not because of lack of resources: the post had been making substantial profits since the mid-1880s. The government decided, however, that postal revenue was to be directed to purposes other than the extension of the system. Given the fact that in 1912 the country had twice as many police stations as postal stations (7,243 postal stations and 17,188 police stations), it would not be too farfetched to infer that the government valued administration and control more highly than general social integration.

These later shortcomings should not be allowed to obscure the real and important contributions of the postal system to social development. The postal system is also important for the study of organizational development during the Meiji period, in no small measure because the administrative difficulties of the 1880s and 1890s illustrate the problems of adjusting an organizational form emulated from another society to a setting where the level of technological and organizational development, the scale of the society, and the administrative setting differ significantly from those of the original model.

4

The Newspaper

In the second half of the nineteenth century the newspaper was widely seen as a powerful engine of progress, harnessing the technologies of the Industrial Revolution in the service of expanding knowledge and information. This first mass communications organization played a many-faceted role: political, in broadening information on state decisions beyond a small elite and in adding a new set of actors, the "fourth estate," to the political process; economic, as an advertising vehicle and as a major industry and employer in its own right; and—more elusive but perhaps most significant—social and cultural, in contributing to the standardization and elaboration of popular culture.

As an organization, the mass circulation newspaper was extraordinarily complex. The production of the content of the newspaper by reporters and editors and its physical reproduction by printers and their apprentices involved two very different types of technology and work structures. Moreover, a distinctive feature of the mass circulation newspaper as a product was that the consumer paid only a part of the cost of its production and distribution. The rest was financed by advertising, and the selling of the newspaper itself and the selling of advertising space required very different marketing methods. This array of activities demanded an increasingly large and complex organization. One early twentieth-century commentator went so far as to assert that "A newspaper is of all modern private institutions the most comprehensive in function and complicated in principle."[1] The newspaper enterprises in any given society therefore reflected the development of the social technologies of commercial organization as well as the physical technologies of transport, communication, and printing.

The newspaper is a major departure from the systems covered in the previous two chapters. Instead of the expansion of subunits of a single organizational system, the organizational history of the newspaper involves a changing population of competing organizations. Instead of following a specific model, such as the French police and the English postal system, newspapers built on a general and often vague model derived largely from the foreign press imported into Japan and from the knowledge that specialized organizations existed to produce them.

No real counterpart of the newspaper existed in Japan before the 1860s. Although Japan had a highly developed publishing sector in the Tokugawa period, official prohibition of the public dissemination of information concerning current political and social events precluded the emergence of anything like the Western newspaper. When foreign newspapers came into Japan with the opening of the country, however, the concept quickly took root. Japanese entrepreneurs began to publish newspapers even before the Meiji Restoration, and by the end of the Meiji period the newspaper was an established part of urban life. The metropolitan press compared in quality and circulation with that of Europe and the United States, and no provincial center in Japan was without its competing local dailies. Indeed, the Japanese went so far as to follow the Western pattern of transplanting the newspaper into their communities overseas; by late Meiji, Japanese-language newspapers had been started in their Korean colony and in the Japanese concessions in China.[2]

The Japanese newspapers of the late 1860s and early 1870s bore very little resemblance to the metropolitan newspapers of the day in the West. Yet over the first three decades of the Meiji period the Japanese press went through much the same transformation in format, organization, technology, and social role as the English and the U.S. press, the world leaders in the newspaper industry. By the end of the Meiji period the similarities with the Western press were very strongly marked. The processes that shaped this convergence and the contrasting pulls toward more distinctive patterns are the principal themes of this chapter.

Historical Background

THE NEWSPAPER IN THE WEST

The newspaper was not, strictly speaking, a product of the Industrial Revolution. The first daily newspapers in Europe appeared in the late seventeenth century, and the first British daily in 1702. However, the formative period of the modern press was the second half of the nineteenth century, especially the 1870s through the 1890s, when the technologies of the Industrial Revolution transformed the newspaper and placed it at the heart of the nineteenth-century information explosion. The telegraph and the telephone speeded up the gathering of information, while the expansion of the railways changed the speed and economy of newspaper distribution. Within the newspaper enterprise itself, the industrialization of printing exemplified the dynamics of innovation of the Industrial Revolution, in which improvement in one facet of production put pressure for innovation on another.

The fundamental factor was the growing capacity of the presses. The first major departure from the basic printing technology developed by Gutenberg in the fifteenth century occurred in 1814, when the *London Times* installed the first steam-powered press. The pace of invention accelerated with the invention of the rotary press in 1846. Its great speed and volume of production generated urgent demands for innovations elsewhere in the printing process. The development of stereotype in 1854 improved reproduction; the development of continuous web paper in 1865 solved the problem of accurately feeding the presses; in 1870 machines were developed to cut and fold newspapers; the use of wood-pulp to product newsprint in the 1870s made paper available in quantity and at a low price. By the 1870s, therefore, the technological base for the cheap, mass-produced newspaper was in place. The one remaining bottleneck was typesetting, still laboriously carried out by hand, until the development of typesetting machines in the 1880s finally loosened the last major technological constraint on the speed and volume of publication. The newspaper was by no means a passive beneficiary of the technological innovations of the Industrial Revolution. Many key inventions, including the typesetting machines, were conceived and developed by men working within the newspaper industry.

The growing production capacity of the technology was exploited and indeed fostered by bigger and more complex organizations. The newspapers of the eighteenth century were generally produced by printer-owners and those of the early and mid-nineteenth century by editor-owners. By the late nineteenth century the metropolitan press in Britain, France, and the United States was run by large organizations that utilized the emerging business control systems of budgeting and bureaucracy to manage an increasingly complex internal division of labor.[3] The expansion in the size and complexity of newspaper enterprise did not necessarily mean the separation of ownership and control, however, as Hearst in the United States and Northcliffe and Beaverbrook in the United Kingdom demonstrated. But control took new forms, based less on direct involvement in daily operations and more on bureaucratic structures and processes.

Because newspaper enterprises drew heavily on the commercial and management practices of their surrounding business environment, the speed of management change varied from country to country. Generally speaking, the "rationalization" of newspaper enterprise—specialization of functions, methods of coordination and control such as double-entry bookkeeping, joint-stock incorporation, and so on—was more rapid in the United States than in Britain, and more rapid in Britain than in France.

As part of the change in management, newspapers in all three societies took an increasingly aggressive approach to the market. Newspaper enterprises benefited from a number of factors outside their control that expanded their potential market: rising incomes, the growing urban and suburban population, and improving literacy rates. But newspapers were no more simply passive beneficiaries of a growing market than they had been of external technological developments. Newspaper owners and managers aggressively devised strategies to enlarge their market, both by expanding their distribution systems to make the paper easier to obtain and by pursuing advertising revenue to lower its price. Even more important was a set of strategies that has been collectively dubbed "the new journalism." It included a simplified style and a more visually appealing format, more entertainment and general information, and a closer relationship with the reader through contests, public welfare campaigns (such as Fresh Air Funds), and columns that responded to readers' queries or comments. Practitioners of the new journalism also acted to create news by sponsoring and publicizing special events, especially sports and entertainment. Indeed, national spectator sports were largely a creation of the late nineteenth- and early twentieth-century newspapers.[4]

As the internal tasks of the newspaper enterprise became more complex and demanding, an array of specialized organizations developed around it. The most important of these were the news service, the advertising agency, and the distribution agency. All three emerged in mid-century, and grew in number, size, and importance in the subsequent decades. The news service used the telegraph to transmit summaries of major stories, national and international, to newspapers that subscribed to the service. France's Agence Havas was established in 1832, Germany's Wolff'sche Telegraphen Büro in 1849, and Britain's Reuters in 1851.[5] The advertising agency purchased blocks of advertising space from the newspaper and then sold it to advertisers. The first such agency was established in Philadelphia in 1841, and since both advertisers and newspaper firms benefited from having a specialized organization handle the growing volume of advertising, ad agencies spread rapidly, especially in the United States and Britain. The distribution agency handled the delivery of newspapers to the network of retailers and delivery agents. The distributors grew largest in Britain and France, where by the late nineteenth century the bulk of the newspapers passed through their hands.

The leading innovators in newspaper technology and organization were the major metropolitan dailies in Great Britain, the United States, and France. Outside the central cities, a flourishing local press drew its models and much of its content from the metropolitan dailies. Innovations in technology and format spread not only within the newspaper industry of each society; they also crossed borders with comparative ease. The first rotary press, for example, was invented by an American (Hoe, in 1846), but his first sale was to a leading Parisian daily. Changes in format and content, such as the key features of the new journalism, also spread from country to country.

Such diffusion was inevitable. The newspaper industry was one of the most international industries of the late nineteenth and early twentieth centuries, at least in the flow of its "products" (newspapers) and its personnel, if not in the structure of competition. The Parisian daily did not compete with the London or New York daily for readers, but its editors did scan the leading London and American journals for news.[6] The news services increased the standardization as well as the internationalization of news, and they relied primarily on the press of various societies for their news summaries. Reporters were posted abroad in growing numbers, and they developed a first-hand familiarity with the metropolitan press of other societies.

The changes in the political role of the Western press in the second half of the nineteenth century also exhibited certain broadly similar trends. As newspaper circulation and the scale of advertising expanded, and as newspapers themselves became more profitable commercial investments, the importance of subsidies from political parties or individual political leaders decreased. This does not mean that newspapers and their owners and editors eschewed political commentary, only that newspapers became more independent of direct connections with political parties and politicians. Political leaders found the press less predictable as a result, and they deplored the change. Such complaints blended with growing reservations about the quality of the popular press and its fostering of an increasingly standardized popular culture through its emphasis on entertainment, sports, consumption, and formula fiction.

The newspaper was introduced to Japan, therefore, at a time when in the West it was undergoing dramatic changes in virtually all aspects: production technology, organization and management, format, and social role. Despite the fact that the birth of the newspaper in Japan lagged behind its emergence in the West by nearly two hundred years, the Japanese metropolitan press during the last three decades of the nineteenth century paralleled developments in the Western newspaper to a striking degree.

PRE-MEIJI DEVELOPMENTS IN JAPAN

Although the newspaper had no direct counterpart in Tokugawa Japan, the social, technological, and economic developments of the Edo period provided a solid base for its introduction after the opening of the country. By the 1860s the literacy of the population and the degree of its concentration in urban centers produced a potential market surpassing any in the eighteenth-century European societies in which the newspaper first took root. Moreover, the Edo period had witnessed the growth of a flourishing publishing industry whose printing techniques were readily adapted to the production of Japan's first newspapers in the 1860s and early 1870s.

Long before Gutenberg produced his famous Bible, printing was introduced into Japan from China. One of Japan's national treasures is an eighth-century religious work believed to be the world's oldest extant printed text.[7] Print remained a rarity, however, until the expansion of literacy and the flowering of popular urban culture in the seventeenth century led to the emergence of a substantial publishing industry. Japan's extremely complex script led to the abandonment of movable type in favor of the hand-carved woodblock, which had the advantage not only in the speed with which the master impression could be produced, but also in the ease with which illustrations could be incorporated into the text.

Shogunal officials encouraged publishing in approved fields, such as neo-Confucian treatises, educational texts, and agricultural manuals; tolerated the printing of novels and poetry; and took steps to prevent the reproduction of political commentary, Christian texts, and the discussion of current events. Booksellers in each of the three major publishing centres (Tokyo, Osaka, and Kyoto) had to belong to official trade associations. Once a year their members assembled to hear a Shogunal official read the regulations on printed materials.[8] This close official supervision led booksellers and printers to practice a considerable amount of self-censorship; the safest strategy was to avoid printing anything that might be deemed objectionable.

From time to time news-sheets *(kawaraban)* describing a single event such as an earthquake or a local crime were printed and sold on the streets. These are regarded by historians of the Japanese press as the indigenous forerunners of the modern newspaper.[9] However, Japan's first real newspapers began in the 1860s. In 1862 the Shogunate authorized an Edo printer to reproduce and sell the *Kamban Batavia Shimbun* (Official Batavia Shimbun), a newspaper published in the Dutch colony of Indonesia, which the Shogunate had been receiving and translating for official use since 1854. But that was not the first newspaper produced in Japan. In 1861 an Englishman, John R. Black, began publishing a biweekly in Nagasaki that covered local, commercial, and international news. A number of other English-language newspapers soon joined it. These were eagerly purchased and translated by Japanese officials in the Shogunate and the domains, who saw the treaty port press both as a source of information about the West and as a barometer of how the foreigners perceived Japan.

The foreign concessions in Yokohama were also the home of the earliest privately published Japanese-language newspapers. These early publications used traditional Japanese printing technology—the hand-carved woodblock—and followed the format established by the *Batavia Shimbun,* which used standard Japanese book-size paper and resembled the newsbooks of the sixteenth century in Europe rather than the English-language treaty port newspapers. Most of the contents consisted of translations of items from newspapers published in the treaty ports of Asia.

The same technology and format were employed by partisan newspapers that emerged during the Meiji Restoration (1867–68). The loosening of political controls and the growing urgency of internal political debates produced a number of proloyalist publications in Kyoto and Osaka and pro-Shogunate publications in Edo. Although they called themselves newspapers, their newsbook format and lack of periodicity had little resemblance to the Western newspaper format of the day.[10] After the consolidation of the new regime in 1869, the government invoked the traditional prerogative of control over information flow, and with Japan's first press law in 1868 it revived the Tokugawa prohibition of criticism of political affairs and officialdom, effectively eliminating the Japanese-language "Restoration press."

The foreign-language press, however, continued to flourish, especially in Yokohama, and it was there that the first recognizably modern Japanese-language daily newspaper was started in 1870. An atmosphere of relative freedom prevailed in the treaty port, under the eyes of a vocal Western community. Yokohama also had access to modern printing technology, and a number of young Japanese printers trained there as apprentices at the presses of the English press.[11] With the establishment of the *Yokohama Mainichi Shimbun,* which used a press imported through the good offices of the *Japan Gazette,* the development of the modern Japanese newspaper began.

Variation and Expansion, 1870–1885

Newspaper enterprises did not long remain confined to the treaty ports. Within a decade of the founding of the *Yokohama Mainichi,* weekly or fortnightly newspapers were being published throughout

Japan, and a number of dailies competed for readers in most of Japan's major cities. The center of Japan's newspaper industry in the 1870s, however, was Tokyo. Between 1872 and 1886 only two years (1878 and 1880) failed to witness the birth of at least two newspapers in the capital. By 1884 an average of nearly 86,000 newspapers were being published each day in Tokyo. This represented 54.5 percent of Japan's daily newspapers, in a prefecture that had 2.3 percent of the country's population.[12]

From the early 1880s on Osaka became a second major center of newspaper publishing and a leader in several aspects of newspaper development. Osaka in 1884 accounted for 21 percent of the nation's newspaper output, with 3.7 percent of the population. By the late 1880s the leading Osaka and Tokyo newspapers were invading each other's territory and competing for readers and for prestige. This two-city rivalry had no direct parallel in the West, where the development of the newspaper industry tended either to be dominated by a single metropolitan center like London and Paris, or to have a localized structure distributed among a number of regional centers, as was the case in the United States and Germany.

Tokyo's first three dailies, established in 1872, exemplify the wide variety of motivations and capacities underlying the founding of newspapers in the early Meiji period. The first paper, the *Tokyo Nichi Nichi*, was produced by three commoners—a writer of fiction, a printmaker, and a shop employee—whose major goal was to make some money.[13] Their choice of newspaper publishing as the avenue for their entrepreneurial efforts was probably influenced by the fact that two of them had worked for one of the short-lived Restoration newspapers.[14] The second Tokyo daily, the *Nisshin Shinjishi*, was owned and edited by John R. Black. Black's motives in publishing a Japanese-language newspaper undoubtedly included profit-seeking, but it is clear from his memoirs that he also sincerely wanted to create a model for the Japanese of what a newspaper should be.[15] Black himself wrote the editorials (the first in Japanese newspaper publishing) and most of the articles, and had them translated by a team of Japanese writers.[16] The third, the *Yūbin Hochi Shimbun*, was the brainchild of Maejima Hisoka, the "father of the Japanese post," who wanted a newspaper that would educate the populace in the ways of the era of civilization and enlightenment. He also aspired to generate a sense of nationhood in its readers by using the post to draw information from all over Japan (postal employees were enlisted as "voluntary" correspondents) to produce a genuinely national newspaper.

While most of the motivations for starting newspapers are represented in these three cases (profit-seeking, providing a model, educating the citizenry, and using resources acquired in other kinds of activities), the three newspapers themselves were atypical in their longevity. Black's newspaper was the first to fold, in 1875. Certain government leaders who did not relish his outspokenly critical editorials first hired him as an adviser (thereby taking him away from active involvement in the paper) and then passed a new press law making it illegal for foreigners to own Japanese newspapers. The *Tokyo Nichi Nichi* passed through several changes of ownership until it was acquired in 1910 by the *Osaka Mainichi* to become that newspaper's Tokyo flag-carrier, a role it maintains to the present day. The *Yūbin Hochi* survived until the Pacific War. Most metropolitan newspapers were much shorter-lived: more than half of the over one hundred recorded newspaper enterprises established in Tokyo in the Meiji period failed to survive for more than two years.[17] Only thirteen Tokyo newspapers survived for more than two decades.

The volatility of the newspaper industry in these early years is itself a measure of the difficulties enterprises faced in trying to establish a market, develop a revenue base, adapt Western printing technologies, and develop internal management systems. The influence of the Western newspaper model and the competing influence of the traditional publishing industry (which supplied key personnel, distribution systems, and technology), combined with low barriers to entry during these early years, made for enormous variation within the newspaper industry during the first decade and a half of the Meiji period, especially in the metropolitan centers.

COMPETING MODELS

The Western conception of the newspaper as a "journal of record" and a source of information for the citizens of the modern state was an ideal that appealed to many government officials in the early Meiji period. They prodded the government to encourage the establishment of "enlightened" newspapers and to reinforce the newspaper's supportive and information-spreading role.

One means of doing so was to make the information that the government wanted disseminated readily and cheaply available. The main vehicle for doing this in many nineteenth-century societies was the official government gazette. The Japanese government began publishing one in 1868. After an interruption from 1877 to 1883, during which each ministry put out its own reports, the government's newsletter became a daily publication, reporting official appointments, regulations, and policies.[18] The gazette was produced primarily for officials, but newspapers and interested citizens could also subscribe for a small fee (the 1883 monthly subscription price for the *Kanpō* was 50 sen, about 30 sen cheaper than the subscription price for the leading Tokyo dailies). For the newspapers, it quickly became a handy source of news of the kind of which the government approved.

Throughout the 1870s and 1880s the government also sought to impose its model of the press through a mix of the carrot and the stick. The inducements included access to information (such as the right to report on trials);[19] paid advertising for government services, including the postal service, the telegraph, government railways, postal savings, and police services;[20] bulk subscriptions to certain approved newspapers for distribution to government offices in Tokyo and in the prefectures; and direct subsidies, either in the form of government printing contracts or under the table cash payments. Press regulations applied the stick to reinforce the approved model. A contemporary observer, Georges Bousquet, who served as a legal adviser to the Meiji government in the early 1870s, put these regulations in their context:

> Journalism offers an unusual picture of the trends operating within this country: the independence of its language contrasts strikingly with the obsequiousness encountered by authority everywhere else; in its columns the freedom banished from the rest of the empire seems to have found refuge; there a spade is called a spade, and certain ministers are called incompetents. So much so that the government has seen itself obliged to search in the well-furnished arsenal of French law to extract therefrom the weapons it needs against this completely unexpected new arrival, the liberty of the press.[21]

The 1875 Press Regulations marked a turning point from the tradition-based controls of the 1868 regulations to the kind of restrictions employed in nineteenth-century Europe: fines and imprisonment for offenses against the standards of acceptable political comment; cease-publication orders to offending newspapers (added in 1876); and the institution of a licensing and deposit system (in 1883). The 1889 Constitution guaranteed the freedom of the press only "within the limits of the law," which meant within the limits of the existing press laws. These laws were gradually relaxed over time, with revisions in 1887, 1900, and 1909, but the concept of the fundamental right of the freedom of the press was not guaranteed in Japan until after World War II. The fact that the press itself drew its models primarily from Britain while the government drew its models of press regulation from the European systems of the 1870s exacerbated the tension between the officially favored role of the press and the models invoked within the industry itself.

How successful were the government's attempts to foster its model of the press? In one respect, at least, it enjoyed some success: throughout the 1870s and most of the 1880s a substantial section of the front page of most major newspapers carried reports of government pronouncements, regulations, and policies, often taken in part or in whole from the official gazette. Despite the battery of inducements and negative sanctions that the government was able to mount, however, the official "engine of progress" model of the press steadily lost ground to an alternative Western view of the newspaper as a proselytizer of a particular political viewpoint.

The creation of political organs, subsidized by loyal adherents or by politicians themselves, was a major force in the rapid proliferation of daily newspapers outside the major metropolitan centers in the late 1870s and early 1880s. Politics also produced a second burst of newspaper formation in the late 1880s and early 1890s, around the beginning of national Diet elections in 1890. The political newspapers of the late 1870s and 1880s faced severe repression: editors and writers were jailed under the press laws, newspaper presses were broken up by government-tolerated thugs,[22] and newspapers were forced to close down for press law violations. And yet the political press proved remarkably resilient. Provincial as well as metropolitan newspapers developed a variety of ingenious dodges, such as appointing a figurehead editor to serve prison terms, leaving the core staff to reopen the paper under another name. They also took steps to arouse public sympathy: when the *Kōchi Shimbun* was ordered to close in 1882, for example, the staff protested by holding a public funeral procession for the paper.[23] Unquestionably, the official government repression imposed high costs on the party press, and yet as an upsurge in party-affiliated newspapers in the early 1890s indicated, it did not succeed in banishing the political organ newspaper from the Japanese press.

How did the political press survive the government's onslaught? For one thing, the positive inducements that the government could bring to bear—advertising, subsidies, special privileges—were limited: they could and did have a powerful influence on some newspapers, but as the number of newspapers grew, the government faced a choice between spreading its inducements evenly and thereby considerably reducing their importance for any one newspaper, or concentrating them on favored newspapers and provoking a competitive response from the less favored. A second factor was the powerful legitimating effect of the Western model: especially in Britain, the political organ press was in the 1870s the dominant element of the newspaper industry.

Most important for the industry's survival, however, were the development of the resources that supported the organ press and the emergence of a strong demand for its services. The growth of the People's Rights Movement and the establishment of elected prefectural assemblies in 1878 gave a number of fairly wealthy, educated men an interest in supporting newspapers so as to broaden their ability to communicate their viewpoints beyond the political meeting (ironically, government controls on political meetings increased their need for the press). The movement also created what was probably the first national labor market outside the government service: young political writers moved around the country, taking positions as editors and writers on party organs. In the process they not only spread the ideas of the People's Rights Movement, but also helped in the diffusion of newspaper technology and organization. The election of prefectural assemblies, which began in 1878, stimulated local notables to turn to the newspaper as a means of building electoral support. And the formation of political parties provided an even more organized base of support, with the Jiyūtō in 1881, the Rikken Kaishintō in 1882, and the spate of parties that formed when the national Diet was created in 1890 (the *Nihon Kindaishi Jiten* lists fifteen political parties established between 1890 and 1900).

Another important influence on the development of the Japanese press was the traditional world of Japanese printing and publishing, from which a number of newspaper owners and staff were drawn in the 1870s and which provided key elements of the early organization-set for the newspapers of the 1870s. The printers and booksellers who had flourished in the Tokugawa period found their market shrinking dramatically in the early Meiji period.[24] Some of these publishers and writers then switched to the production of what were dubbed the *koshimbun* (small newspapers). These were produced in the early years of Meiji with the simple text and lavish illustrations of the earlier serial novels. Their contents, however, expanded to include contemporary events and serialized and semifictional crime and human interest stories. Some of these publications gradually moved to daily production, and as their circulations grew they turned to new Western-derived production technologies.

The party press, the government-approved "civilization and enlightenment" newspapers, and the independent dailies were called *ōshimbun* (large or great newspapers), both because of their larger printed sheets and their loftier orientation. In Tokyo during the 1870s and early 1880s the two types of newspapers did not regard themselves as direct competitors: the *koshimbun* aimed at a less educated audience than the *ōshimbun,* and they sold for less than half the price. In general, the *koshimbun* were staffed by printers, writers, and illustrators from Tokugawa publishing circles, and the *ōshimbun* by former samurai who regarded the newspaper as a vehicle for participation in public affairs. The distinction between the apolitical, entertainment-oriented, tradition-shaped *koshimbun* and the Western-modeled, politically oriented *ōshimbun* is usually portrayed as a major feature of the early Meiji newspaper industry.

Some of the early Meiji newspapers combined aspects of the *ōshimbun* and the *koshimbun.* They aimed for a simplified version of the *ōshimbun* to bring news of political and social developments to the less educated audience. The most successful newspaper of this type in Tokyo was the *Yomiuri Shimbun,* founded in 1874 by a publishing firm run by three former samurai. Two of them (Koyasu Takashi and Shibata Shokichi) had worked for the Bureau of Foreign Affairs translating Western publications, including newspapers; the third, Motono Morimichi, had spent time in England. They established a publishing firm, the Nisshūsha, in 1869 in Yokohama, the early seedbed of newspaper development.[25] Its presses were imported from Shanghai and a foreigner was hired to train the Japanese apprentices in their operation. Thus when the company moved to Tokyo in 1873 and began preparations for launching its newspaper, its printing plant had the most advanced technology of any of Japan's newspapers to date. Throughout the 1870s it continued to be a technological innovator: the first newspaper to use a steam-powered press (1876), the first to use a gas-powered press (1877), and the first to use stereotype (1877). By 1875 the *Yomiuri* reached an average daily circulation of 17,000, the highest in the country, and more than twice the circulation of the largest of the *ōshimbun,* the *Tokyo Nichi Nichi.*

Because the *Yomiuri* resembled the popular *koshimbun* in the size of its paper, its price, and the colloquial style of its articles, it is usually described as the most successful of the small newspapers. But in its early years it did not use illustrations or carry the serialized novels so important to the more usual *koshimbun,* and it did give extensive coverage to public affairs and government activities. Many of its staff came from the same stratum of samurai and scholars who produced the *ōshimbun.* One analyst suggests that an important model for the early *Yomiuri* was the prestigious *London Times,*[26] but in fact the *Yomiuri* was actually closer in some respects to the new journalism emerging in Britain and the United States in the 1870s than to the older Western model followed by the *ōshimbun.*

Like many organizations that do not follow the models dominant in their environment, however, the *Yomiuri* experienced some strains in maintaining its distinctiveness. In the increasingly politicized environment of the mid-1870s, with the splits in the Meiji leadership, growing resistance to the government's policies, and the formation of political parties, it was difficult for a newspaper that concerned itself with public affairs not to be drawn toward a more politicized model. The pull was especially strong in Tokyo, the center of government and consequently of political debate, and by the early 1880s virtually all of Tokyo's daily newspapers had a clear political affiliation. In 1882 the *Yomiuri* also succumbed, becoming an organ of one of the two national political parties, the Rikken Kaishintō.

The early success of the *Yomiuri* invited emulation. The party press of the early 1880s turned to a modified *koshimbun* format to take its political message to a less educated audience. In 1882, for example, Tokyo witnessed the publication of two new dailies published in support of the Jiyūto, one of the early political parties. One, the *Jiyū Shimbun,* followed the *ōshimbun* format; the other, the *E-iri Jiyū Shimbun* (Illustrated Jiyū Shimbun), adopted the format and style of the *koshimbun,* carrying serialized "political novels" with strong political messages and more light-handed political reporting. However, the most successful of the emulators was the Osaka-based *Asahi Shimbun.* In the first decade of the Meiji period Osaka newspaper entrepreneurs followed the trends of the Tokyo press closely, including the differentiation between the popular *koshimbun* and the public affairs-oriented *ōshimbun.* In 1879, however, the *Asahi Shimbun* was founded in Osaka on the model of Tokyo's *Yomiuri*—nonpartisan, information-oriented but popular in style, and low-priced—and it avoided more successfully than its Tokyo model the pull toward the political model. The *Asahi* eschewed any overtly partisan political stance and managed through shrewd marketing, fierce competitiveness, and extensive distribution not only in Osaka but also in the nearby cities of Kyoto and Kobe to achieve a dominant position in the Kansai market.

ESTABLISHING AND EXPANDING THE MARKET

Newspaper enterprises faced several problems in selling their product in the Meiji period: they had to increase the number of people who knew what a newspaper was; they had to convince buyers that the newspaper was something they wanted every day, not just intermittently; and they had to develop distribution systems to make regular purchase as convenient as possible for the buyer. In the early years of the Meiji press, newspaper enterprises were able to turn to an organization-set inherited from the Tokugawa publishing industry to help tackle these problems, but by the mid-1880s the limitations of the older patterns were becoming obvious.

An anecdote from John R. Black's memoirs describes the early difficulties of cultivating a market for the newspaper. One of the duties of the staff of his Japanese-language *Nisshin Shinjishi* was to canvass the city for subscribers, and Black himself accompanied his business manager, a Portuguese who spoke Japanese, on some of these visits, including the following call on a large commercial establishment in the heart of Tokyo:

> My companion, possessing remarkable fluency in the Japanese colloquial, was the spokesman. Addressing himself to the proprietor he told him the object of our visit. He heard all with great complacency, and we fancied with marked attention. Alas! we found that he had understood nothing. What we meant by a newspaper he had no idea. At length one of the *bantos* (clerks) said, "Oh yes, Sir! You have seen the paper. You have it by you somewhere—the *Nisshin Shinjishi*. Surely, you remember." "Ah! so I have," he said, "here it is." And he produced a copy of it. He then proceeded to pay some compliments on its getting out, and the interesting news it contained from foreign countries; and we thought that one who appreciated it so much would be a certain subscriber; but when he came to the end of his praises he said nothing about taking it regularly. Mr. Da Roza suggested, therefore, that as it had given him so much satisfaction he should place his name on the list of annual subscribers. "Why?" he asked, "I've got it—what more do I want?" "Yes, you have one day's issue, and it comes out every day." "So I understand," he replied, "but having it already, why should I take it every day?" And all the *bantos* laughed, thinking it an excellent stroke of wit, no doubt. Mr. Da Roza was about to explain, but the little boy (sitting beside him holding his account books) did it for him. "Master!" the little fellow said, "You don't quite understand. It is not in the same words every day, but it comes out every morning with the news of the day before, always something new." "What?" asked the master, opening his eyes doubtfully, "As much as this changed every morning? I cannot believe it possible!" He said he would not subscribe; but send to his booksellers for it as he wanted it. One could not have supposed that such ignorance of the uses of a newspaper would have been found among such generally intelligent, substantial people.[27]

This story reveals the difficulty posed by the general unfamiliarity of newspapers and points toward one element of the solution: the traditional distribution channels developed for publications in the

Tokugawa period, the booksellers of the urban centers. Many well-to-do merchants and samurai in the Edo period had a standing arrangement with their neighborhood bookseller to have interesting new publications delivered to them, on a running account that would be paid two or three months later.[28] As that practice continued in the early Meiji period, it resulted in the distribution of copies of newspapers to individuals who, like the merchant in Black's story, would not have taken the initiative to buy them on their own.

The traditional route of the booksellers was not the only means for making the public aware of the newspaper. The Meiji government in 1872 authorized the purchase of several hundred copies of three metropolitan dailies for distribution to government offices throughout Japan, a move that opened an important channel for exposing people to the newspaper as a product, especially outside Tokyo and the treaty ports. Both the army and the school system (especially the normal schools) made certain approved newspapers available to their members. And of course newspaper enterprises themselves worked to expand the awareness of the newspaper as a product, efforts that included the door-to-door canvass described in Black's anecdote. In the early 1870s, for example, the *Tokyo Nichi Nichi* built ten brightly painted newspaper kiosks (like those in Paris) at key intersections in the city, but had to abandon them because too many passers-by used them as toilets.[29] Several papers adopted the practice of using street-hawkers and of dressing their delivery people in eye-catching jackets. One new paper, which targeted the theater as its key specialty (the *Miyako Shimbun*), hired newsboys to scatter copies among the seats at Tokyo's major theaters.[30]

Fostering awareness of the newspaper as a product was of course only one aspect of creating a market. Equally important was making its regular purchase as convenient as possible for the buyer through the development of distribution systems. And in the early Meiji era the metropolitan newspapers depended heavily on the willingness of booksellers to act as distributors as well as sales agents. Even when home delivery was introduced in the mid-1870s,[31] many booksellers were willing to use their clerks as delivery people, or even to hire part-time help. In the major metropolitan centres some of the larger agents became, in effect, wholesalers of newspapers: that is, middlemen between the newspaper and the retail sales agent. By the mid-1880s five major distributors had emerged to act as the liaison point in Tokyo between the newspapers and the network of retailers that put the newspaper directly into the hands of the customers.

In building this kind of distribution chain the newspapers were following a prevailing commercial practice, and having a ready-made distribution system through the booksellers was a boon to the small-scale newspaper enterprise. Newspaper distribution, especially after the introduction of home delivery in 1875, was not an easy process to manage. It required a large and reliable but part-time labor force. To begin its home delivery service in 1875, for example, the *Tokyo Nichi Nichi* hired fifty delivery people whose previous occupations had required early rising, such as tofu sellers and rickshaw pullers.[32] Hiring and keeping such people on a part-time basis proved difficult, and newspaper enterprises quickly turned to external, nonexclusive distributors to handle both home delivery and the delivery of newspapers to the growing number of retailers willing to add the newspaper to their wares. The newspaper enterprise continued to maintain a small distribution force (usually only about a dozen people) to take care of some distribution, but as circulations expanded the proportion of delivery handled directly by the newspaper steadily decreased.

The postal system provided another distribution channel. The post had adopted the special cheap rates for newspapers and magazines of its British model, and early Meiji newspaper enterprises were quick to take advantage of them. The *Tokyo Nichi Nichi*, for example, mailed out 2,700 copies to prefectures outside Tokyo in 1874, at a time when its total circulation was under 8,000.[33] The prefectural history of Gifu (in central Japan roughly halfway between Tokyo and Osaka) records that as early as 1872 one village leader had a mail subscription to Black's *Nisshin Shinjishi*.[34] A list compiled in 1882 of newspapers distributed within Gifu prefecture contains forty different titles, including Tokyo, Osaka, Kyoto, and regional papers (such as the *Fukui Shimbun* from a neighboring prefecture), as well as locally produced newspapers.[35] The relatively easy circulation of newspapers through the postal system provided models for local papers, a source of news, a basic familiarity with the newspaper as a commodity—not to mention a means for the metropolitan newspaper to extend its distribution into areas where it was impossible to deliver the newspaper directly and where no reliable distributor had been identified.

Even the task of mailing newspapers was eventually handed over to sales agents. Given that each distributor handled all the major dailies, his efforts were not particularly vigorous on behalf of any single newspaper. Indeed, by the early 1880s the newspaper enterprises in Tokyo were themselves less aggressive in trying to attract new readers. Perhaps their preoccupation with their growing role as political organs and the related threat of government repression were in part responsible; perhaps, as the history of Osaka's *Asahi Shimbun* suggests, Tokyo's newspaper owners and managers tended to neglect the commercial side of the newspaper industry. Whatever the reason, building a market for the newspaper took a back seat to the focus on political discussion in the Tokyo press of the early 1880s.

It was an Osaka newspaper, the *Asahi Shimbun* (founded in 1879), that became the earliest innovator in the effective use of distribution channels. Like the Tokyo papers, the *Asahi* was distributed primarily through sales agents (over 70 percent of its circulation in the early 1880s was through distributors). Its relations with those distributors, however, were much closer than those that existed in Tokyo. The *Asahi* had chosen one major distributor for each of the three cities in which it was sold (Osaka, Kyoto, and Kobe), and it gave that distributor the responsibility for expanding the market and building a network of retail agents within that city. Given the *Asahi*'s commanding market position (by 1881, only two years after its establishment, its circulation outstripped that of all other Osaka papers combined), the enterprise was in a much stronger position vis-à-vis its distributors than were the newspapers in the much more competitive Tokyo market. One explanation for the *Asahi*'s relatively early strength in distribution techniques—the most commonly encountered in newspaper histories—is cultural: the more commercial orientation of Osaka favored greater attention to the business side of the newspaper than did the more political culture of Tokyo.[36] Another has to do with the nature of the environment: the greater dispersion of the Kansai market, especially across three major cities (Osaka, Kyoto, and Kobe) that were close together but not contiguous, meant that to reach effective production scale the newspaper had to cultivate its distribution system more consciously than did the Tokyo press.

TECHNOLOGY

The woodblock technology of the traditional publishing industry had several major strengths for the production of newspapers in the early Meiji period, in addition to its comparative cheapness and the ready availability of the requisite expertise. One was the ease with which the blockmaker could add small phonetic symbols alongside complex characters to indicate the pronunciation and thereby make the text easier to read. Another was the close integration of text and illustration on the same woodblock, a technique that could easily be adapted to the production of illustrated newspapers in early Meiji.

However, the traditional technology had two serious limitations: the number of copies that could be reproduced from one set of blocks was limited, and the technique lacked flexibility. In Tokugawa times, when five hundred copies of a work constituted a large printing,[37] the fact that the blocks wore down after a thousand copies or so mattered little. However, even the earliest dailies began with printings of over a thousand copies; the 2,000 copies that constituted the first edition of the *Tokyo Nichi Nichi* in 1872, for example, strained the reproduction system to its limit. Moreover, once a block had been cut, it could not be edited or updated; to change the text even slightly required the carving of a complete new block. Both factors, but particularly the first, quickly pushed newspapers whose circulation was growing to turn to Western printing technologies.

The transition was not easy. There were three major problems: obtaining and learning to use printing presses, switching to the more expensive Western-style paper and ink, and developing type that could accommodate the multicharacter Japanese writing system. The experience of Tokyo's first daily, the *Tokyo Nichi Nichi,* epitomizes the difficulties. Its first two-page issue in 1872 was printed with woodblocks: a woodblock carver sat beside the writer and carved the sentences into the block as they were written, and two printers ran off the 2,000 copies. With the second issue, an attempt was made to switch to metal type and a press, both purchased in Shanghai, but the printing required too many *kana* (Japanese syllabary) that were not available in the Chinese type case, and the reproduction was unclear (probably because of the paper used, a Japanese-style paper on which the ink tended to run). The newspaper switched back to woodblocks with the twelfth issue and continued to use them through the 117th issue.[38]

For many newspapers an important transitional step toward Western technology was the use of movable wooden type with a flatbed press. Wooden type had greater flexibility and somewhat greater durability than the woodblock, and a skilled printer could carve a character on the premises as it was needed. Once the printing skills had been mastered with the wooden type, the transition to metal type was comparatively easy. And at least for the metropolitan newspapers, the switch to metal type was easier because they could expand their inventory of type piecemeal. John R. Black records that when the *Nisshin Shinjishi* switched from wooden to metal type, the typesetters could quickly obtain any additional character by sending a messenger to the foundry and paying the equivalent of one cent per character.[39]

By the 1880s hand-operated flatbed presses were being manufactured within Japan, and Japan's domestic paper industry was able to produce Western-style paper.[40] This reduced the cost and the difficulty of obtaining and using printing presses, and most newspaper enterprises in the metropolitan centers and the major prefectural cities had switched to metal type and Western-style paper. Moreover, throughout the 1880s it was possible to set up a newspaper enterprise in the major cities without directly investing in a printing plant at all; the actual printing could be contracted out. One newspaperman who began his career in the 1880s, Asahina Chisen, recounted in his autobiography that in 1888 he and some of his friends, unable to get a job with one of the established newspapers, began publishing their own newspaper, the *Tokyo Shimbun*, and subcontracted out the printing. The newspaper was shortlived, but it served its purpose, at least for Asahina; his work with the paper won him a job with the prestigious *Tokyo Nichi Nichi*.[41]

Newspaper enterprises were not alone in desiring improved printing technology. It was the government's printing bureau, with its greater access to foreign technology and the heavy demand for rapid and high-volume printing, that was the leader in the introduction of faster presses throughout the Meiji era. The printing bureau imported Japan's first cylinder press in 1874. The cylinder press was considerably faster than the hand-operated flatbed presses (not very different from Gutenberg's press of the fifteenth century) that were most commonly used in Japanese newspaper enterprises throughout the 1870s. Although the cylinder press made for much speedier operations, especially when it was powered by a gas engine (first used in the newspaper industry by the circulation leader, the *Yomiuri,* in 1877), the flatbed presses had the advantage of being relatively inexpensive, especially after manufacture in Japan began in 1877.

Even with the cylinder press, however, it took twelve and a half hours to print 10,000 copies of the four-page newspapers of the late 1870s. For the few enterprises whose circulations exceeded 10,000 (there were only three of them in 1877, the *Yomiuri,* the *Tokyo Nichi Nichi,* and the *Chōya Shimbun*), the solution was to use stereotype to get multiple impressions from a single typesetting, and to multiply the number of presses used. In 1882, for example, the *Asahi*'s printing plant consisted of one English-made cylinder press, one foot-operated press, and seven hand presses; by 1885, it had eight cylinder presses, one foot press, and one hand press.[42]

ORGANIZATION AND MANAGEMENT

The aspect of Western newspaper enterprise on which Japanese newspaper entrepreneurs had the least information in the early Meiji period was internal organization: the division of labor, reward structures and career patterns, the information-gathering process, ownership and control patterns, and the financial structure and control systems. In the absence of a specific model, and given the variation in general models, marketing, and technology described above, it is hardly surprising that early Meiji newspaper firms would exhibit considerable variation in their internal structures.

Newspaper enterprises during these years were small-scale organizations by the standards of the Western metropolitan press of the day, or by those of late Meiji newspaper firms. The *Yomiuri,* for example, began in 1874 with one editor and three writers, and the *Asahi* in 1879 with a staff of eleven. The metropolitan *ōshimbun* were somewhat larger: the *Tokyo Nichi Nichi* in 1875 employed twenty-seven people on its editorial staff.[43] The provincial news-papers were even smaller: the *San'yō Shimbun* in Okayama began operations in 1879 with an editorial staff of three.[44] Because printing was so labor-intensive in Japan, the editorial employees were out-numbered by the printing staff. In 1879, for example, the *Asahi* employed forty-two people in printing, compared to its eleven jour-nalists.[45] Since most marketing and distribution activities were car-ried on by the outside distributors, neither the business staff nor the delivery staff was very large.

By the mid-1880s daily newspaper enterprises were becoming somewhat larger. One contemporary estimate of the costs of starting a *koshimbun* in the mid-1880s put the total minimum investment at four to five thousand yen, and the minimum staff at thirteen full-time people and one part-time illustrator.[46] Although the total amount of capital required to start a newspaper was not great, the uncertainty of the investment, particularly the vulnerability of newspapers to financial stress from closures for press law violations, encouraged multiple ownership and discouraged sole proprietorships, even in the provincial press. The larger metropolitan newspapers such as the *Tokyo Nichi Nichi* and the *Jiji Shimpō* favored the private partnership form of organization, with several stockholders of wealth and influ-ence.

The internal organization of the newspaper was shaped to a con-siderable degree by the state's press regulations. The 1873 regula-tions required each newspaper to identify its owner(s), editor, and printer when it filed its application for permission to publish, and assigned to the editor the primary responsibility for content.[47] The press regulations had a marked effect on the position of the editor. Because he was subject to imprisonment for violations of the ex-tremely restrictive press code, the position tended to be a *pro forma* one in the early Meiji press. As Jay Rubin has put it, "A newspaper had only to set up dummy editors and keep replacing them as they were jailed to continue printing subversive material. Nine such ar-rests occurred in 1875, followed by forty in 1876."[48] One common characteristic of the Meiji newspapers, therefore, was that the po-sition of the editor was lower in importance and status than it was on Western newspapers.

The *ōshimbun* of the metropolitan centers and the political press of the provinces accorded the highest status to the chief writer (*shūhitsu*). He wrote the most important articles, and usually had the loudest voice in the key decisions about what other major items would be included in each day's edition. On the large metropolitan newspapers, the chief writer also enjoyed a fairly high salary. Fukuchi Genichirō, for example, the head writer for the *Tokyo Nichi Nichi* (and a major shareholder as well, who therefore garnered a share of the profits in addition to his salary) was paid a monthly salary of 250 yen in 1875; this was the same as the salary of the head of the national Police Bureau, who was one of the Home Ministry's higher-ranking officials.[49] On the other hand, salaries diminished rapidly as one descended the status hierarchy: of the other sixteen people on the editorial staff at the time, ten earned only ten yen a month, which was a barely adequate wage.[50] Pay was even lower on the *koshimbun,* which often did not even have a chief writer: the *Yomiuri,* for example, did not institute such a position until 1886. Specialization was virtually nonexistent; writers on the staff were expected to turn their hands to novels, feature articles, and serialized stories as the need arose. In the early 1880s the top salary in many of the *koshimbun* was fifty yen, and the lowest five yen.[51]

During these years the reporter's role was divided between two distinct groups on the editorial staff: the staff writers who spent their time producing the text, and a smaller group of lower-status employees (the *saguri-gata*) who hung around police stations, fire stations, and government offices to pick up information to bring to the writers.[52] The differentiation between those whose erudition turned information into news and those who merely fetched the information may have traditional roots in the concept of the aloof Confucian scholar, but it was probably influenced in part by the treaty port press and Black's *Nisshin Shinjishi,* where the proprietor-editor relied heavily on Japanese subordinates to bring him information for write-up and presentation.

For an enterprise that employs fewer than twenty people, informal recruitment channels are more than adequate. Entry into the early Meiji newspapers was based primarily on some personal connection with the owners or chief employees: personal or family acquaintance, common geographical origin, common experience in the same office or organization before joining the newspaper, or, for the political press, shared involvement in a political party. There is no typical career pattern for early Meiji reporters, and one example can illustrate why. Takabatake Ranzen was born in 1838, and became a print-maker and writer of serial romances. Because his brother owned the bookshop managed by Nishida, one of the founders of the *Tokyo Nichi Nichi*, Takabatake joined the staff of the fledgling newspaper. After three years he left to join a *koshimbun* (the *Hiragana E-iri*) as chief editor. Thereafter he moved into and out of a number of publications. In 1876 he joined the Nisshūsha (the enterprise that published the *Yomiuri*) to work on a new magazine they were launching. In 1878 he was one of the founders of Tokyo's first evening newspaper, the *Tokyo Mai-yū*, but he left it after a few months. Over the next three years he worked for three different newspapers, including the *Osaka Shimbun*. In 1880 he returned to the Nisshūsha, this time as the head of printing for the *Yomiuri*, a position he left in 1882. His subsequent career was one of frequent job changes among newspaper enterprises.

In the sheer number of his employers Takabatake was probably untypical, but his switches from one newspaper to another, and the change in roles from writer to editor to newspaper entrepreneur and back are patterns frequently encountered in the biographies of early Meiji journalists. In the first two decades of the Meiji period the short life of many newspapers, the low barriers to starting one's own newspaper, and the frequent changes of management and direction even at established papers all encouraged a high degree of mobility. So did the small size of many newspaper enterprises; often the only way to move into a higher-paid and higher-status position was to move to another enterprise.

Takabatake's initial entry into journalism—through a personal connection with someone in authority on a newspaper—was also common, and not only in Meiji Japan. Eugène DuBief, writing in 1892, described how to get into journalism in Europe: by going to the editor or proprietor with a letter of recommendation from an influential person; by throwing an article into the paper's mailbox (like Charles Dickens, who got a job as a parliamentary reporter in precisely this way); and by starting one's own paper.[53] Both in Europe and in Japan the personal connection, direct or indirect, was probably the most common, although the other two modes of entry were also used.

In the 1880s, however, a new ladder into journalism began to emerge in Tokyo; it led from the new institutions of higher education into the newspaper enterprises. The linkages were especially strong between the newspaper industry and the private academies such as Keiō Gijuku (founded by Fukuzawa Yukichi in 1868), the Tokyo Semmon Gakkō (later Waseda University, founded by Okuma Shigenobu after his expulsion from the government in 1882), and Dōshisha University (founded by Niijima Jō in 1875). The first two in particular developed close ties with the newspaper world.

The connection began in the 1870s and was in part indirect, operating through the linkages between the academies and the political parties. The Tokyo Semmon Gakkō was closely connected with its founder's political party, the Kaishintō, and Keiō with the Nisshūsha. Therefore the schools served as ladders into the political press as well as into the parties themselves. More directly, in 1882 Keiō's founder, Fukuzawa Yukichi, began publishing a general-audience metropolitan daily, the *Jiji Shimpō,* from the school's printing bureau. The public commitment to journalism that this represented influenced more students than those who submitted articles to the *Jiji* and who went on to join its staff after graduation. Students were encouraged to send drafts to other newspapers. Asahina Chisen, for example, had his work published by the *Hochi Shimbun* while he was an undergraduate at Keiō in the 1880s.[54]

What was the attraction of journalism for graduates of these schools? In Meiji Japan, as in most countries even today, journalism was an occupation that had glamour. It also had the prestige of being intellectual work, which was especially important in a society with a Confucian tradition. For writers on politics and public policy, it had the added attraction of being a form of involvement in politics and public service. For those covering the arts or producing novels and serialized articles, it was a means of earning a steady living through the pen and of moving freely and with some prestige in the world of the artist and performer. And in the early Meiji period, when entry into the bureaucracy was still based on whom one knew and where one came from, it provided employment for those who lacked the necessary connections to get into state organizations.

The small scale of newspaper enterprises in early Meiji limited their capacity for gathering information. Aside from the news brought in by the *saguri-gata* or collected through the chief writer's informal contacts, the major source of news in this early period tended to be other newspapers. Foreign and treaty port newspapers supplied international news; newspapers from other cities were the source of most regional news; the official gazette carried much of the information about state activities; and rival newspapers were the source of additional items. In taking news from the pages of other newspapers, the Japanese press was far from unique. As Stephen Koss said of the Victorian press, "The press, a ravenous animal, has always fed on itself, not always with appropriate acknowledgement."[55]

In addition to other newspapers, the press of the 1870s relied heavily on informal connections to get information from more distant sources. The *Tokyo Nichi Nichi,* for example, listed eight "foreign correspondents" in its columns between 1875 and 1880, in such exotic places as Persia, Vienna, and Hartford, Connecticut.[56] None of these people were regular employees of the newspaper: they were businessmen or students who were persuaded to send dispatches to the newspaper, presumably for some remuneration. Irregular correspondents also wrote articles in various parts of Japan, either at the request of a friend on the newspaper staff or at their own volition. Again, this pattern is very like that prevailing in the British press of the day and in the British-dominated treaty port press. John Dawson, writing in 1885, pointed out that "The paragraphs in a London daily paper come from all manner of sources and from all quarters, and only a very small proportion of them are done by salaried men on the staff."[57]

What this meant for early Meiji newspapers was that gathering information did not cost them very much. Gradually, however, the newspapers expanded their own networks of newsgathering, and as they did so the financial needs of the enterprise grew. The first special-assignment reporter was probably Fukuchi Genichirō, the chief writer for the *Tokyo Nichi Nichi,* who went in person to cover the Satsuma Rebellion of 1877 in the south of Japan. By the time of the 1884 Sino-French conflict in China, in which Japan naturally had a keen interest, most of the major metropolitan papers dispatched their own reporters to China to cover developments.[58] Even with its limited newsgathering capacity, the metropolitan press was able to break some important stories during these early years. The revelations of official graft in the sale of government-owned enterprises in Hokkaido in 1881 constituted an important example of early investigative journalism: it forced a revision of government policy and proved that during these years before the election of a national assembly the newspaper provided the main arena for political debate.

The emphasis most historians have placed on the political role of the early Meiji press has tended to obscure the important but gradual changes in the revenue structure of the newspaper that had begun to take place. One of the distinctive characteristics of the mass circulation newspaper is that it is a product for which the consumer bears only a part of the cost of production and distribution. The cheap daily, accessible to a mass audience because of its low price, covers the rest of its costs through advertising revenue. In both Britain and the United States the mass press was made possible by a rapid increase in advertising, and the growth of a mass market in brand name consumer goods was made possible by the growth of the mass circulation newspaper. A similar pattern can be seen in Japan, although there the newspaper played a much more aggressive role in stimulating the growth of an advertising industry.

In the Meiji period the market for advertising, like the market for the newspaper itself, had to be created. In the early years it was virtually nonexistent, and newspaper enterprises looked elsewhere for the revenue to support the establishment of the newspaper. Many enterprises found it in printing.

The early Japanese newspaper publishers, like their eighteenth-century British predecessors, were generally printing establishments for whom the newspaper was one of their printing activities. Printing capacity was the major initial investment in starting a newspaper, and building a circulation large enough to support it took time and effort. For some of the early newspaper enterprises, like the Nippōsha which published the *Tokyo Nichi Nichi,* the newspaper was the core activity of the enterprise, and other printing activities were undertaken only to support the newspaper while its market was being established. Other enterprises, like the Nisshūsha which published the *Yomiuri,* had well-established publishing activities before they turned to newspaper production as one way of using their printing plant. One of the most profitable of the newspapers of the first two decades was the *Jiji Shimpō,* which could utilize the contributions of Keiō's own students for much of its material in its early days. As a result, its expenses were low and its profits high. An 1883 book about newspapers, cited in *Shimbun Taikan,* reported the *Jiji*'s monthly revenues at 3,050 yen and its expenses at only 650 yen.[59]

The major source of printing revenue was of course the national and the prefectural government. The various government ministries, bureaus, and offices put out multiple copies of regulations, notices, and handbooks of instruction, both for internal use and for circulation to the public. Much of this printing was contracted out to local enterprises, thereby providing an important source of revenue to some of the printing establishments that were producing the early newspapers. The government was also the first major advertiser.

Newspaper enterprises, even in the earliest years of the Meiji period, were well aware of the role of advertising. The treaty port newspapers carried a considerable number of ads, and so did the earliest translated newspapers, which carried the text of these ads, painstakingly translated into Japanese along with the feature articles. The *Tokyo Nichi Nichi* carried a listing of its advertising rates for its first twelve issues; its first ad ran in the fifth.[60] In the following year, 1873, the *Shimbun Zasshi* carried a feature article on English newspapers emphasizing the importance of advertising and urging Japanese newspaper enterprises to pay more attention to procuring it.[61] An advertising agency was actually established in Tokyo in 1873, but it quickly disappeared, leaving little record of its activities except its name.[62]

The first advertisers were shops carrying Western or specialty items; they tended to advertise irregularly. The government, however, proved to be a more generous advertiser. The postal savings system began running advertisements in 1875; the Keishi-cho took out ads to advertise lost property; the telegraph bureau placed ads for its service.[63] Throughout the 1870s the volume of commercial advertising in the metropolitan press increased gradually, primarily for new, Western-style commodities, such as beer, milk, lemonade, coffee, photographs, pens, and Western-style clothes. The provincial newspapers had to rely primarily on government advertising to supplement their sales and printing revenue. How much of a newspaper's income—even in Tokyo—came from advertising during these years is not easily determined. Newspapers were privately owned and did not make their revenues public. However, it seems that for most newspapers in the 1870s advertising remained a minor source of revenue.

The pursuit of advertising seemed unnecessary for the major metropolitan newspapers of the 1870s and early 1880s. Especially the *ōshimbun,* with their higher purchase price, enjoyed a healthy level of profits from sales alone. The *Jiji Shimpō* may have been unusual in the scale of its profits, but others too gained respectable returns. One of the *Tokyo Nichi Nichi*'s founders later reported that in 1873 his newspaper received average daily revenues of 56 yen and 40 sen and had expenditures of 38 yen 77 sen, a profit level of some 45 percent.[64] By the late 1870s rising costs and increased competition had lowered these profit levels considerably, although they were still quite respectable: profits for the leading Tokyo dailies ranged from 3 to 7 percent of sales.[65]

The *Jiji*'s Fukuzawa Yukichi was ardently committed to the model of the Western press, including advertising. He was involved in the founding of Tokyo's first successful advertising agency in 1882, which was set up to provide advertising support for the *Jiji,*[66] and he cooperated with Mitsui's chief manager, Nakamigawa, to set up a general advertising agency in 1884.[67] By 1883 approximately one-quarter of the *Jiji*'s revenues came from advertising, but this was probably higher than the average even for the metropolitan press.

In summary, by 1885 newspaper enterprises had grown considerably, but they remained small by Western standards. Japan's largest daily was Osaka's *Asahi,* with 32,000 copies. In the much more competitive Tokyo market, with its sixteen daily newspapers, the largest was the *Yomiuri,* with 15,450 copies.[68] To a Western eye, both the newspaper itself and the organization that produced it would have still been far removed from the metropolitan press of Britain, the United States, and France. Yet in the second half of the 1880s, a major transformation of the Japanese industry began to take place.

Expansion and Convergence, 1886–1912

In the mid-1880s the Tokyo newspaper enterprises that had led the industry in circulation and in profitability over the previous decade faced increasing problems. Between 1884 and 1885 the total circulation of daily newspapers in Tokyo grew by only 7 percent, and between 1885 and 1886 by only 3 percent.[69] Expenditures were increasing; the costs of telegraph messages during the 1884 Sino-French conflict, for example, had added considerably to the outlay of the metropolitan newspapers in that year. The continuing recession (triggered in 1881 by the Matsukata deflation and continuing through the mid-1880s) meant that the efforts to expand advertising revenues were meeting with little success. And yet new newspapers continued to come onto the Tokyo market: four in 1884, two in 1885, three in 1886.

However, as Table 10 indicates, newly established newspapers were increasing their circulations not by attracting new readership, but by drawing away the audience of the older newspapers. Only five newspapers founded in the 1870s continued to be published in 1885, and all but one of these experienced a decline in circulation between 1884 and 1885.

The president of one of the troubled newspapers, Yano Fumio of the *Yūbin Hochi,* responded to its declining circulation and profitability in a way that was not uncommon at times of crisis in Meiji organizations. He went on an extended tour to the West to look for solutions. Yano, one of the many graduates of Keiō Gijuku to enter the newspaper business, spent almost two years investigating the journalistic and management practices of the major Western metropolitan dailies. The changes he instituted on his return were so successful in reviving the fortunes of the *Yūbin Hochi* that other newspapers quickly followed suit. His innovations set the path of development of the Meiji press firmly in line with the new journalism in leading Western nations.

TRANSITION POINT, 1886–1891:
THE "NEW JOURNALISM" IN JAPAN
Yano's innovations were virtually identical to those which Alan Lee has identified as the components of the "new journalism" of the

Table 10. Circulation of Tokyo daily newspapers, 1885
(overall circulation: +7%)

Rank in circulation	Newspaper	Year founded	Percent change from previous year
1	Yomiuri	1874	−8
2	Jiyū no Tō	1884	+40
3	E-iri Chōya	1883	+65
4	Kaishin Shimpō	1884	+40
5	Jiji Shimpō	1882	+35
6	E-iri Jiyū	1882	−21
7	Konnichi	1884	+186
8	Tokyo E-iri	1876	−32
9	Yūbin Hochi	1872	+.5
10	Chōya	1874	−25
11	Nihon Taimusu	1885	—
12	Tokyo Nichi Nichi	1872	−19
13	Tokyo-Yokohama Mainichi	1870	+6
14	Keisatsu Shimpō	1884	+427
15	Meiji Nippō	1881	+4
16	Jiyū	1882	−91

1880s in Great Britain.[70] They covered changes in price, format, content, and language, as follows:

Like the other *ōshimbun,* the *Yūbin Hochi* had charged more than twice as much as the *koshimbun.* Yano lowered its monthly rate first to 30 sen from 83, and then later the same year to 20 sen, below even the price of the leading *koshimbun* (the monthly subscription rate of the *Yomiuri* was 33 sen).[71]

The size of the newspaper sheet was reduced by half (to virtually the same size as today's newspaper).

The serialized novel came to the pages of the *Yūbin Hochi* (Yano wrote the first one himself), as did the items of social interest and entertainment that had been the preserve of the *koshimbun.* Yano also insisted on a new emphasis on information over opinion, and for the first time enforced a general editorial policy to which writers were expected to conform.

Writing style and vocabulary were simplified considerably, in order to widen the accessibility of the newspaper.

Yano's innovations were not drawn wholly from the British press. Britain's new journalism had in its turn drawn heavily on the American press, where these trends were even farther advanced, and much the same innovations had begun in the Paris press in the 1860s. In all three societies the new journalism was seen as the wave of the future, for better or for worse. It did not lack for critics, who derided its emphasis on information rather than opinion and regarded its use of entertainment and human interest stories as a betrayal of the older golden age of journalism.

While Yano's innovations paralleled those of the Western new journalism virtually *in toto,* they also incorporated many elements of the tradition-based *koshimbun.* This raises an interesting question: was the transformation of the Tokyo press in 1886 "Westernization," or was it rather a form of "traditionalization"? The move to the new journalism in the West clearly inspired and legitimated Yano's moves to popularization. The *koshimbun,* however, with its roots in traditional popular culture and its decade-long experience with the tastes of a nonelite audience, provided a handy model for the substance of that popularization, in terms of the kind of language and the kind of human interest story that would appeal to the Meiji public. The answer to the Westernization versus tradition argument is that Japan's new journalism was the product of a pull toward a Western model of format and strategy, with a content defined in large part by Japanese popular culture.

As a result of Yano's innovations, the *Yūbin Hochi* went from its 1885 ranking of ninth in circulation among the sixteen dailies being published in Tokyo in that year to first in 1888. Its average daily circulation rose from approximately 5,700 in 1885 to over 15,000 in 1887 and over 22,000 in 1888.[72] Not surprisingly, the other *ōshimbun* imitated its example with considerable speed.[73] The *koshimbun,* including the *Yomiuri,* found that for the first time they were competing directly with the *ōshimbun,* and responded by incorporating elements of the old *ōshimbun* into their contents, especially increased emphasis on politics and public affairs. Some of the *koshimbun* had been moving in this direction even before the *Yūbin Hochi*'s transformation (the *Yomiuri,* for example, had begun to include an editorial from January of 1886), but the intensified competition hastened the changes. The *Asahi* gave a further impetus to competition when in 1888 it moved directly into the Tokyo market by purchasing a faltering daily which it rehabilitated as the *Tokyo Asahi Shimbun*.[74] Total newspaper circulation in Tokyo nearly doubled between 1884 and 1889.[75] And the advent of a number of new papers made for unprecedented volatility as new and old vied to attract the new audience. From 1874 to 1885, the *Yomiuri* remained Tokyo's circulation leader; between 1887 and 1890, the circulation leader changed each year.

The distinction between the *ōshimbun* and the *koshimbun* quickly disappeared from Tokyo's newspaper industry—or rather, it was internalized within the newspaper enterprise, which blended elements of each into a new model. More important, the new journalism necessitated (or speeded up considerably) changes in the newspaper's organization-set. As in the West, the drive to increase circulation to compensate for the drastic reductions in the newspaper's cover price led to changes in the distribution system and pressure to expand advertising revenue. And the growing demand for news led to the formation of wire services. Yano himself was instrumental in the creation of Japan's first general news wire service in 1890 (the *Shimbun Yōtatsu Kaisha*).

The various models in the Meiji newspaper industry are summarized in Table 11. As in the West, the older forms, particularly the elite press and the political press, continued to coexist with the newer forms for almost two decades. But by the end of the Meiji period the new journalism was clearly the dominant force in the Japanese daily newspaper industry. For many Japanese press historians, as for many in Britain, the commercialization of the new journalism was a falling away from the newspaper's calling as a political organ. But with this transformation the newspaper became a genuine mass medium and was able to develop as a complex organizational system that had strong similarities to the leading Western newspaper enterprises of the day.

TECHNOLOGY

The rapid expansion of circulation created serious strains on the production system of the publishing enterprise. Here, as in the

Table 11. Types of Meiji newspapers

Characteristic	*Ōshimbun*	*Koshimbun*	Political organs	Papers featuring new journalism
Origins	Western elite press	Traditional Japanese publishing	Western party press	"New journalism" of Britain and the United States
Peak	Early 1870s to mid 1880s	Mid 1870s to mid 1880s	Late 1870s to 1890s	Mid 1880s
Contents	Public affairs, commentary	Entertainment, human interest	Partisan portrayal of public events	Information and entertainment
Target audience	Highly educated	Moderately educated	Moderately educated	All readers
Format	Large sheet, dense typography, no illustrations	Small sheets, often illustrated	Small or large format	Standard newspaper size, illustrated
Price (per month)	60–85 sen	33–50 sen	Priced according to format	20–30 sen

introduction of the cylinder press in the 1870s, the key innovator was the government's printing bureau. Anticipating that the opening of the national Diet in 1890 would place increased demand on the government's printing office, the authorities sent the head of the official gazette to Europe in 1889 to learn about the latest printing technology. He arranged for the purchase and delivery of two French Marinoni presses. Because of his friendship with the head of the *Tokyo Asahi,* Murayama Ryūhei, he allowed an *Asahi* employee to accompany him on the trip. The newspaperman too ordered a Marinoni press, and spent a considerable amount of time at one of the leading dailies of Paris, *Le Petit Journal,* mastering the techniques of its operation.

As an interesting footnote to this story, the *Asahi*'s chief rival, the *Mainichi,* quickly followed suit and ordered its own Marinoni press in 1893, through the Mitsui Trading Company. However, nobody in either the *Mainichi* or Mitsui had actually seen the press in operation, and the *Mainichi* therefore owned a press it could not use. The *Asahi,* as a matter of course, zealously guarded its press rooms from the curious eyes of its rival. The *Mainichi*'s printing chief therefore asked the paper's stockholders for an introduction to the head of the government's printing bureau. Unfortunately, this gentleman, whether because of his personal ties to the *Asahi*'s owners or for some other reason, refused him access to the government's machines. The poor man finally found an employee of the bureau who was from the same village and prevailed upon his fellow-villager to smuggle him into the premises to observe the presses for three hours, on condition that he did not make his presence conspicuous by taking notes. The *Mainichi*'s printing chief then had to rush home and make notes from memory; he managed to make one more clandestine visit to clarify the techniques before he returned to Osaka with enough information to bring the press into operation.[76] The government was not always an open-handed initiator of new technology, but it was less able than a private enterprise to guard its knowledge.

The Marinoni press came to dominate the Japanese newspaper industry. The *Osaka Asahi* itself began to manufacture the presses in 1904, and two other Japanese manufacturing firms quickly followed suit. This brought the price of the presses down to a level affordable by the larger regional newspapers, which began in the first decade of the twentieth century to acquire their own Marinoni presses.[77]

It was not until the 1920s that metropolitan newspapers in Japan were able to acquire the high-speed presses that had been introduced into Western newspaper enterprises before the turn of the century.[78] The principal reason for this lag was that the major technical problem in the Japanese press between 1890 and 1920 was not the speed of the presses but the speed of typesetting. Just as in the West, the last link in the industrialization of the press in Japan was the typesetting machine, which automated the setting of type and redistributed the type for reuse. In the West, effective and affordable typesetting was finally provided by the *London Times*'s rotary caster in 1881 and Morgenthaler's Linotype machine in 1890. Even then, as Anthony Smith has pointed out, "the Linotype machine was an invention after its time. It had been urgently needed for years."[79]

In Japan, however, the complexity of the language made automatic typesetting a major challenge, one that was not solved until the invention in 1920 of the first Japanese-language typesetting machine by the company that had produced the first commercial Japanese-language typewriter. Until then, typesetting continued to be the bottleneck in the Japanese newspaper production system that it had been until the 1880s in the West. Indeed, it was an even more serious problem in Japan, because typesetting there was so much more labor-intensive and time-consuming. The difficulty was not only the greater number of characters and the resulting size and complexity of the print matrices;[80] it was also the practice of adding *furigana*, the small phonetic characters placed beside complex characters to indicate the appropriate reading. The *koshimbun* had started using *furigana* in the 1870s, and most major newspapers had adopted the practice by the 1890s. To use *furigana* with metal type meant that the typesetters had to switch to another type matrix to add the small symbols after they had set the type for the main text.

In 1901 the head of printing of the *Osaka Asahi*, by then Japan's largest-circulation newspaper, developed a system for adding *furigana* simultaneously with the characters by using type that carried both the character and its phonetic reading. Given that Japanese characters virtually all have multiple readings (some of the more common characters have as many as nine or ten), this made for much larger and more complex type matrices. Once the typesetters had mastered the system, however, it gave the *Asahi* a significant competitive advantage, especially during the Russo-Japanese War, when the Osaka paper was consistently faster than its competitors in getting its extras onto the streets. As with its earlier mastery of the Marinoni press, the *Asahi* endeavored to keep its technology secret, this time with greater success. The *Mainichi*, despite cooperative efforts with one of Japan's major type foundries, did not succeed in developing an effective working matrix that incorporated *furigana* with the characters until 1911.[81]

This innovation, while it helped speed up typesetting, certainly was far from solving the problem. Until 1920 the technological limitation on typesetting had an important influence on the newspaper's style and content and its internal organization. From the beginning of the Meiji period newspaper writing tended to be compressed and dense to save space. More important, however, was the limitation on how much information could be included in the daily paper. This became especially troubling for the new journalism, with its move to broaden the range of coverage and expand its advertising.

In the West the consolidation of the new journalism coincided with changes in the technology of newspaper reproduction, which allowed considerable expansion in the number of pages.[82] In Japan, however, the transition preceded the introduction of higher-speed presses and the large-scale production of cheaper newsprint by several years, and of automatic typesetting by two decades. In the late 1880s, when the *Yūbin Hochi* pioneered the trend, most newspapers were four to eight pages long; increasing the number of pages substantially was difficult, given both the constraints on press capacity and on typesetting. In the 1890s the owners of Marinoni presses were able to increase the size of their daily newspapers to ten pages, but that remained the maximum feasible size for the daily newspaper for the rest of the Meiji period.[83]

Newspaper enterprises therefore turned to a number of strategies to get around the technological constraints. One strategy was the inclusion of supplements that could be printed in advance: advertising supplements, special features, and self-advertising commemorative issues. As early as 1880, for example, the *Tokyo Nichi Nichi* was putting out an advertising supplement at least twice a month; in the last six months of 1880 it published 84 supplements (some only a page, others several pages) of extra news, price reports, and so on that would not fit into its regular four pages.[84] Some newspapers produced regular specialized supplements; in 1891, for example, the *Miyako Shimbun* added three illustrated sixteen-page inserts on the theater each month.[85] And major newspapers in the Meiji period lost few opportunities to produce special commemorative issues celebrating certain milestones—for the 2,000th issue, for example, or the tenth anniversary of the first issue. The *Yomiuri* issued thirteen such commemorative issues in the Meiji period, and it was not untypical.[86] These made an excellent public relations vehicle and a useful advertising supplement. The *Osaka Mainichi's* 1912 special issue commemorating its 10,000th number took nearly a year in the planning and had a hundred pages, eighty of which were devoted to advertising.[87]

The strategy that had the longest-lasting effect on Japan's newspaper industry, however, was the production of two distinct editions of the same newspaper: a morning edition, typeset during the late night hours, and a smaller evening edition, with a greater emphasis on features and entertainment, that could be typeset during the morning and early afternoon hours. This meant two shifts of use for the type matrices, allowing more pages to be produced each day without doubling the size of the matrices. The *Tokyo Nichi Nichi* first attempted to produce two editions in 1884; the *Jiji Shimpō* and some provincial papers, including Okayama's *San'yō Shimbun,* in 1885; the *Yūbin Hochi* in 1889.[88] The distribution system, however, could not manage the increased load; the evening edition arrived at too many houses after the family had retired for the night. These efforts therefore lasted only a few months.

In 1906 the *Hochi Shimbun* made a second attempt to produce two separate editions, and this time its distribution system, with its newly constructed network of exclusive distributors, was able to deliver the evening editions effectively.[89] The *Asahi* and the *Mainichi* finally followed suit in 1915. Their emulation of the practice marked the general institutionalization of the distinctive Japanese production of the two-edition set. Even after the introduction of typesetting machines in 1920, the major newspaper enterprises remained wedded to the production of morning and evening editions, sold to subscribers as a package. The uniquely Japanese institution of the set continues to this day, causing endless headaches for those engaged in international comparisons of per capita newspaper circulation (is the set one newspaper, or two?) and making newspaper distribution more labor-intensive and time-consuming in Japan than elsewhere.

EXPANDING THE MARKET

The new journalism aimed at expanding readership not only by changes in format and content, but also by innovations in marketing and distribution. In the decades after the transition to the new journalism newspaper enterprises put much more effort and more of their own resources into persuading people to buy newspapers and getting their papers into the hands of their readers.

The growing emphasis on marketing and distribution in the Tokyo metropolitan area began with Yano's reforms of the *Yūbin Hochi* in 1886. Among his innovations that year was the aggressive expansion of the number of sales agents in the Tokyo area, so that the entire city was covered by newspaper distributorships.[90] Since these were nonexclusive, other newspapers were quick to utilize the bigger distribution network. The pressure on marketing and distribution was dramatically intensified in 1888, when Osaka's *Asahi* purchased a faltering Tokyo daily (the *Mezamashi Shimbun*) and reorganized it as the *Tokyo Asahi Shimbun*.

The *Asahi* brought to the Tokyo market a new level of competitiveness and competence in marketing and distribution. Backed by the considerable profits and resources of its Osaka parent, the *Tokyo Asahi* could undercut the price of its Tokyo rivals and could indulge in such opening-day dramatics as renting Tokyo's municipal trams to give free rides (under *Asahi* banners), and printing in its first issue a handsome portrait of the Emperor and the Empress, at a time when representations of the imperial countenances were still unusual. The Tokyo newspapers reacted by organizing a boycott of the *Asahi* by the five major distributors in Tokyo. The *Asahi,* with its accumulated expertise in marketing and distribution, simply bypassed the main distributors and went straight to the local retailers and news agents, and the boycott failed. The *Asahi*'s entry into

Tokyo accelerated the trend toward more aggressive marketing of the newspaper.

One important marketing approach borrowed from the Western press was to increase the reader's involvement with the newspaper through a variety of techniques: fund-raising drives for victims of disaster or distress, contests and lotteries, and newspaper-sponsored concerts or sports events. The precise forms which these new interaction patterns took in Japan of course differed somewhat from the Western ones, but the general mode was similar. Tracing the exact provenance of these schemes is not an easy task; newspaper enterprises were unlikely to acknowledge the source of their inspiration in devising circulation-building tactics, whether their model was a foreign newspaper or a domestic competitor. Once a newspaper tried a particular tactic, however, and it proved effective, other newspapers would pick it up very quickly—without acknowledgment.

One of the first participation-building schemes picked up by the Japanese press was the charity drive, in which the newspaper first publicized a cause or emergency for which money was needed and then acted as a fund-raiser and intermediary. This served the dual purpose of arousing the readers' concern and presenting the newspaper as an effective agent for translating that concern into useful activity. The first such drive in the Japanese press was prompted by the *Normanton* disaster in 1886, when five major Tokyo dailies sponsored collections for the families of the victims of a dramatic shipwreck. An English cargo ship, the *Normanton,* had foundered in a storm off the Japanese coast; the English captain and crew took to lifeboats and were rescued, while the twenty-three Japanese on board drowned. Under the unequal treaties the Japanese courts had no jurisdiction over the English seamen, despite their obvious negligence in Japanese territorial waters. The ship's captain was prosecuted in an English consular court in Yokohama, and, the strong protests of the Japanese government notwithstanding, received an extremely light sentence, with no compensation given to the victims. The newspapers gave major coverage to the wreck and the subsequent debate over the injustices of extraterritoriality. The story combined the appeals of nationalism, discussion of a major government policy issue (the ending of the unequal treaties) in a way supportive of the government, and human interest in the victims of the tragedy and their families. So successful was the fund-raising drive that the provincial press joined in, including Okayama's *San'yō Shimbun,* which appears to have been an assiduous follower of the trends of the metropolitan press.[91]

The charity drive also fit well with the public service rhetoric that newspapers invoked in their efforts to defend the press against government repression. At least some papers continued to resort to it at fairly regular intervals. The *Osaka Mainichi,* for example, had fund-raising drives in 1889 for the victims of the Kishū flood, in 1890 for the victims of the Saitama flood, in 1891 for the victims of the Gifu-Aichi earthquake, and in 1896 for the victims of the Miyagi tidal wave (the disaster-prone geography of Japan was a boon to the newspapers in providing regular opportunities for using this particular involvement-raising tactic).[92] One of the effects of these efforts was to reinforce the growing sense of national identity in Japan, cutting across regional and local loyalties to make the plight of tidal wave victims in northern Japan, for example, a reality for the inhabitants of the Kansai.

A less elevated and more controversial mode of inducing reader involvement in the newspaper was the popularity contest, which became a staple of the metropolitan press from the late 1880s through the rest of the Meiji period. The newspaper would contain ballots for the readers to vote on the best kabuki actor, the best play, the most estimable businessman, or—in wartime—the most popular general.[93] Participation was extremely enthusiastic: the winner of the *Kokumin Shimbun*'s 1908 poll on Japan's most outstanding businessman received 858,180 votes and the runner-up had 704,021, at a time when the newspaper's total daily circulation was around 100,000.[94]

The 1890s and 1900s also saw growing use of contests that offered prizes for the winners. By and large, in Japan as in the West, the newspapers that were not the circulation leaders were the most ingenious and dedicated practitioners of this particular marketing technique. For example, in 1905, the *Osaka Mainichi* sent two reporters around Japan to see which ones could cover the most miles by railway in ten days, and offered prizes to the readers who came closest to guessing the winner's mileage (a tactic that undoubtedly raised reader interest in the daily dispatches filed by each reporter).

The use of lotteries and contests was, however, fairly closely controlled, and the police stepped in from time to time to ensure that the prizes were not excessively valuable. In 1893, for example, the *Miyako Shimbun* was locked in a fierce competitive struggle with the newer *Yorodzu Shimbun* (which had been established by a former *Miyako* writer), and as a circulation-builder decided to celebrate its fifth anniversary with a lottery offering valuable prizes including a gold watch. The Keishi-cho intervened and insisted that less expensive prizes be substituted.[95] But it was the chance of participating—and of becoming news—that appealed to the reader, as much as the prize itself.

This observation deserves special emphasis, although it is perhaps obvious. These marketing techniques—the charity drive, the polls, the contests and lotteries—themselves created news for the columns of the newspaper. The newspaper's growing recognition of its capacity for generating as well as gathering news was one of the more controversial features of the new journalism. Using its own marketing campaigns as fodder for feature stories was only one aspect of this capacity—albeit one of the most self-serving. Another example, common to all societies, was the creation of a mass audience for sports.

Traditional Japanese sumo wrestling was the first sport taken up by the press. By 1900 newspapers were competing fiercely to be the first to get the results of the major sumo tournaments onto the streets.[96] The first decade of the twentieth century saw the beginning of newspaper coverage of baseball: in 1906, the *Yomiuri Shimbun* began a sports column featuring the baseball rivalries of Tokyo's high schools and colleges.[97] Some of the more enterprising newspapers took to creating sports events. The first was the *Osaka Mainichi*'s 1901 sponsorship of a five-mile swim; in 1907, the paper sponsored Japan's first marathon.[98] The creation of newspaper-sponsored events went beyond sports. In 1911 the *Mainichi*'s rival, the *Asahi*, organized Japan's first air show by bringing over an airman from the United States to demonstrate his "flying machine."[99]

The creation of news was matched by the creation of features. The first general feature to appear in the Japanese press was the theater column. By 1890 every major Tokyo newspaper had its own theater critic; several of them were (or became) major figures in Tokyo's literary circles. At the turn of the century most major papers also started columns aimed at housewives, and literary columns aimed at students and the more educated readers. By the closing years of the Meiji period, the attempt to develop closer relationships with readers had led many major newspapers to offer a range of reader services such as newspaper-sponsored excursions, concerts, and lecture tours.

In short, newspaper enterprises in the metropolitan areas were increasingly generating as well as reporting on popular culture. They did so not with any conscious effort at shaping society or of importing Western activities into Japan. Their efforts were simply a part of their increasingly intense competitive strategies to capture public attention and to keep readers coming back regularly to their particular newspaper. Anything that succeeded was imitated; less successful efforts were quickly dropped. The Western press of the day inspired many of these efforts, but, as in the case of sumo wrestling or the kabuki theater, existing Japanese traditions were also exploited, with mutual benefits. In the process of building a larger mass audience for the traditional arts, the newspapers became part of a new organization-set that surrounded and supported those arts.

In addition to increasing the attractiveness of the newspaper itself, newspaper enterprises sought to increase their control over the distribution process. The distribution system inherited from the Tokugawa publishing industry, despite the expansion it went through during the early Meiji period, had certain disadvantages that centered on the issue of control. One problem was that of pricing. In the Tokugawa period publications had not had a fixed price: the bookseller would charge a price that covered his expenses and included a reasonable profit, plus whatever increment could be obtained from the customer—or in some cases, minus whatever was necessary to keep the customer from falling into the hands of a rival bookseller. Newspaper enterprises in the early Meiji period sold their issues to their agents at a lower price than they charged directly to the customer, on the understanding that the agent would cover his expenses and make up his profit on the difference between the price he paid to the newspaper (or to its wholesale distributor) and what he charged the customer. If the newspaper was mailed out, an additional charge would be levied on the customer to cover postal charges. However, newspaper enterprises had no direct means of controlling or even monitoring the prices actually charged to their customers. The *Asahi*'s own history claims that the enterprise was able to control the purchase prices within Osaka from the very beginning, but that beyond the boundaries of the city the price could vary considerably.[100] Presumably other newspaper enterprises had similar problems and dealt with them in the same way: by drawing up ever more specific sales contracts with their agents, by advertising regularly in the columns of the newspaper the price the customers should be paying, and by sending sales staff on regular visits to the distributors to monitor their operations.

A second problem was the structure of the distributorships. In its earliest years the newspaper signed up sales agents not on the basis of a carefully constructed sales plan but for their willingness to take on the task of distribution. One agent was often reluctant to hand over a customer to another, even one who was closer. Consequently by the mid-1880s there was a haphazard pattern of distribution agencies, with overlapping territories, often competing with each other to serve existing customers.

Part of the new journalism, then, was the effort to rationalize the newspaper distribution system, expand its geographic scope, and increase its control over its agents, without having to assume directly the burden of distribution. As the volume of sales grew, the most appealing solution, the exclusive distributorship, became economically feasible. Once again the *Hochi Shimbun* (the *Yūbin* was dropped from the title in 1894) was the leader among the Tokyo newspapers. In 1901 it set up four exclusive distributors in Tokyo to act as its major liaison agents with retailers, and in 1903 it established a network of exclusive distributorships on the retail level. The fierce competition to maintain circulations in the wake of the Russo-Japanese War compelled the other major metropolitan papers to follow suit.[101] The exclusive distributorship erected a major barrier to entry into the newspaper industry. It is perhaps not surprising that after 1903 the Meiji period saw only three new entrants into the Tokyo market, and they were very short-lived.

As marketing and distribution grew in importance, men who

worked on the business side of the newspaper came to have greater status within the company and were duly recognized as key elements of an enterprise's success. They also came to have larger and better-paid staffs and more influence on the format of the newspaper.

ORGANIZATION AND MANAGEMENT

When the *Yūbin Hochi* raised its circulation to 25,000 copies a day in 1886, it became the largest circulation newspaper in Tokyo. Two decades later it was producing 300,000 copies a day and was one of six Japanese newspapers (four in Tokyo and two in Osaka) to be selling over 100,000 copies.[102] The growth in the organizations that lie behind these figures is less easy to chart with precision, but it was almost equally dramatic. The growth in scale of production and sophistication of marketing kept pace with the growing capacity for gathering information, for building the revenue base, and for recruiting and organizing personnel. Smaller establishments that could not keep up were gradually eliminated from the metropolitan press, although smaller-scale enterprises that looked much like the metropolitan newspapers of the mid-1880s continued to flourish in many provincial cities.

The second half of the 1880s was a major turning point for the organization of newsgathering within the newspaper enterprise. The practice of having lowly staff assistants fetch information from police headquarters or government offices was replaced by the Western practice of having full-fledged reporters write up their own stories from the information they collected themselves.[103] By the time of the Sino-Japanese War in 1894, newspaper enterprises had expanded to the point where 66 newspapers sent a total of 114 reporters, 11 artists, and 4 photographers to China. Hundreds more reporters were dispatched to the military headquarters at Hiroshima to get the latest pronouncements from the army and navy.[104]

The large number of reporters involved in covering the war was a reflection of the growing size of newspaper staffs. Indeed the growing number of reporters led to the beginnings of the reporters' club attached to each ministry or government office, a practice that has evolved into what many regard as a distinctively Japanese phenomenon. Its beginnings in the Meiji period do not seem to be very different from similar arrangements in the West, where police headquarters and government offices put aside a room for the use of reporters covering that institution and provided regular briefings for them. The first Japanese institution to do so was apparently the Keishi-cho, which provided a space for reporters in the late 1880s. With the election of the first Diet, a *Jiji* reporter organized a Diet Accredited Reporters Association (Gikai De-iri Kisha Dan), which brought together the reporters assigned by the various newspapers to cover the Diet. In 1902 the reporters attached to the Ministry of Agriculture and Commerce formed their own association, and in 1904 the Army Ministry and the leading political party, the Seiyūkai, set up reporters associations. To what extent this formalization of the interaction of reporters and their subjects prejudiced the kind of information that reached the pages of the newspaper is a topic that is extremely controversial today. In the Meiji period, however, it seemed to signal a welcome acceptance of the newspaper's information-gathering role by the state's major institutions.

Newspapers expanded their part-time staff as well as their full-time staff. The *Mainichi,* for example, by 1905 had a total employment of 410, of whom 53 were editorial staff, 111 were domestic correspondents, and 13 were foreign correspondents.[105] Not all the 111 domestic correspondents were full-time employees of the *Mainichi.* Most worked for provincial newspapers or in other jobs, and dispatched news to the *Mainichi* by telegraph when it crossed their desks.

The newspaper enterprise supplemented its own newsgathering capacity by resorting to the news service, an organization that routinized the collection of information from the various newspapers and information sources in a society, and sold the package to subscribing newspapers, either by telegraph or (for much cheaper rates) by mail. The first news service to operate in Japan was Britain's Reuters. Under the "ring combination" agreement among the world's major news services, Reuters had a monopoly in China and Japan. In the 1870s the treaty port newspapers received Reuters dispatches by boat from Shanghai; Japanese newspapers picked up the resulting information by translating their stories, rarely with any formal acknowledgment. The first Reuters byline in a Japanese newspaper appeared in the *Tokyo Nichi Nichi* in 1879, although it does not seem to have been the result of any formal arrangement with Reuters.[106] In the 1880s, however, the Japanese government arranged to provide the English-language newspaper, *Japan Daily Mail*, with a subsidy so that it could subscribe to Reuters telegraphic news service, on the understanding that the Japanese press could avail itself of the information that was used in the *Mail*. Because the *Japan Daily Mail* was an evening paper, this enabled the Japanese dailies to pick up and translate the stories in time to get them into their morning editions. The government thereby encouraged the Japanese press to cover foreign news more adequately and managed to avoid playing favorites by not subsidizing any one Japanese newspaper. Perhaps the government also hoped that easier access to foreign news would decrease the newspapers' attention to domestic politics.[107]

The model provided by Reuters led in the late 1880s to the creation of domestic Japanese news services. The first one, in 1887 (the Tokyo Kyūhō Sha), was a specialized commercial service: it carried rice market news from Osaka to Tokyo for the commercial columns of the daily papers. The first general news service began in 1888, the Jiji Tshūshin Sha. One of the leading managers of Mitsui, Masuda, organized it with backing from the government. A rival service was established in 1890 by Yano at the *Yūbin Hochi*. The competition between the two proved to be too costly, and they amalgamated to become the Teikoku Tsūshin Sha. By 1901, however, the demand had accelerated to the point where the newspaper industry could support rival national news services, and the *Nihon Dempō Tsūshin Sha* (the forerunner of today's advertising giant, Dentsu) was founded. In 1906 it joined forces with an advertising agency to provide both advertising and news services and signed an agreement with Reuters to distribute Reuters telegraphic news service to its customers. In 1907 it spread its international newsgathering net (and by extension that of the Japanese press as a whole) with similar agreements with United Press in the United States and with Germany's Wolff'sche Telegraphen Büro.

The erosion of the cozy arrangement by which the Japanese newspapers picked up Reuters material from the *Japan Daily Mail* was the stimulus for this international expansion of the Japanese news service. In 1893 the *Jiji Shimpō* signed the first agreement between Reuters and a Japanese-language newspaper; the *Osaka Asahi* became the second in 1897. The full impact of the *Jiji*'s move did not apparently hit its rivals until the turn of the century, when heightened Japanese interest in international affairs (stimulated by the Boxer uprising and the growing tension with Russia) meant that *Jiji*'s ability to print its dispatches from Reuters a full day ahead of its rivals gave it a significant competitive advantage. As a result, the managers of two of Tokyo's leading newspapers, the *Yorodzu* and the *Kokumin Shimbun,* visited the editor of the *Jiji* to protest against its agreement with Reuters and to suggest a return to a more cooperative strategy—without success.[108] In the wake of the fierce competition to maintain readership that followed the Russo-Japanese War, the solution of making Reuters available through the major national news service was welcomed by the Japanese press in general—though presumably not by the *Jiji* or the *Asahi.* It did set off a major competition among the largest Japanese dailies to enhance their coverage of foreign affairs by other means. In 1907 the *Osaka Asahi* signed an agreement with the *London Times* for a telegraphic link between the two papers. Its main rival, the *Mainichi,* turned to developing a larger network of correspondents abroad by recruiting Japanese studying in Europe and America, some of whom returned to become *Mainichi* reporters.[109]

By the end of the Meiji period, the Japanese press was firmly embedded in the international network of newsgathering. Its news services were linked to those of Britain, the United States, and Europe; its reporters were stationed in most major capitals of the West and rubbed shoulders with the growing numbers of Western correspondents in China. Its coverage of the domestic scene had also reached levels comparable to those in the United Kingdom or the United States: the leading newspapers stationed correspondents in the key metropolitan centers (the *Mainichi,* for example, although based in Osaka, had full-time correspondents in Kyoto, Kobe, and Tokyo by 1905).

The process of expanding the newsgathering capacity of the press, both internationally and domestically, raised considerably the cost of newspaper operations. The days when five staff members could put out a newspaper based on information culled from other papers were over by the early 1890s. And as the scale and costs of newspaper operations increased, so did the search to expand the revenue base.

In 1885 the Ministry of Agriculture and Commerce issued Japan's first set of trademark regulations, facilitating the switch from promoting products to promoting brands that was the foundation of modern mass advertising. And in the following year, the *Yūbin Hochi*'s radical price reduction made the profitability of the newspaper dependent on advertising. One of the consequences of the new journalism—with its expansion of news coverage and greater variety of contents—was that the expenses of the newspaper enterprise rose at the same time that its price fell. It had to increase its volume of sales to remain profitable—hence the great efforts to strengthen marketing and distribution that began in the mid-1880s—and it had to expand its major alternative source of revenue, advertising.

Newspaper enterprises expanded their business staffs and used their columns to tout the virtues of advertising. The *Miyako Shimbun,* for example, in 1892 ran a five-day serialization of Henry Samson's *History of Advertising* (in translation). Newspaper enterprises also played a role in setting up advertising agencies. The *Jiji* had established Tokyo's first advertising agency. In 1890 one of the directors of the *Osaka Mainichi* was among the founders of a general agency in Osaka, which, like that in Tokyo, was intended to have a special relationship with the newspaper. Other newspapers followed suit, and the number of advertising agencies increased considerably. By 1895 agencies controlled most of the advertising in Tokyo, acting as "space brokers," like the early agencies of North America and Britain: they purchased blocks of newspaper space, and then sold it at a markup to clients. The *Miyako Shimbun,* in an attempt to increase its revenues, tried in 1895 to bypass the agencies and sell space directly to the advertisers. The agencies in consequence boycotted the *Miyako,* and after eight months the paper was forced to concede.[110] Although the newspapers managed to achieve direct control over distribution, through the exclusive distributorship, they did not gain control over advertising.

One form of advertising over which the newspaper could have direct control was the classified ad. The *Hochi Shimbun* was the first to adopt this Western-derived practice in 1898, and other newspapers quickly followed suit.[111] Another advertising innovation, also borrowed from the West, was introduced by the *Mainichi* in 1912.

That paper's advertising department head returned from a trip abroad with copies of the *London Times* that carried a series of articles on various American railroads, all of which had been paid for by the railroad companies. In the following year the *Mainichi* followed suit with its own profitable line in *kiji kōkoku,* or article-ads.[112]

Although the impetus for the change was given in the mid-1880s, the turning point in the revenue structure of the Japanese press appears to have been the Sino-Japanese War. The enormous increase in expenses in war coverage, the added cost of putting out numerous "extras" to break news from the battlefield, and the rise in the price of newsprint all made newspapers look to advertising to raise their revenues. For the *Osaka Asahi,* for example, 1895 marked the year when sales revenues no longer covered the costs of putting out the newspaper, and advertising revenue was a necessary element of making a profit.[113]

Fortunately, the growing demand for advertising meant that the price the newspaper could charge for advertising space also went up rapidly. Between 1886 and 1908 the purchase price of the *Osaka Asahi* doubled, from 25 sen to 50 sen, but the cost of a unit of advertising space increased by nearly six times, from 13 sen to 75 sen. Not only did the advertising charges increase, but so did the space which the newspaper devoted to advertising. In the *Osaka Asahi* this nearly doubled in less than a decade, from 547,422 units in 1902 to 1,000,999 units in 1910.[114] It was advertising that paid for the rising costs in newsgathering and in distribution. And the growing sophistication of advertisers meant that circulation became a more important element of how much a newspaper could charge for its ad space. In 1886 a new newspaper, the *Miyako Shimbun,* printed its advertising rates in its first issue: they were identical with those of Tokyo's established circulation leaders, the *Yomiuri* and the *Yūbin Hochi.* By the turn of the century advertising rates varied considerably, depending on circulations, and newspaper enterprises were beginning to publish their circulations, although official circulation data collected by an impartial agency was still several decades away. This in turn exacerbated the competition among newspapers in marketing and distribution.

The changing importance of the advertising, marketing, and distribution functions can clearly be seen in the changing structure of the newspaper's labor force. In 1875 the *Tokyo Nichi Nichi* employed seventeen people in the editorial department, and five in its business department, which handled internal accounts and purchasing as well as distribution, marketing, and advertising.[115] In 1905 the *Osaka Mainichi* had fifty-three people in its editorial department, and forty-eight in its business department.[116]

In the early 1900s the growing complexity of the newspaper's activities led the larger newspaper enterprises to build a structure of departments *(bu)* very like those of the government offices. The *Osaka Mainichi,* for example, distributed its fifty-three editorial employees among six departments (politics, society, overall editorial, dispatches, economics, and education and culture) and three branch offices (Kyoto, Tokyo, and Kobe), and set up four departments in its business bureau (advertising, sales, accounts, and printing).[117]

One important feature of newspaper enterprise in Japan was the direct entry of the Osaka newspapers into the Tokyo market. From their earliest days the major Tokyo newspapers had found a market in Osaka: the oldest recorded newspaper sales agreement in Japan was between the Nippōsha (the firm publishing the *Tokyo Nichi Nichi*) and two Osaka merchants who were to distribute copies of the *Tokyo Nichi Nichi* in Osaka. The Nippōsha bore the costs of sending the copies by mail from Tokyo; they arrived two or three days after publication.[118] In 1886 the *Asahi* reversed the flow by opening a branch office in Tokyo to deliver copies sent by post from Osaka.

The *Asahi*'s entry into the Tokyo market in 1888 with the *Tokyo Asahi,* however, was a major change in strategy. The *Tokyo Asahi* was in effect a separate establishment, headed by one of the *Asahi*'s founders, Motoyama Ryūhei; it could draw on the experience, the personnel, and the financial resources of its Osaka parent, but the distance between the two cities was such that it had to generate and reproduce its own contents. It was a different newspaper, so much so that in 1892 the *Osaka Asahi* began distributing its Tokyo sister paper in the Kansai.[119] The *Tokyo Asahi* was subsidized for many years by its Osaka parent. Apparently its newsgathering capacity and the prestige of competing effectively in the national capital was worth the financial outlay. The *Mainichi,* the *Asahi*'s chief Osaka rival, followed the same pattern. In 1893 it opened a distribution office in Tokyo to handle delivery there, and in 1904 it began serious efforts to enter the Tokyo market by acquisition. Its first attempt, the purchase of the *Dempō Shimbun,* was unsuccessful: the newspaper did little to develop a distinctive identity and it was a major financial drain on its parent.[120] In 1910 the *Mainichi* negotiated the purchase of Tokyo's oldest daily, the *Tokyo Nichi Nichi,* on condition that its name not be changed, and folded the *Dempō Shimbun* into its operations. As with the *Asahi,* the returns on the investment were in terms of newsgathering and prestige rather than profits.

One Tokyo paper responded to the invasion in kind: the *Jiji Shimbun* set up the *Osaka Jiji* in 1905 to compete with the Osaka papers on their home ground. It had comparatively little success in the Osaka market, which was dominated by the fierce competition between the solidly established *Asahi* and *Mainichi.* And for a Tokyo newspaper an Osaka operation lacked the payoff in prestige and newsgathering that an establishment in the national capital had for the Osaka papers. But with this mutual invasion we can see the beginnings of the national newspapers with their multiple publication centers that dominate the Japanese press today.

By the end of the Meiji period the economic structure of the Meiji metropolitan press strongly resembled that of its Western counterparts. The environment of the provincial press, however, did not provide either the infrastructure of advertising agencies or the population of advertisers that the major cities afforded. With some notable exceptions, the circulations of the provincial press remained closer to those of the metropolitan press of the late 1870s (around 10,000), and their revenue structure also resembled that of the political press of the earlier era. The gap between the two sectors of the press was wider in Japan than it was in the United Kingdom, where even for the smaller provincial papers of the 1860s and 1870s, "the proportion of total revenue made up by advertising was between one-half and three-fifths."[121]

The personnel that carried out and managed the changes in newspaper enterprise came from the metropolitan academies in growing numbers. The interaction between the press and the schools that dated back to the beginning of the Meiji period was cemented in the late 1880s as several leading journalists moved into academic positions. Three of the eight men who served as chief writers for the *Yomiuri* between 1887 (when the post was first established) and 1914 joined the faculty of the Tokyo Semmon Gakkō (later Waseda University). One, Ichijima Shunjō (chief writer from 1892 to 1894), who had been an associate of Okuma's in the founding of the school, became its head librarian and a key administrator. The second, Matsudaira Yasuo (chief writer in 1901–1902), became a professor of history and Chinese studies. The third, Gōrai (chief writer in 1914–1915), left the *Yomiuri* to set up a journalism department and to become its first head. Such men attracted students who aspired to become journalists and could provide introductions to their former newspapers or to other contacts in the newspaper industry.

The illustrious Tokyo University also contributed some luminaries to the Meiji newspaper industry. The most famous is probably Katō Kōmei, an 1881 graduate of Tōdai who entered the industry at the top: he bought the *Tokyo Nichi Nichi* in 1904 and became its president, striving mightily to turn it into an elite paper on the model of the *London Times*.[122] At a less lofty level, the staff biographies in the *Yomiuri*'s hundred-year history reveal that three of its eight chief writers in the Meiji period were Tōdai graduates, and two others had studied in the early 1870s at institutions that later became parts of Tōdai.

Increasingly graduates of such institutions of higher education had an advantage in entering the world of journalism. But many other routes still led into the newspapers. Some newspaper historians have endeavored to trace the roots of the entrance examination system, which the major newspaper enterprises introduced in the 1920s on the model of the civil service examinations. Takagi Takeo suggested that the first newspaper entrance examination was held in 1881, when the *Osaka Asahi* recruited three staff members through a competition in which aspiring journalists submitted drafts of articles.[123] The competition did not set a precedent, and it seems to be stretching to interpret the event as the first *nyūsha shiken* (entrance examination) in the Japanese newspaper world. A similar competition—again a single rather than a regular event—took place in 1893 at the *Yomiuri*. In 1904 the *Yomiuri* again held a contest for written essays, followed by an interview for the more successful candidates. That event attracted 358 applicants, of whom only one was hired.[124] None of these screening devices became institutionalized during the Meiji period.

The attractions of a career in journalism came to be augmented by what it could lead to as much as by what it was. In Meiji Japan, as in Europe, the newspaper could be a rung on the ladder into political life. Sixteen members of Japan's first Diet were newspapermen, and a larger number were elected to prefectural assemblies and to local government. Journalism could even be a ladder into officialdom: the Meiji government was not above coopting its critics by offering them government posts. It could also, as we have seen, be a route into academic positions, even in the early twentieth century. To return again to the *Yomiuri's* chief writers (largely because their careers have been well-documented), two of the eight were eventually elected to the Diet (and a third was an unsuccessful candidate); two entered the government service in official positions; three (as we have seen) became academics; and only one ended his career in the *Yomiuri*, rising to become the vice-president of the company. The Meiji newspaper world produced at least one prime minister, Hara Kei, who began his career as a journalist and became chief writer for the *Mainichi*. In an era when the paths into many major institutions were not yet formalized, the contacts that one could make in the newspaper industry and the visibility one could attain made it an attractive occupation for ambitious young men. Few opportunities existed for young women. By the turn of the century several metropolitan newspapers had begun regular columns for housewives, and some of them took the bold step of hiring women to write them. At a time when most careers remained firmly closed to women, it was significant that positions in journalism were available at all. By and large, however, the Japanese newspaper industry was a male bastion in the Meiji period—as it still is today.

In the new journalism, the internalization of the differentiation between the *koshimbun* and the *ōshimbun* made for a serious clash of cultures, one that was not resolved until long after the end of the Meiji period, if indeed it ever was. Some newspaper historians see even today a tension between the *seiji-bu*, the political affairs department, the heir to the concerns of the *ōshimbun*, and the *shakai-bu*, the inheritor of the mantle of the *koshimbun*. As the former *ōshimbun* hired people who had worked on the *koshimbun* to write their serial novels and cover the human interest stories they were incorporating into their pages, the established reporters apparently regarded the newcomers as performing a necessary but definitely inferior set of tasks. And as the *koshimbun* hired journalists to cover politics and foreign affairs whose background was in the world of the *ōshimbun,* the existing employees tended to regard the newcomers as snobbish and demanding interlopers. The two groups— often dubbed "hard" and "soft"—differed in lifestyle (the *ōshimbun* reporters favoring the latest in Western fashions and concerns, the *koshimbun* writers holding to more traditional interests) as well as in writing style, and the hostility was evident. The internal competition, however, was probably good for the newspaper as a whole, as the two groups vied to make the most effective contribution.

The hostility did not abate when some of the "soft" reporters successfully invaded the "hard" reporters' turf. In both the Sino-Japanese and the Russo-Japanese wars, some of the most effective and popular reporting on the war came from men from a "soft" background, who wrote human interest stories personalizing the war and the experiences of individual soldiers and sailors, heroes and ordinary men alike. The emotional impact of such stories was considerable, and they were very popular among readers.[125] This approach, though very good for newspaper circulations, bears not a little of the responsibility for the emotional reaction after both wars to the peace treaties, which were seen as having betrayed the sacrifices of Japan's fighting men by conceding too much to the enemy. The personalizing of the sacrifices made the betrayal all the more dramatic.

The newspaper reporter's career continued to involve considerable mobility of employment. Data on movement out of the newspaper enterprise can be derived from the lists of staff the *Yomiuri* published in two years: 1903 and 1909. The same chief writer presided over the paper in both years, but of the thirty-nine reporters listed in 1903, only fourteen (36 percent) remained in 1909, although the staff had grown to ninety-four members. The high turnover and the unstructured recruitment and career patterns of the Meiji newspaper enterprises are far removed from the recruitment directly from the school system and the lifetime employment of the model "Japanese employment system," which came to characterize the metropolitan press in the 1920s.

SUMMARY

One of the advantages of followership in industrialization is that a society need not recapitulate the experience of the firstcomer. The organizational histories of the police and the post exemplify the ability of organization-builders in a follower country to adopt social technologies that were the product of decades of development in the original societies, without going through the same sequence of changes that produced them. The organizational history of the Japanese newspaper, however, recapitulates the essential elements of two centuries of evolution in the countries that provided its primary inspiration. The first Japanese newspapers were produced with a woodblock technology that predated Gutenberg, in small-scale enterprises that would have seemed familiar to a newspaper proprietor of early eighteenth-century London. Over a twenty-year period newspaper enterprises moved from woodblocks to hand presses to foot presses to gasoline-powered cylinder presses to the high-speed Marinoni press. Over a thirty-year period the newspaper industry moved from domination by an expensive elite press to a period of domination by a political organ press and then into the era of the cheap mass press supported by a high volume of sales and by advertising. Over the forty-five years of the Meiji period, the small printing shop producing a newspaper with fewer than ten people gave way to increasingly complex organizations that eventually employed several hundred people and were supported by an organization-set of advertising agencies, distribution agencies, and domestic and international news services. In other words, the organizational history of the Japanese daily newspaper enterprise compresses into forty years the developments in material and social technologies that took over two centuries in the countries in which the newspaper originated.

The contrast between the "stage-skipping" development of the police and the post and the incremental evolution of newspaper enterprise was rooted in two major factors: the level of independence from environmental constraints and the availability of models. Whereas state subsystems could draw on the public treasury to support them while they established themselves in their new environment, private organizations such as the newspaper enterprise had to build more incrementally. Japanese newspaper enterprises in the early 1870s faced conditions that were very similar to those of the early newspapers in the West: a limited number of people who had the knowledge and the inclination to purchase a newspaper, virtually no demand for advertising space, and slow and restricted access to information. They had to begin on a small scale, as their counterparts had done in the West two centuries earlier. But as institutions emerged in Meiji Japan that provided a context similar to that which had supported each stage of development of the Western press—the political parties and the growth of an educated urban populace—newspaper enterprises moved to take advantage of and even to speed up those changes.

The availability of models also differed from unified state systems such as the French police and the British post, where the social technologies of earlier phases of development were replaced as newer ones emerged. In Western newspaper industries earlier forms of organization and even technology survived in the local press and in the expatriate treaty port press, even when they had been replaced in the metropolitan press. The earliest model of the Western newspaper accessible to the Japanese was the treaty port newspaper produced by an owner-editor with the assistance of a very small staff. It was, and it looked like, the equivalent of the small town newspaper still being produced in Britain. As newspaper enterprises grew and became increasingly knowledgeable about the Western newspaper, the range of models from which they drew expanded.

Even more important, although the main features of the new journalism were evident in the British and U.S. press of the 1870s, general recognition even in the West of the totality of the new model and of its triumph in the major metropolitan centers was a phenomenon of the 1880s in the United States (with Pulitzer's *The World*) and the 1890s in Great Britain (with Alfred Harmsworth's *Daily Mail*). The wonder is not that Japanese newspapers lagged behind the West in picking up the new journalism but that they were able to adopt it so quickly. In the United States and Great Britain the transition came after the circulation of the leading metropolitan dailies had passed the 100,000 mark, printing technologies had moved to higher-speed rotary presses and automated typesetting, and an organization-set of advertising agencies and news services was firmly in place. In Japan the move to the new journalism occurred when the largest Tokyo daily had a circulation of under 20,000, reproduction technologies were comparable to those of the 1850s in the West, and the organization-set of the modern press had only begun to develop. While the Japanese metropolitan press did not skip stages, its development clearly compressed them.

The speed with which the major metropolitan newspapers in Japan made the transition to the new journalism owes much to the rapidity with which they were able to establish themselves in the early Meiji environment. This in turn was built on an organization-set inherited from the traditional Japanese publishing industry, which provided a basic technology and an initial distribution channel. The newspaper also benefited in its early years from the rapid development of other organizations, such as the early extension of the post, the technological leadership of the government printing bureau, the expansion of the political parties (which provided both revenue support and a market), and the educational institutions that provided key personnel.

However, with the move to the new journalism the newspaper enterprises took a major role in speeding up the changes in circulation, technology, and organization-set that enabled them to break out of the limitations imposed by the earlier organization-set. The powerful example of the Western model of the newspaper provided both the inspiration and the legitimation for these moves, and the success of the first Japanese newspapers to adopt the new model prompted rapid imitation in the competitive metropolitan press. The very speed of the newspaper's development in Japan may well have contributed to the rapidity with which it made the transition to the new journalism; the patterns of the older models were less deeply entrenched in the newspaper enterprises and in their audiences than they were in Great Britain and the United States.

Just as the dominant trend in the Meiji period was toward the Western-modeled new journalism, so over time the Japanese newspaper was becoming more like its Western counterpart. At the end of the Meiji period, however, there remained some important distinctive features that continue to characterize the Japanese press to this day. One was the close linkage between the newspaper world and the educational elite, with the early institutionalization of a recruitment ladder from the leading institutions of higher education into the newspaper. A second was the creation of the morning and evening "set," in response to the technological limitations of the day—a pattern that had a major impact on distribution systems. And a third was the emergence of two centers of newspaper development, Osaka and Tokyo. The publishing of Tokyo editions of the two leading Osaka papers (the *Asahi* beginning in 1888, the *Mainichi* in 1906) and the establishment of the *Osaka Jiji* in 1905 by Tokyo's *Jiji Shimbun* mark the emergence of a national press with multiple publication centers that is so marked a feature of the Japanese newspaper industry today.

In both the move toward the Western model and the ongoing distinctiveness of some of the Japanese patterns the newspaper was not simply passively responding to environmental pressures, or even taking advantage of opportunities provided by the environment. The newspaper provides a case of a population of organizations many of whom were actively striving to change the environment— to create, rather than to find, a niche (in the words of the population ecologists). In so doing, they changed that environment in ways that were surely largely unanticipated by the early founders of the newspaper, or even by the later innovators themselves.

The Newspaper and Its Social Environment

The focus of most of the work on the Meiji press in English has been the political role of the newspaper.[126] This emphasis is hardly surprising; for the first decade and a half of the Meiji period, the newspapers were the major forum for criticism of a government that was increasingly dominated by the Satsuma and Choshu *hanbatsu*. And as the audience of the newspapers grew after the late 1880s, the potential of the press for expanding the basis for political participation also increased dramatically.

However, many newspaper historians feel that it was a potential that was not realized. As Albert Altman has pointed out, the years between the 1873 government split over policy toward Formosa (a split made public in the Tokyo newspapers, much to the displeasure of those who remained in the government) and the late 1880s "are often looked upon in the standard histories of the Japanese press as a golden age of journalism. Journalists, we are told, then pursued their calling in the name of social ideals, very often suffering imprisonment and fines for what they wrote . . . These journalists are the 'true' journalists, and these newspapers the 'true' newspapers, by which others are to be judged."[127] The commercialization of the newspaper in the late 1880s resulted, in this view, in a betrayal of the true role of the press in favor of building circulation and making a profit by giving the public what it wanted rather than what it needed. This did not mean that the political impact of the press was reduced, only that both the motivation and the orientation shifted significantly. In the late 1880s, for example, newspaper campaigns criticizing the concessions to the major powers in the proposed revisions of the unequal treaties produced what one historian has called "a typhoon of hostile public opinion" that derailed the negotiations.[128] Newspaper criticisms of the treaty ending the Russo-Japanese War in 1905 led to widespread protests and popular outrage. Newspaper campaigns on various social issues caught the attention of policy-makers, even though their impact on policy is often difficult to trace. Nevertheless the sensationalism of much of this coverage and the suspicion that it was driven more by a desire to expand circulation than to deepen public awareness of major policy issues has led many historians to share the critical tone of a comment in a 1914 guidebook to Japan: "While some of them (Japanese newspapers) compare favorably with the great journals of Europe and America, others constitute the real 'Yellow Peril' of international relations."[129]

The political orientation of the new journalism did indeed mark an important departure from the older approach of the elite and the political press. It followed the model of the new journalism in the West, in which patriotism (which offended no one) offered a safer approach for the mass market than partisanship. The newspapers of the new journalism often took clear stands on public issues, but whenever possible they took them on the moral high ground of the public interest and the nation, beyond the realm of partisan politics. In Western nations such as Britain and the United States, where the political system and political parties had a legitimacy that newspapers themselves could hardly match, the effects of the depoliticization of the press had less impact than in Meiji Japan, where political parties were in their infancy and struggling for public acceptance. Carol Gluck's analysis of "the ideological denial of politics" in the late Meiji period traces several factors that led in the late 1880s and early 1890s to a denigration of politics and political parties, such as the government's efforts to circumscribe political activities, traditional Confucian ideals of governance, and the attempts of the press "to eradicate its [politics'] baser parts and thus to ennoble it."[130] That the establishment of the Diet coincided with the move to the new journalism, with its emphasis on patriotism over partisanship and information over opinion, was an equally important factor.

Whatever the gap between what the newspaper could have done in Meiji Japan and what it did do, it was clearly the most important vehicle for disseminating information about the political and social changes in the society. As the first mass communications medium, the newspaper was an intermediary between individual citizens and a range of organizations. In other words, the newspaper became an important part of the organization-set of a variety of organizations. The theater, the arts, and the book publishing industry all found the newspaper a critically important means of getting and maintaining the attention of potential customers. So did the rapidly expanding number of producers of consumer goods, although these organizations had to pay for all the space they received in the newspaper and the cultural organizations got most of their exposure in the features columns.

The newspaper was also an organization-creating organization, playing an active role in the creation of advertising agencies, news services, and distribution agencies. However, these organizations, while they were critical for the newspaper enterprises, did little in their turn to support the immediate emergence of new kinds of organization: they were specialized and oriented primarily to the support of the newspaper. Only later, as magazines turned more to advertising for their revenues, did the agencies expand their clientele beyond the newspaper industry. On balance, the newspaper's role as a direct creator of new organizations was less important for the development of organizations in Japan than its role as a communications medium, which made it an important element of the environment for cultural organizations, consumer products firms, and political and state organizations. In short, the newspaper in Japan, like its counterpart in the West, became a key element of the institutional map of its society.

Conclusion

The relevance of the experience of "follower nations" for the societies from which they drew their models, and for general views of social change, has long elicited comments like the following:

> Great Britain should not be above learning a few lessons from Japan . . . The evolution in this country (Great Britain) has been comparatively slow, and many of our industrial developments are due to conditions which are rapidly disappearing . . . Other countries, notably France, Germany, and the United States, and above all Japan, have developed their educational arrangements and applied the results to national affairs in such a way as to affect profoundly economic and social conditions at home and trade abroad.[1]

This passage could easily have come from last week's *Economist;* in fact it was written eighty years ago by a Scots engineer, Henry Dyer. As early as the beginning of the twentieth century some Westerners had begun not only to realize how profoundly Japan had changed since opening to the West less than half a century earlier, but also to suggest that some of the institutions that it had modeled on those of the West might have something to teach its original mentors.

Implicit in Dyer's comments, probably unrecognized even by him, are three assumptions that have been elaborated, analyzed, and debated hotly by subsequent generations of social scientists. One is that a society's organizations and institutional arrangements reflect the conditions of the period in which they emerged and may be slow to adjust to changing conditions.[2] Consequently later developing societies, which need not retrace the steps of the firstcomers but which can adopt the newest material and social technologies, may have systematic advantages over the first industrializers. However, just as later developing societies can learn from the experiences of the firstcomers, so the firstcomers can in turn learn from the latecomers.

Dyer's assumptions were grounded less in the social science of his day than in personal experience. He had gone to Japan at the request of the Japanese government in the early 1870s as the principal of Japan's first school of engineering. In 1904 he looked back on his reaction to the invitation and his excitement at the prospect of shaping the new course of study:

> For some time I had made a special study of all the chief methods of scientific and engineering study in the different countries of the world and of the organization of some of the most important institutions, with the intention of devoting myself to the advancement of engineering education in Britain, so that I had fairly definite ideas both as to what was desirable and what was possible. I little thought that my first experiments would be made in far Japan, a country which at that time was almost unknown to foreigners, but which is now leading the way not only in education but also in many of the arts of peace and war.[3]

After his return to Scotland, he was involved in the reorganization of the Glasgow and West Scotland Technical College, and as he says, "I was able to transfer from Japan the programme of studies of the Imperial College of Engineering to the Glasgow institution which is the successor of the College in which the Vice-Minister of Public Works [Ito Hirobumi, who had hired Dyer in the 1870s] and I had studied as apprentices in the evening classes."[4]

While the rapidity of the reverse transfer of learning may make Dyer's case unusual, his role in setting the curriculum of Japan's first engineering school exemplifies one type of late development effect: the potential for a society to take from another country the most advanced social technologies for building its new organizations, even when those technologies are not yet widely used within the originating society. Ronald Dore contrasts this type of late development effects (due to "modernity factors" such as the range of available alternatives) with those caused by "underdevelopment factors," that is, by "the structural characteristics of late developing countries themselves or of interactions between them and the advanced countries."[5] Examples include the greater strength of nationalism and the greater resort to formal training to cope with the technological gap.

Late development effects, by definition, produce patterns that are common across a group of societies that embark on industrialization in the same time period. These effects stand between the influences on organizations and behavior that are unique to one particular society and therefore make for almost infinite variation, and those that exert similar pulls everywhere and therefore make for convergence across societies. As Ronald Dore and Robert Cole have made explicit in their debate over the relevance of late development effects in explaining Japanese industrial relations,[6] the main forces for divergence across industrial societies have been widely identified as culture and tradition. The case for convergence has largely been made on the basis of the "universal concomitants of the industrialization process,"[7] that is, the internal logic of industrialization and state-building, both of which require technologies and large-scale organizations that have common imperatives, whatever the social setting.[8] The debates over convergence are often framed at the level of the society as a whole, but the dynamics invoked to explain societal patterns are very much those at the organizational and interorganizational levels.

Japan, the first non-Western industrializer, has long been regarded by social scientists as a case with particularly important implications for social change theory and for other late developing societies. Japanese organizations today exhibit many characteristics that differentiate them from their North American counterparts, and this has been widely seen as evidence against convergence theories and hence *for* the predominance of culture and tradition in shaping Japanese organizations.

The three case studies in this book cover only four decades, and therefore the time span may be too short to address adequately the long-term direction of organizational change. But given this constraint, do the findings of the three organizational histories contribute anything to the debate over the relative importance of late development effects, culture, and the universal concomitants of industrialization? What late development effects identified in the existing theories or in other Japanese organizations can be found in the police, the postal system, or the newspaper? What were the main pulls toward the Western model in each organization, and are they adequately portrayed as "universal concomitants of industrialization" or are there other important categories of convergence factors? Conversely, what were the main pulls away from the Western models, and are they adequately covered by the concepts of culture or tradition?

Late development effects. An inventory of late development effects identified in the social science literature would include the following:

The later development begins, the greater is the direct role of the state in economic organization[9] and therefore the more likely are state organizations to become models for later-developing organizations;[10]

the less likely is the ideology of market individualism to be firmly established, and therefore the more likely that rewards and incentives will be organization-oriented rather than market-oriented;[11]

the more likely is the formal educational system to precede or to develop concurrently with other new types of organizations, and therefore schools are likely to be a more important part of their organization-set, as a routine source of recruits;[12]

the greater the resort to in-house training to deal with the knowledge gap between the advanced models and the new organization's members;[13]

the greater the likelihood that organizational patterns designed in the advanced countries to cope with specific problems will be adopted before those problems actually arise, in order to preempt and contain them.[14]

The police and the post confirm the suggestion put forward in Chapter 1 that the state role in economic organization is only one aspect of a more general activism in organization-creation. And the case of the newspaper suggests an even more general hypothesis: the later modernization begins, the greater the likelihood that organizations modeled on those of the advanced countries will engage in organization-creation, and the greater the level of resources and activities that will be allocated to "niche-building," that is actively developing the output side of the environment.

That the state bureaucracy was an important model for the two organizational subsystems of the state (the police and the post) is hardly surprising, although the connection seems to have been stronger in Japan than in either of the two original settings. For the newspaper the state bureaucracy apparently had some influence on the internal structure of departments. The influence of the state organizational models can be traced in the control and incentive structures of the police and the post, both of which exhibit the characteristics of organization-oriented rather than market-oriented incentive structures. They took from their original models a number of organization-oriented systems of bureaucratic controls (routinized reporting, a structured promotion system, and inspection), but both also reacted to high organizational turnover and inadequate individual performance by exhortation and training, neither of which had their origins in the Western models. The newspaper, on the other hand, seems throughout the Meiji period to have been characterized by a market-oriented system.

Both the police and the newspaper exhibit the tendency to turn to institutions of higher education as recruiting grounds well before such a practice became standard in the original models. Such institutions, with their Western-modeled courses of study, were graduating students who wanted to work in modern organizations, but the business world was not yet prepared to absorb them. Opportunities in mainline government bureaucracies were limited, so they took jobs where they could find them, including the newspaper industry and the police. There is an important distinction to be made between the two organizations, however: the newspaper recruited primarily out of the private academies, whose graduates found very limited opportunities in government. The police could recruit out of the national universities, because they had the advantage of being closely identified not only with the government in general but with one of the most powerful government ministries, the Home Ministry.

Another apparent late development effect is the reliance on formal training in the police and the postal system: both set up schools to train their recruits and provide advanced training for veteran employees. However, we should note that formal training was introduced in the postal system not as a consequence of "underdevelopment factors," in order to overcome an initial knowledge gap, but as a consequence of the amalgamation with the telegraph nearly two decades after the post began operations. Training in postal management was incorporated into the curriculum of the long-established telegraph school. And in the police the training schools were set up on the model of the army schools; here too they were not an immediate response to a perceived knowledge gap but an emergent response to organizational problems. Whether the formal training is truly a late development effect in these cases is therefore open to question.

In the police, the post, and the newspaper there are some examples of late development effects attributable to "modernity factors," in which social technologies that were relatively new in the originating society were adopted into the Japanese organizations. The adoption of postal savings is the primary example from the postal system, and the resort to the new journalism in the newspaper. The police system achieved a level of centralization that was only an ideal in Europe, both because it was able to preempt the emergence of local municipal forces and because it could draw on new communications technologies like the telegraph and the telephone to maintain effective levels of centralization as it expanded its geographic scope. Police training in techniques of monitoring and controlling socialism years before the formation of a socialist party provides an example of preemptive adoption of advanced patterns in order to control the environment, and the post's formation of an employee welfare association exemplifies a preemptive move to prevent the emergence of internal control problems.

One additional type of late development effect can be observed in all three organizations, although it is not of the usual "the later, the more" format and might therefore more accurately be labeled a "period effect," in the term proposed by Robert Cole.[15] What Theda Skocpol has called "world time" affects organization-building in a discontinuous fashion. The post provides an important example. In the second half of the nineteenth century, the post remained the backbone of the national communications system in the advanced industrial societies, and Japan, like the other nineteenth-century modernizers, followed their example and built a routinized and widely accessible postal system. When the telephone became economically feasible, Japan could incorporate it into an established communications organization. Twentieth-century late developers faced more difficult choices across communications systems, and were often able to satisfy the administration and control needs of the government without giving priority to the cheap, generally accessible and reliable post.

In the case of the daily press, the latter part of the nineteenth century was the era of the newspaper; it was unchallenged by the more accessible but also more controllable electronic media. Japan's mass media system today resembles, in its journalistic norms of news and newsgathering and in the configuration of its media organizations, much more those of other nineteenth-century modernizers than later developing societies. And in the case of the police, foreign demands for a standardized Western-style police force as a condition for renegotiating the extraterritoriality provisions of the unequal treaties enhanced the salience of the police in the state-building activities of mid-Meiji; each prospective round of negotiations signaled a reorganization of the national system aimed at increasing its capacity and standardization. In the twentieth century, when the unequal treaties system gave way to economic imperialism, the pressures of the international system on the developing countries shifted their focus.

Late development effects are clearly observable in all three organizational histories. However, only one such effect is observable across all three organizations—the organization-building role of foreign-modeled organizations—and at least one organizational feature widely believed to be a consequence of late development (formal training) has a more complex lineage than the existing literature would suggest.

Late development effects are primarily oriented to explaining systematic differences between the patterns of the more and less advanced countries that arise in the initial stages of development. They are grounded on the assumption that the subsequent path of development will diverge from that of the advanced countries. And yet we saw that in the case of the post and the newspaper the organizations tended to become more like their Western models over time. The high point of resemblance between the Japanese police system and its French model, on the other hand, was in the early 1880s; thereafter it developed distinctive patterns of dispersion, training, and control. Andrew Gordon has identified a similar pattern in his study of Japanese labor relations in heavy industry from 1853 to 1955: "Japanese labor relations resembled those of the West more at the outset, in the nineteenth century, than today."[16] Had the organizational histories of the post and the newspaper pursued developments past the end of the Meiji period, the same pattern might have been observed there as well. As Gordon has pointed out, such a development path is not explained well either by late development effects, theories of convergence, or by resort to tradition and culture. What other factors can account for the pulls toward and away from the Western models?

Pulls toward the model. The major source of continued pulls toward the Western models in all three organizations was continued interaction with or exposure to the foreign model. In the case of the post and the newspaper, interaction occurred in part because the foreign organization directly provided inputs to its Japanese counterpart: the Western newspaper provided news, and the Western posts provided (and took) mail. Indeed, in the case of the post we can see that those interactions resulted in the postal system taking on functions for foreign mail that it assumed later on the domestic scene. Japan introduced a parcel post for foreign mail, accessible in Tokyo and the open ports, thirteen years before the domestic parcel post. And it assumed full responsibility for lost foreign mail in 1883, seventeen years before it did so for domestic mail. The postal system was the only one of the three organizations to belong to an international organization that involved regular interaction with representatives from other systems: the Universal Postal Union, which Japan joined in 1877. The newspaper firm, however, looked to Western newspapers and Western news services for a significant part of its content. In other words, two of the three organizations had foreign organizations as members of their organization-set.

Having Western organizations in the organization-set is only one aspect of the interaction between the advanced countries and the latecomer. More direct influences were at work in the development of the Japanese police. In both the police and the post exposure to the Western models was routinized through the creation of a department with the mandate to collect and disseminate information on developments in Western systems. And in the police a series of investigative missions (the most important in 1879) provided more detailed first-hand information.

A second major pull toward the model over time came as the organization-set of the original emerged in the Japanese environment. For both the post and the newspaper the completion of the organization-set was a key element of the process by which the organizations moved closer to the patterns of their models over time: the railroads, the transport companies, and major commercial and administrative users for the post, the advertising agency, the news service, and the distribution agency for the newspaper.

Pulls away from the model. The most powerful pull away from the original model came from other Western-modeled organizations in the environment. The original models were far away, and the continued acquisition of information on their structures was often less influential than the models provided by powerful organizations in the immediate environment of the emerging organization. The army provided a powerful model for the police, and the central government ministries provided models not only for the two state subsystems but also for the newspaper.

A second source of divergence came from idiosyncratic, function-linked adaptations in response to the challenges of specific societal conditions. The dispersion of police posts throughout the urban areas is one example; the production of separate morning and evening editions of the same newspaper in response to technological constraints is another.

What departures from the Western models can be linked directly to culture or tradition? In the post, the refusal of the early post to employ women, the use of the free post to carry petitions from citizens to the government, the restrictions on access to postal savings can all be traced to cultural factors. However, all three were relatively short-lived. In the police, the invocation of the samurai model of loyalty and paternalism toward the citizenry are the most striking examples of traditional influence, and these lasted much longer. The contrast in the longevity of traditional patterns in the two organizations suggests two hypotheses. First, specific organizational structures and functions derived from traditional patterns are less likely to survive than general attitudinal patterns. Second, in an organization built on a specific foreign model, traditional patterns are more likely to have a sustained influence when they are legitimated by the existence of similar patterns in the model. In the case of the police, for example, the samurai legacy was explicitly seen as the analogue to the military background of the continental police. And the well-known arrogance of the police toward the citizens in France and in Germany rivaled and legitimated the Japanese patterns.[17]

One of the areas where culture and tradition has been seen as most important in the analysis of industrial relations has been the use of training, socialization, and exhortation to elicit performance, rather than offering material inducements. This pattern is strongly in evidence in the police. However, two important factors explain much of the institutionalization of this incentive structure in the police: the model of the army, another Western-modeled organization, and the severe constraints on police financial resources throughout the Meiji period. Nevertheless, the possibility remains that cultural and traditional legitimation made this a more congenial incentive structure in Japan than in the West, even though tradition was not the primary driver.

For the most part, however, the extensive and important emergent innovations in the three organizations cannot be attributed primarily to the conscious or unconscious accommodation of the Japanese tradition. What we see in these three organizations is a reshaping of the Japanese traditions to fit the needs of the organizations rather than a reshaping of the Western models to fit the traditions of Japan.

The reshaping of the tradition was a phenomenon of the late Meiji period; that is, it followed the adoption and adaptation of the new organizations, rather than preceding them or occurring simultaneously. Organizational models serve two important roles: inspiration and legitimation. Inspiration is providing the ideas for innovations in organizational patterns: it centers on the question, "How have other organizations solved this problem?" Legitimation involves generating a convincing precedent for innovations: it centers on the question, "Who else (that we respect) solved the problem this way?" To put the changing functions of Western models in somewhat oversimplified form, we can see a gradual shift in their role between the early Meiji period and late Meiji. In the early Meiji period, Western models provided both inspiration and legitimation; later, they continued to supply inspiration, but the grounds for legitimation were increasingly sought in the Japanese tradition and environment.

This change is dramatically illustrated in a remarkable collection entitled *Fifty Years of New Japan,* edited by Okuma Shigenobu, one of the Meiji elder statesmen, and published in 1910 in both English and Japanese editions. Each of its more than fifty chapters describes the development of one of Japan's major organizational systems: the army, the police, the railways, the post, and so on. The list of contributors reads like a *Who's Who* of Meiji Japan's institution-builders: Okuma himself, Yamagata Aritomo, Maejima Hisoka, Ōura Kanetake, Yamamoto Gombei, and a host of other illustrious names. How much these putative authors actually wrote of the chapters that bear their names is a moot point, but the symbolic significance of the roster of names is almost as important as the content of the chapters. It indicates the importance these men attached to codifying and formalizing the organizational histories of these institutions, for a Western audience as well as for the Japanese.

Each chapter presents the organization on which it focuses as a modern, effective institution that is the equal (or on the verge of becoming the equal) of its counterparts in the "advanced" West. Ōura's chapter on the police, for example, summarizes its development as follows:

> In the beginning of the Meiji era the Japanese Government commenced an investigation of the police systems of various countries of Europe and an inspection of their actual working. By the acquisition of this knowledge it was enabled to establish a new police system suited to the national and traditional state of affairs in our country; this has since undergone modifications as occasion necessitated, and has now attained a condition of comparative perfection.[18]

This passage is representative in that most of the authors recognize the Western inspiration of the organizations and many of them acknowledge the important contributions made by individual foreign advisers, but they are somewhat less inclined to recognize overtly the organizational models and the degree of their specificity.

Rather, they seem more concerned to demonstrate the essential continuity between the new organizations and the past, to establish the essential "Japaneseness" of the organization in question. Most chapters trace the lineage of the system far back into Japanese history: the chapter on the police, for example, claims that "a system of constabulary was in force even in ancient times."[19] The early Meiji advocates of the police and the post, in contrast, not only did not involve such precedents, but at least in the case of Maejima Hisoka and the post overtly expressed contempt for them.

By the late Meiji period tradition was distant enough to be selectively defined in order to justify patterns that had their actual inspiration in Western sources. Specific traditional organizational patterns, such as the Tokugawa practice of appointing multiple incumbents to administrative offices in order to limit the power of any one person, quickly disappeared wherever they were in conflict with the modern patterns. Traditional values, on the other hand, had much greater generality and flexibility than the specific patterns they had legitimated; they could be framed so as to justify a wide range of structures and behaviors.

This is not to deny that the Western-based patterns had to adapt to the Japanese environment. However, the Japanese environment of the Meiji period was rapidly being transformed by the wide ranging introduction of Western organizational forms. To use the vivid metaphor of Meyer and Rowan, there was a dramatic change in "the building blocks for organizations [that] come to be littered around the societal landscape."[20] In early Meiji, when the organizations examined here were introduced, the strongest pulls in the environment did not come from tradition but from other Western-modeled organizations.

If neither culture nor the universal concomitants of industrialization capture the essence of the pulls toward and away from the Western models in Meiji Japan, what concepts might be of more help? The three case studies in this book have drawn heavily on recent work in organizational sociology that has generated two additional perspectives on the forces pushing organizations to become more alike: the population-ecology focus on competition, selection, and retention, and the organizational isomorphism concern with emulation. Both are products of the organization-environment paradigm that has come to dominate organizational sociology over the last decade, driven in large part by the difficulties that researchers in the 1950s and 1960s experienced in their attempts to construct general theories of organizations based solely on the relationships among internal organizational variables. Researchers and theorists widened their frameworks to encompass the relationships between an organization and its immediate environment, and then, increasingly, to look at populations and groups of organizations in interaction with the social environment.

Recent developments have been dominated by two powerful analogies: organizations as physical organisms, and organizations as social actors. The "organization as organism" analogy draws on biological models of variation, selection, and retention of certain organizational characteristics in populations of organizations.[21] In its simplest form, the population ecology perspective holds that the organizational form that is most effective in getting the resources it needs from its immediate environment, and most efficient at using them, will prevail within any "resource pool."[22] Because this approach assumes a population of competing organizations, it applied only to the newspaper among the three organizational histories. It provides an explanation for the growing importance of the subunits within the newspaper engaged in handling the business side of distribution, marketing, and advertising, and of the increasing dominance of the new journalism.[23]

The "organization as a social actor" model draws on social psychology, theories of social interaction, and social network theory. The organization seen as a social actor can both react to and anticipate changes in its interactions with its environment, not simply in terms of resources but also in terms of social relationships.[24] DiMaggio and Powell have suggested that organizations emulate the patterns of other organizations for a number of reasons: a more powerful organization or set of organizations exerts pressure toward certain changes ("coercive isomorphism"); an organization often emulates the patterns of "successful" organizations even when the connections between success and those patterns are not established ("mimetic isomorphism"); and professional training and socialization may push organizations that hire those professionals into becoming more like each other ("normative isomorphism").[25]

The universal concomitants of the industrialization process are therefore not the only reason for convergence in organizational patterns across societies. The convergence can be generated by a selection process in which organizations in different societies are competing for the same resources or for resources whose configuration in their respective environments is very similar. It can also occur where more powerful societies demand the emulation of organizational forms in weaker societies; where the uncertainty of how to achieve desired goals encourages the resort to successful foreign models; or where common patterns of professional training encourage it. On the other hand, we can expect divergence across societies not only because of cultural differences but also because the configuration of resources in the environment differs, and therefore the organizational patterns that are effective at acquiring the resources and efficient at using them differ, or because of strong isomorphic pulls across organizations within the society that outweigh the pulls across societies.

The alternative perspectives provided by population ecology and especially by organizational isomorphism provide the frameworks for identifying the relevant elements of the environment and the processes by which they affect the development of organizational patterns that produce development paths like those of the police and of labor relations, where an initial period of emulation of foreign models gives way to a period of divergence. These approaches hold one of the keys to moving beyond the longstanding debates over Japanese tradition versus Western rationality, and the uniqueness of Japanese culture versus the universal requirements of industrialization, to a clearer understanding of the general social processes of the interaction of organizations and social environment by which institutions develop in every society.

What remains is the thorny issue raised by Henry Dyer eight decades ago: can the patterns of late developers be transferred to earlier developing societies? The case studies in this book refer to only one kind of cross-societal transfer of social technologies: the establishment of new organizations (or new organizational subunits such as subsidiaries of multinational enterprises). When firstcomers consider learning from latecomers, the context is much more likely to be the selective emulation of certain organizational patterns into existing organizations (like the adoption of Japanese inventory management systems or quality control circles).

Selective emulation in existing organizations will be even more complex than setting up a new organization on a foreign model. Many factors are common to both processes: the nature of the information about the model, the factors influencing decisions about selective emulation, the adaptation to an environment where the organization-set that supports the particular patterns being emulated is not present, and indigenization.[26] There is, however, an additional factor that becomes significant: the internal organizational structures and processes that in the original setting support the patterns being emulated. They are unlikely to be wholly present in the emulating organization, and three of the four choices that confront organization-builders concerning the external organization-set also apply to the internal supporting patterns: find an alternative functionally equivalent pattern; do without and try to adapt; or emulate the supporting patterns. That the result will not be a replica of the original model is certain; as the organizational histories in this book have demonstrated, emulation produces innovation. In the emulation of selected elements of foreign organizational patterns, as in the creation of new organizations on foreign models, cross-societal emulation simultaneously involves pulls toward and away from the chosen models. The effect is both convergence that does not produce uniformity and divergence and variation that is neither random nor infinite.

Notes

Index

Notes

Introduction

1. See Conrad Totman, *The Collapse of the Tokugawa Bakufu 1862–1868* (Honolulu: University of Hawaii Press, 1980).

2. Albert M. Craig, "The Central Government," in *Japan in Transition: From Tokugawa to Meiji*, ed. Marius B. Jansen and Gilbert Rozman (Princeton: Princeton University Press, 1986), pp. 49–52.

3. Some examples of the very extensive literature on this topic are: Marion J. Levy, Jr., "Contrasting Factors in the Modernization of China and Japan," in *Economic Growth: Brazil, India, Japan,* ed. Simon Kuznets, Wilbert Moore, and Joseph Spengler (Durham: Duke University Press, 1955); William W. Lockwood, "Japan's Response to the West: The Contrast with China," *World Politics* 9 (October 1956): 37–54; Thomas Smith, "Japan's Aristocratic Revolution," *Yale Review* (Spring 1961): 370–383; Marius Jansen, *Sakamoto Ryōma and the Meiji Restoration* (Princeton: Princeton University Press, 1964); Everett C. Hagen, *On the Theory of Social Change* (Cambridge, Mass.: MIT Press, 1964); Seizaburo Sato, "Response to the West: The Korean and Japanese Patterns," in *Japan: A Comparative View,* ed. Albert Craig (Princeton: Princeton University Press, 1979).

4. Among the major works on this topic are: Thomas C. Smith, *The Agrarian Origins of Modern Japan* (Stanford: Stanford University Press, 1959); John Whitney Hall and Marius Jansen, eds., *Studies in the Institutional History of Early Modern Japan* (Princeton: Princeton University Press, 1970); Ronald Dore, *Education in Tokugawa Japan* (Berkeley: University of California Press, 1965); Edwin Dowdy, *Japanese Bureaucracy* (Melbourne: Cheshire Press, 1973); Gilbert F. Rozman, *Urban Networks in Ch'ing China and Tokugawa Japan* (Princeton: Princeton University Press, 1973); Cyril E. Black et al., *The Modernization of Japan and Russia* (New York: The Free Press, 1973).

5. One of the exceptions to this statement is the recent volume edited by Marius Jansen and Gilbert Rozman, *Japan in Transition: From Tokugawa to Meiji* (Princeton: Princeton University Press, 1986), whose contributors specifically address the issues of the continuities and discontinuities across the decades from 1850 to the 1880s.

6. The major exception is Ernst Presseisen's study of the army, *Before Aggression: Europeans Train the Japanese Army* (Tucson: University of Arizona Press, 1965). The use of Western models in framing the Constitution in the 1880s has been the subject of two studies: Joseph Pittau, *Political Thought in Early Meiji Japan, 1869–1889* (Cambridge, Mass.: Harvard University Press, 1967) and George Akita, *Foundations of Constitutional Government in Modern Japan, 1868–1900* (Cambridge, Mass.: Harvard University Press, 1967). There have been smaller-scale studies of the initial adoption of an organizational model, such as Toshihiko Yoshino, "The Creation of the Bank of Japan—Its Western Origin and Adaptation," *Developing Economies* 15–4 (December 1977): 381–401; George Oakley Totten III, "Adoption of the Prussian Model for Municipal Government in Meiji Japan: Principles and Compromise," ibid.: 487–510. These last two studies do not follow the institutions after the adoption of the model. Much of the debate over the influence of Western organizational models has centered on the development of the factory and the emerging system of industrial relations, but this has rarely entailed systematic historical comparisons of the similarities and differences between Japanese and Western factories as they developed over time.

7. William F. Whyte, "Imitation and Innovation: Reflections on the Institutional Development of Peru," *Administrative Science Quarterly* 13 (1968): 372.

1. The Processes of Cross-Societal Emulation

1. Kenneth E. Boulding, *The Organizational Revolution: A Study in the Ethics of Economic Organization* (New York: Harper and Row, 1953), p. xi.

2. Alfred P. Chandler, *The Visible Hand: The Managerial Revolution in American Business* (Cambridge, Mass.: Harvard University Press, 1977), p. 1.

3. See Peter Mathias, *The Retailing Revolution* (London: Longmans, 1967), and Benedict Anderson, *Imagined Communities: Reflections on the Origin and Spread of Nationalism* (London: Verso, 1983).

4. See Rondo E. Cameron, "Founding the Bank of Darmstadt," *Explorations in Entrepreneurial History* 8–3 (February 1956): 113–120.

5. F. H. Hinsley, Introduction to *The New Cambridge Modern History* (Cambridge: Cambridge University Press, 1976), vol. XI, p. 21.

6. Miyagi-ken shi hensan iinkai, *Miyagi-ken shi 7* (Sendai: Miyagi-ken shi kankōkai), p. 256.

7. Togai Yoshio, *Nihon Sangyō.Kigyō shi Gaisetsu* (Tokyo: Zeimu Keiri Kyōkai, 1969), p. 26.

8. Hinsley, in *The New Cambridge Modern History,* vol. XI, pp. 17–18.

9. William H. McNeill, *The Pursuit of Power: Technology, Armed Force, and Society Since A.D. 1000* (Chicago: University of Chicago Press, 1982), pp. 223–306.

10. Yasuo Horie, "Modern Entrepreneurship in Meiji Japan," in *The State and Economic Enterprise in Japan,* ed. William Lockwood (Princeton: Princeton University Press, 1965), p. 197.

11. Cited in Hazel J. Jones, *Live Machines: Hired Foreigners and Meiji Japan* (Vancouver: University of British Columbia Press, 1980), p. 41.

12. Ibid., p. 108.

13. One interesting exception was the use of the Banque Nationale de Belgique as the model for the Bank of Japan in 1882. Although Finance Minister Matsukata wanted to take the French central bank as his model, the French economist Leon Say recommended that the newer, more rationalized Belgian bank be adopted instead. See Yoshino Toshihiko, "The Creation of the Bank of Japan," *Developing Economies* 15 (December 1977): 386–389.

14. Ernst Presseisen, *Before Aggression: Europeans Train the Japanese Army* (Tucson: University of Arizona Press, 1965), p. 8.

15. Henry Dyer, *Dai Nippon: A Study in National Evolution* (London: Blackie & Son, 1904), p. 176.

16. James T. Conte, "Meiji Ryūgakusei: Overseas Study in the Development of Japan," Ph.D. diss., Princeton University, 1978.

17. Georges Bousquet, *Le Japon de nos jours* (Paris: Librarie Hachette, 1877), pp. 283–284. (Translation mine.)

18. See Carol Gluck, *Japan's Modern Myths: Ideology in the Late Meiji Period* (Princeton: Princeton University Press, 1985).

19. Quoted in Paul J. DiMaggio and Walter W. Powell, "The Iron Cage Revisited: Institutional Isomorphism and Collective Rationality in Organizational Fields," *American Sociological Review* 48 (April 1983): 151.

20. This distinction evolved in the course of a conversation with Rosabeth Kanter on the legitimating role of organizational models.

21. D. Eleanor Westney, "The Military," in *Japan in Transition: From Tokugawa to Meiji,* ed. Marius B. Jansen and Gilbert Rozman (Princeton: Princeton University Press, 1986), pp. 185–186.

2. The Police

1. See, for example, the summary of prevailing theoretical perspectives in Robert Liebman and Michael Polen, "Perspectives on Policing in Nineteenth Century America," *Social Science History* 2–3 (1978), and David Snyder's "Theoretical and Methodological Problems in the Analysis of Governmental Coercion and Collective Violence," *Journal of Political and Military Sociology* 4–2 (1976).

2. David Bayley, "The Police and Political Development in Europe," in *The Formation of National States in Europe,* ed. Charles Tilly (Princeton: Princeton University Press, 1975), p. 345.

3. Ibid., pp. 329, 370.

4. The first major work in this area was David Bayley's *Forces of Order: Police Behavior in Japan and the United States* (Berkeley: University of California Press, 1975). It was followed by Walter L. Ames, *Police and Community in Japan* (Berkeley: University of California Press, 1981), and L. Craig Parker, Jr., *The Japanese Police System Today: An American Perspective* (Tokyo: Kodansha, 1984).

5. Quoted in E. H. Norman, *Japan's Emergence as a Modern State,* in *Origins of the Modern Japanese State: Selected Writings of E. H. Norman,* ed. John W. Dower (New York: Pantheon Books, 1975), p. 121.

6. Ibid., pp. 332–333.

7. Nihon no keisatsu hensankai, *Nihon no keisatsu* (Tokyo: Nihon no keisatsu hensankai, 1969), p. 26.

8. Oka Tadao, *Meiji jidai keisatsukan no seikatsu* (Tokyo: Yūsankaku shuppan, 1974), p. 61.

9. William Kelley, *Deference and Defiance in Nineteenth Century Japan* (Princeton: Princeton University Press, 1985), pp. 112–113.

10. These included the progenitor of the modern Japanese army, Ōmura Masūjiro, and one of the early advocates of a Western-style police system, Hirosawa Saneomi.

11. Yokohama Shi, *Yokohama Shi shi 3* (Yokohama: Yokohama Shi, 1961), pp. 25–41.

12. Keishi-chō shi hensan iinkai, *Keishi-chō shi* (Tokyo: Keishi-chō shi hensan iinkai, 1959), p. 29.

13. The police literature paints a touching picture of the entire barracks standing patiently beside barrels of sake, waiting for midnight to strike and signal their release from abstinence. Tanaka Tetsuo, *Keishi-chō monogatari: mitsuwa no hyakunen* (Tokyo: Kasumigaseki shuppankai, 1974), p. 41.

14. Fukushima Shi shi hensan iinkai, *Fukushima Shi shi Kindai 1* (Fukushima: Fukushima Shi shi hensan iinkai, 1972), p. 41.

15. *Keishi-chō shi,* p. 46.

16. Takahashi Yūzō, *Meiji nendai no keisatsu buchō: Meiji keisatsu-shi kenkyū* (Tokyo: Ryosho Fukyukai, 1976), p. 216.

17. Takahashi Yūzō, *Meiji keisatsu shi kenkyū 4 Zenpan* (Tokyo: Ryōbunsha, 1972), p. 24. Hereafter cited as Takahashi, *Meiji keisatsu shi 4a.*

18. *Nihon no Keisatsu,* pp. 56–57.

19. Takahashi, *Meiji keisatsu shi 4a,* pp. 22–23.

20. Oka, *Meiji jidai keisatsukan,* pp. 80–82.

21. Oikata Sumio, "Nihon kindai kokka ni okeru keisatsu ryoku no kisei," *Rekishigaku Kenkyū* 470 (July 1979): 21.

22. *Keishi-chō shi,* p. 39.

23. Howard C. Payne, *The Police State of Louis Napoleon Bonaparte 1851–1860* (Seattle: University of Washington Press, 1966), p. 20.

24. Ibid., p. 25.

25. Ibid.

26. *Keishi-chō shi,* pp. 116–117.

27. Takahashi, *Meiji keisatsukan 4a,* p. 115.

28. Philip John Stead, *The Police of Paris* (London: Staples Press, 1957), pp. 137–138.

29. Naimusho Keihōkyoku, *Cho-fu-ken keisatsu enkaku shi 1* (Tokyo: Hara shobo, 1973), p. 16.

30. Tanaka, *Keishi-chō monogatari,* p. 66.

31. Ibid., p. 65.

32. Niihira Katsunosuke, "Keisatsu shikō," in *Keisatsu Jihō* (February 1978), p. 74.

33. William R. Miller, *Cops and Bobbies: Police Authority in New York and London 1830–1870* (Chicago: University of Chicago Press, 1973), p. 26.

34. Raymond B. Fosdick, *European Police Systems* (New York: The Century Company, 1915), p. 200.

35. *Keishi-chō shi,* p. 56.

36. Tanaka, *Keishi-chō monogatari,* p. 42.

37. *Keishi-chō shi,* p. 51.

38. Basil Hall Chamberlain, *Things Japanese* (London: Kegan Paul, 1927), pp. 145–146.

39. Payne, *The Police State of Louis Napoleon,* p. 130.

40. L. Andrieux, *Souvenirs d'un préfet de police* (Paris: Jules Rouff, 1885), pp. 287–288.

41. Ibid., pp. 284–293.

42. Stead, *The Police of Paris,* p. 143.

43. *Keishi-chō shi,* pp. 240–243.

44. Later in the Meiji period this procedure was changed. Only on designated inspection days did the constables report first to the station; otherwise they went straight to the police box. Ibid., p. 467.

45. Isabella L. Bird, *Unbeaten Tracks in Japan: An Account of Travels on Horseback in the Interior* (New York: G. P. Putnam's Sons, 1881), vol. I, p. 316.

46. Fosdick, *European Police Systems,* p. 142.

47. *Keishi-chō shi,* pp. 154–155.

48. These were Kyoto and Saitama in 1881, and Wakayama, Fukushima, Nagano, and Hyogo in 1884.

49. *Keishi-chō shi,* p. 51.

50. Ibid., pp. 112, 121.

51. Oikata Sumio, "Seinan sensō ni okeru 'junsa' no rinji chobo," *Nihon rekishi* 362 (July 1978): 50–67.

52. Tanaka, *Keishi-chō monogatari,* 36–37.

53. Taigakkai, *Naimusho-shi 1* (Tokyo: Chiho zaimu kyokai, 1971), p. 733.

54. Payne, *The Police State of Louis Napoleon,* p. 245.

55. *Hyogo-ken keisatsu shi,* p. 134.

56. In 1874, for example, in a communication with the Home Ministry, the Kobe police chief used the character for the Keishi-cho when he referred to his own headquarters; this drew a sharp rebuke from the ministry, which saw it as a symptom of aspirations to unacceptable levels of autonomy.

57. *Nihon no keisatsu,* p. 59.

58. *Hyogo-ken keisatsu shi,* p. 112.

59. Ibid., pp. 43–45.

60. The 1875 recruitment criteria included height and physical fitness standards, age restrictions, "good moral character," and literacy.

61. Stead, *The Police of Paris,* p. 138.

62. Oka, *Meiji jidai no keisatsukan,* p. 28.

63. The principal development came with the reorganization of prefectural administration in 1878, which raised the subunit charged with police administration to the status of a section *(ka)* directly reporting to the governor; it was subdivided into four subsections *(kakari)*: administrative police, judicial police, records, and accounts.

64. Iwai Tadakuma, "Gunji keisatsu kiko no seiritsu," *Iwanami kōza Nihon rekishi 15* (Tokyo: Iwanami Shoten, 1976), p. 192.

65. Takahashi, *Meiji keisatsu shi,* pp. 131–133.

66. *Statistique annuaire de la France 1885.*

67. Data from *Nihon teikoku tōkei nenkan,* annual series.

68. Zenkoku kenkyūkai rengōkai, hensan iinkai, *Nihon kempeitai seishi* (Tokyo: 1976), p. 127.

69. In the 1880s the Kempeitai made about 2,000 arrests a year (between 63 percent and 88 percent of which were of civilians, except for a "civilian low" in 1887 of 37 percent); in the 1890s this increased to a high of 10,510 arrests, of which 9,350 were of civilians. Data from *Nihon teikoku tōkei nenkan,* annual series.

70. Data from *Nihon teikoku tōkei nenkan,* annual series.

71. Asakura, *Meiji kansei jiten,* p. 182.

72. Takahashi, *Meiji keisatsu shi 1,* p. 97.

73. Takahashi, *Meiji keisatsu shi 4a,* p. 236.

74. Takahashi, *Meiji keisatsu shi 1,* pp. 76–85.

75. Ibid., p. 76.

76. Bayley, "The Police and Political Development in Europe," p. 374.

77. Takahashi, *Meiji keisatsu shi 1,* p. 73.

78. Takahashi, *Meiji keisatsu shi 4a,* p. 327.

79. At the opening ceremonies for the reestablished Academy in 1897, the Home Minister, Saigo Tsugumichi, referred openly to the increased complexity of police tasks occasioned by the impending treaty revision as a reason for the school's establishment. Takahashi, *Meiji keisatsu shi 1,* p. 186.

80. Takahashi, *Meiji keisatsu shi 4a,* p. 107.

81. Fosdick, *European Police Systems,* pp. 73–74.

82. Quoted in Iwai, "Gunji keisatsu kikō," p. 205.

83. Oka, *Meiji jidai keisatsukan,* pp. 61–62.

84. *Hyogo-ken keisatsu shi,* p. 648.

85. *Miyagi-ken shi,* pp. 191–198.

86. Magali Sarfatti Larson, *The Rise of Professionalism: A Sociological Analysis* (Berkeley: University of California Press, 1977).

87. Richard H. Hall, *Organizations: Structure and Process* (Englewood Cliffs, N.J.: Prentice-Hall, 1977), pp. 164–172.

88. In 1890 the average manpower of police stations was 2.06. In 1912 it had only risen to 2.39. In 1893 the prefectural average in Tokyo, the largest in Japan, was 7.5; in the prefecture where the posts were smallest the average was 1.4. Based on data from the *Nihon teikoku tōkei nenkan,* annual series.

89. Samuel Walker, *A Critical History of Police Reform* (Lexington, Mass.: D. C. Heath, 1977), p. 13.

90. In Tokyo the loss rate was 15.7 percent in 1889 and 15.3 percent in 1890 (*Tokyo hyaku-nen shi,* p. 846); in Yamagata, one of Japan's more rural prefectures, it was 21.3 percent in 1894 and 20.2 percent in 1898.

91. Fukushima-ken keisatsu hombu, *Fukushima-ken keisatsu shi* (Fukushima: 1980), pp. 845–848.

92. Oka, *Meiji jidai keisatsukan,* pp. 37–39.

93. *Hyogo-ken keisatsu shi,* pp. 644–645.

94. The official standards for deployment required a greater density of police in urban areas. The standards set up in 1896 mandated one constable for every 300–800 people in urban areas, and one for every 1,000–2,000 in rural areas. *Naimusho-shi,* p. 622.

95. In Tokyo, the ratio rose from 6.1 in 1886 to 25.0 in 1909. Calculations based on data in the *Nihon teikoku tōkei nenkan.*

96. Takahashi, *Meiji jidai no keisatsu 4a,* pp. 253–254.

97. Takahashi, *Meiji jidai no keisatsu 1,* pp. 239–240.

98. *Naimusho-shi,* pp. 668–669.

99. Takahashi, *Meiji keisatsu shi 1,* pp. 230–247.

100. Augusta Campbell Davidson, *Present-day Japan* (Philadelphia: J. B. Lippincott, 1904), p. 254.

101. See for example Samuel Walker: "Professionalization was an attack upon the pervasive influence of partisan politics on American policing in the nineteenth century." Walker, *A Critical History,* p. 3. See also the work of Raymond Fosdick in the second and third decades of the twentieth century.

102. Miyashita Hiroshi, *Tokkō no kaisō* (Tokyo: Tabata Shoten, 1978), pp. 28–29.

103. The riots began when a public meeting, planned to protest what many Japanese felt was the unfair treaty imposed on Japan at the end of the war, was forbidden by the police. Its organizers held it anyway, and when the police tried to break it up violence exploded and lasted for several days.

104. See E. Herbert Norman, "The Feudal Background of Japanese Politics," pp. 458–461.

105. Baron Kanetake Oura, "The Police of Japan," in *Fifty Years of New Japan,* ed. Okuma Shigenobu (London: Smith Elder, 1910), vol. I, p. 294.

106. Bayley, "The Police and Political Development in Europe," p. 350.

107. Arthur Lloyd, *Every-day Japan: Written after Twenty-five Years' Residence and Work in the Country* (London: Cassell, 1919), p. 161.

108. Takahashi, *Meiji keisatsu shi 4a,* p. 381.

109. Oikata Sumio, "Seinan sensō."

110. Data published in the *Nihon teikoku tōkei nenkan,* annual series.

111. Asakura, *Meiji kansei jiten,* p. 185.

112. The police were finally issued firearms in 1918, in response to the Rice Riots of that year.

113. *Hyogo-ken keisatsu shi,* pp. 654–655.

114. R. H. P. Mason, *Japan's First General Election* (Cambridge: Cambridge University Press, 1969), pp. 52–53.

115. Takahashi, *Meiji keisatsu shi 4a,* pp. 271–273.

116. *Nihon no keisatsu,* p. 45.

117. *Hyogo-ken keisatsu shi,* p. 609.

118. Takahashi, *Meiji keisatsu shi 4b,* pp. 379–380.

119. Ibid., pp. 268–269.

120. *Keishi-chō shi,* p. 480.

121. Ono Tatsuzo, *Nihon no seiji keisatsu* (Tokyo: Nihon no keisatsu hensankai, 1973), p. 70.

3. The Postal System

1. These are 1839 data from Great Britain, General Post Office, *The Post Office: A Historical Summary* (London: His Majesty's Stationery Office, 1911).

2. Data from *European Historical Statistics 1750–1970,* p. 163.

3. Edward Bennett, writing on the history of the British Post Office, sees the railway as a necessary condition of the success of Sir Rowland Hill's reforms; *The Post Office and Its Story* (London: Seeley, Service, 1912), p. 31.

4. By 1872 the British Post Office was already handling over one billion pieces of mail; Japan did not pass the one billion mark until 1904. At no point in prewar Japan did its absolute volume of mail equal Britain's.

5. Bennett, *The Post Office and Its Story,* p. 243.

6. I am indebted for this information to Professor Frank Bealey of the University of Aberdeen.

7. Yabuuchi Yoshihiko, *Nihon yūbin sōgyō shi: hikyaku kara yūbin e* (Tokyo: Yusankaku, 1975), pp. 22–23.

8. One may well wonder why there was no development of a system of relay riders comparable to the frontier Pony Express. One reason might well be that horses were more expensive than manpower, and on the hilly roads of Japan were not much faster. The quality of the post horses may well have been a factor here: if the accounts of travelers in the early Meiji period, such as Isabella Bird, provide an accurate description of Japanese post horses in general, they were certainly not built for speed. For example, Miss Bird reports that "Mr. Wilkinson [the British consul] . . . agrees with everybody else in thinking that legions of fleas and the miserable horses are the great drawbacks of Japanese travelling." *Unbeaten Tracks in Japan* (1880; reprinted London: Virago Press, 1984), p. 11.

9. Yabuuchi, *Nihon yūbin,* p. 39.

10. Ibid., pp. 56–57.

11. Sir Rutherford Alcock, *The Capital of the Tycoon: A Narrative of a*

Three Years' Residence in Japan (New York: Harper and Row, 1863), p. 136.

12. Takahashi Zenshichi, *Oyatoi gaikokujin: Tsūshin* (Tokyo: Kajima Kenkyūjo shuppankai, 1969), pp. 14–15.

13. Yūseisho, *Yūsei hyakunen shi* (Tokyo: Yoshikawa Kobunkan, 1971), p. 299.

14. Maejima served as an instructor in the Bakufu's *Kaiseijo* in 1866 and 1867; later in 1867 he was appointed to an administrative post in the administrative offices of Kobe, one of the treaty ports.

15. Oda Takeo, *Maejima Hisoka* (Tokyo: Maejima Hisoka Kenchokai, 1958), p. 85.

16. Ibid., pp. 95–98.

17. *Yūsei hyakunen shi,* p. 68.

18. Oda, *Maejima Hisoka,* pp. 108–110.

19. *Yūsei hyakunen shi,* p. 96.

20. Takahashi, *Oyatoi gaikokujin,* pp. 30–31.

21. Ardath Burks, "Japan's Outreach: The Ryūgakusei," in *The Modernizers: Overseas Students, Foreign Employees, and Meiji Japan,* ed. Ardath Burks (Boulder: Westview Press, 1985), p. 151.

22. *Yūsei hyakunen shi,* pp. 92–93.

23. Ibid., p. 81.

24. Data from Yūseisho, *Yūsei hyakunen shi shiryō 27* (Tokyo: Yoshikawa Kobunkan, 1971), pp. 358–368.

25. *Yūsei hyakunen shi,* pp. 135–136.

26. Ibid., p. 135.

27. Ibid., pp. 141–143.

28. J. C. Hemmeon, *The History of the British Post Office* (Cambridge, Mass.: Harvard University Press, 1912), p. 73.

29. *Yūbin hyakunen shi Shiryō,* vol. XXIX, p. 36.

30. Yamaguchi-ken Bunsho-kan, *Yamaguchi-ken Sei shi, Jōkan* (Yamaguchi-ken: 1971), p. 231.

31. *Yūsei hyakunen shi,* pp. 239–240.

32. Ibid., pp. 432–433.

33. Haruhiko Asakura, ed., *Meiji Kansei Jiten* (Tokyo: Tokyodo Shuppan, 1969), p. 639.

34. Takeuchi Kyōzō, *Meiji zenki yūsōshi no kisōteki kenkyū* (Tokyo: Yūsankaku, 1978), p. 32.

35. Tanaka Tetsuo, *Keisatsu Mitsuwa Hyakunen* (Tokyo: Kasumigaseki Shuppankai, 1974), p. 54.

36. Takeuchi, *Meiji zenki yūsōshi,* pp. 20–28.

37. Yabuuchi, *Nihon yūbin,* pp. 50–51.

38. Data from 1872 in ibid., p. 172.

39. Ibid., p. 179.

40. The total estimated general expenditures of the national government at the time were 33 million yen. Data on total government revenues are from Kyoto Daigaku Bungakubu Kokushi Kenkyūshitsu, ed., *Nihon Kindaishi Jiten* (Tokyo: Tōyō Keizai Shimpō sha, 1970), pp. 912–913, and data on the postal system revenues and expenditures are taken from the *Yūsei hyakunen shi Shiryō*, vol. XXIX.

41. Hugo Richard Meyer, *The British State Telegraphs* (New York: Macmillan, 1907), pp. 18–29.

42. By 1905 telegraph services were available at all offices and the title *Yūbinkyoku*—Post Office—was used for all.

43. The two bureaus eventually turned into three: domestic communications, foreign communications, and engineering.

44. Asakura, *Meiji Kansei Jiten*, pp. 422–424.

45. Yabuuchi, *Nihon yūbin*, pp. 177–178.

46. *Yūsei hyakunen shi*, p. 223.

47. *Yūsei hyakunenshi Shiryō*, vol. XXVI, pp. 338–339.

48. *Yūsei hyakunen shi*, pp. 314–315.

49. The British Postmen's Federation, formed in 1891, was the third attempt to create a labor organization for postal workers. The leaders of the first two (the Postmen's Association of 1886 and the Postmen's Union in 1889) had been dismissed, members were harassed, and the organizations dissolved. *The Interdepartmental Committee on Post Office Establishments* (Glasgow: Postmen's Federation, 1896).

50. Bennett, *The Post Office and Its Story*, p. 85.

51. *Yamagata Shi shi*, p. 424.

52. Yabuuchi, *Nihon yūbin*, pp. 167–171.

53. *Yūsei hyakunen shi*, p. 250.

54. Ibid.

55. Ibid., pp. 218–219.

56. Ibid., p. 157.

57. Ibid., p. 163.

58. Ibid., p. 158.

59. Ying-wan Cheng, *Postal Communication in China and Its Modernization, 1860–1896* (Cambridge, Mass.: Harvard University Press, 1970), p. 5.

60. Ibid., p. 96.

61. Ibid., p. 10.

62. Ibid., p. 36.

63. Ibid., p. 32.

64. Ibid., p. 88.

65. Ibid., p. 89.

66. Geoffrey Clarke, *The Post Office of India and Its Story* (London: John Lane, The Bodley Head, 1921), pp. 109–110.

67. Ibid., p. 110.

68. Ibid., p. 37.

69. Yabuuchi, *Nihon yūbin,* p. 89.

70. Detailed information on all the items sent to the post offices from the center throughout this period is provided in the mammoth thirty-volume *Yūsei hyakunen shi Shiryō;* the information on the clocks is given in vol. XXVI, pp. 227–229.

71. Yabuuchi, *Nihon yūbin,* p. 204.

72. Ibid., p. 69.

73. Takechi, *Meiji zenki yūsōshi,* p. 113.

74. Inferences about the number of depositors based on the number of postal accounts are dangerous, because savers apparently avoided the upper limits on postal deposits by maintaining multiple accounts.

4. The Newspaper

1. G. Binney Dibblee, *The Newspaper* (New York: Henry Hall, 1913), p. 11.

2. Albert A. Altman, "Korea's First Newspaper: The Japanese *Chosen shinpo*," *Journal of Asian Studies* 43–4 (August 1984): 685–696.

3. Robert W. Desmond, *Windows on the World: The Information Process in a Changing Society 1900–1920* (Iowa City: University of Iowa Press, 1980), p. 44.

4. Alan J. Lee, *The Origins of the Popular Press in England* (London: Croom Helm, 1976).

5. Robert W. Desmond, *The Information Process: World News Reporting to the Twentieth Century* (Iowa City: University of Iowa Press, 1978), p. 141.

6. Eugene DuBief, *Le Journalisme* (Paris: Librarie Hachette, 1892), p. 90.

7. Hashimoto Motomu, *Nihon Shuppan Hanbai shi* (Tokyo: Kodan-sha, 1964), p. 4.

8. Ibid., p. 10.

9. Nishida Taketoshi, *Meiji Jidai no Shimbun to Zasshi* (Tokyo: Shi-bundo, 1961), pp. 1–2.

10. Albert A. Altman, "Shinbunshi: The Early Meiji Adaptation of the Western-style Newspaper," in *Modern Japan: Aspects of History, Literature,*

and Society, ed. William Beasley (Berkeley: University of California Press, 1975), p. 55.

11. Okamoto Kozo, ed., *Nihon Shimbun hyakunen shi* (Tokyo: Nihon Shimbun Kenkyukai Remmei, 1961), p. 511. Hereafter cited as NSHS.

12. Ukai Shinichi, *Chōya Shimbun no Kenkyū* (Tokyo: Kabushiki kaisha Misuzu Shobo, 1985), p. 42.

13. Mainichi Shimbun hyakunen shi kankō-iinkai, *Mainichi Shimbun hyakunen shi* (Tokyo: Mainichi Shimbun sha, 1972), p. 1. Hereafter cited as *Mainichi.*

14. The newspaper in question was Fukuchi Gen-ichiro's *Kōkō Shimbun;* Fukuchi was subsequently hired as the *Tōnichi's* chief writer.

15. John R. Black, *Young Japan: Yokohama and Yedo* (London: Trubner, 1881), pp. 367–368.

16. One of the first Western scholars of Japan, Basil Hall Chamberlain, writing in 1905, stated that "The founder of Japanese journalism was an Englishman, Mr. John Black . . . Mr. Black's *Nisshin Shinjishi,* started in 1872, was the first newspaper worthy of the name—the first to give leading articles and to comment seriously on political affairs. The seed once sown, Japanese journalism grew apace." Basil Hall Chamberlain, *Things Japanese* (London: Kegan Paul, Trench, Trubner & Co., 1927), p. 351.

17. Interestingly enough, this finding is close to that of Carroll and Delacroix on the Argentine and Irish newspaper industries. They too found that "the rate of death is very high for the first two years of operating." Glenn Carroll and Jacques Delacroix, "Organizational Mortality in the Newspaper Industries of Argentina and Ireland: An Ecological Approach," *Administrative Science Quarterly* 27 (1982): 177.

18. The first version of the gazette was called the *Dajōkan Nisshi* and was printed by a private subcontractor; from 1872 to 1877 it was put out by the Dajōkan's own printing bureau. The next incarnation, the *Kanpō,* was established in 1883 in response to a petition from Yamagata Aritomo. As a preparatory step, the government consulted leading foreign residents of Tokyo about the format and nature of official gazettes in the major Western countries. Asakura Haruhiko, ed., *Meiji Kansei Jiten* (Tokyo: Tokyōdō Shuppan, 1969), pp. 380, 138.

19. Takagi Takeo, *Shimbun shōsetsu: Meiji-hen* (Tokyo: Kokuhō Kankōkai, 1974), p. 5.

20. Nakanowatari Nobuyuki, *Masukomi Kindai shi* (Tokyo: Yūsankaku Shuppan, 1969), p. 161.

21. Georges Bousquet, *Le Japon de nos jours* (Paris: Librairie Hachette, 1877), p. 280. (Translation mine.)

22. Local policemen and firemen were often the agents of such violence.

In 1883, for example, when a small fire broke out in the office of the *Fukui Shimbun,* the firemen arrived in force and in the process of extinguishing the blaze broke the presses and overturned the type-cases. San'yō Shimbun Sha, *San'yō Shimbun kyūjūnen shi* (Okayama: San'yō Shimbun Sha, 1969), p. 35.

23. Ibid., p. 37.

24. Takagi has suggested that they suffered from the sudden reduction of the number of samurai women in Tokyo and the castle towns; apparently they were a major market for the serialized novels that were the staple of the Tokugawa publishing industry. *Shimbun shōsetsu,* p. 17.

25. Among the early publications the Nisshūsha produced was a 50,000 word English-Japanese dictionary, the most extensive of the day. Yomiuri Shimbunsha, *Yomiuri Shimbun hyakunen shi* (Tokyo: Yomiuri Shimbun sha, 1974), p. 126. Hereafter cited as *Yomiuri.*

26. Takagi, *Shimbun shōsetsu,* pp. 14–15.

27. Black, *Young Japan,* pp. 371–372.

28. Hashimoto, *Nihon Shuppan Hanbai shi,* p. 21.

29. *Mainichi,* 338.

30. Hijikata Masaoto, "Miyako Shimbun shi," (Part 4) *Sōgō Janarizumu Kenkyū* 68 (1975): 63.

31. It was first adopted by the *Tokyo Nichi Nichi* in 1875, and was quickly emulated by the other major metropolitan newspapers.

32. Kawakami Tomizo, *Mainichi Shimbun Hambai shi* (Osaka: Mainichi Shimbun Osaka Kaihatsu KK, 1979), p. 40.

33. *Mainichi,* 339–40.

34. Gifu-ken, *Gifu-ken shi. Tsūshi. Kindai-hen* (Gifu: Gifu-ken, 1972), p. 1,360.

35. Ibid., p. 1,364.

36. NSHS, p. 600.

37. Hashimoto, *Nihon Shuppan Hanbai shi,* p. 19.

38. *Mainichi,* p. 422.

39. Black, *Young Japan,* p. 368.

40. The first press was produced in Japan in 1877; Western paper was first produced in 1874.

41. Asahina Chisen, *Rōkisha no Omoide* (Tokyo: Chūō Koronsha, 1938), pp. 13–14.

42. NSHS, p. 513.

43. Ibid., pp. 658–659.

44. *San'yō Shimbun,* p. 14.

45. Osaka Honsha, *Asahi Shimbun Hambai,* p. 21.

46. Zen Nihon Shimbun Remmei, *Shimbun Taikan 1* (Tokyo: Zen Nihon Shimbun Remmei Shimbun Jidai Sha, 1973), p. 123.

47. Asakura, *Meiji Kansei Jiten,* p. 330.

48. Jay Rubin, *Injurious to Public Morals: Writers and the Meiji State* (Seattle: University of Washington Press, 1984), p. 21.

49. Takahashi Yūzō, *Meiji keisatsu shi kenkyū 4a,* p. 96.

50. NSHS, pp. 658–659.

51. Zen Nihon Shimbun Remmei, *Shimbun Taikan,* 123.

52. This same pattern was picked up, not surprisingly, in the provincial press. The *San'yō Shimbun,* for example, in 1879 had two *saguri-gata* to bring information to the chief writer. *San'yō Shimbun,* p. 19.

53. Eugène DuBief, *Le Journalisme* (Paris: Librairie Hachette, 1892), p. 101.

54. Asahina, *Rōkisha no omoide,* pp. 13–14.

55. Steven Koss, *The Rise and Fall of the Political Press in Britain,* vol. 1: *The Nineteenth Century* (London: Hamish Hamilton, 1981), p. 22.

56. *Mainichi,* p. 26.

57. John Dawson, *Practical Journalism* (London: L. Upcott Gill, 1885), p. 21. The same pattern prevailed nearly three decades later: Dibblee's 1913 book, *The Newspaper,* says, "The ordinary American paper from cover to cover is almost wholly written by professionals, while perhaps one-third of our papers (i.e. in Britain) is the product of an outside sporadic ring of contributors, who are practically half-employed amateurs." Dibblee, *The Newspaper,* p. 29.

58. *Mainichi,* p. 33.

59. Zen Nihon Shimbun Remmei, *Shimbun Taikan 1,* p. 122.

60. *Mainichi,* p. 338.

61. Zen Nihon Shimbun Remmei, *Shimbun Taikan,* p. 74.

62. Nakase Toshikazu, *Nihon Kōkoku Sangyo Hattatsu shi Kenkyū* (Kyoto: Horitsu Bunka Sha, 1968), p. 77.

63. Nakanowatari, *Masu.komi kindai shi,* p. 161.

64. *Mainichi,* p. 339.

65. In 1881 the *Tokyo Nichi Nichi*'s profits were 5.88 percent of sales. Data from Ukai, *Chōya Shimbun no Kenkyu,* p. 17.

66. Nakase, *Nihon kōkoku,* p. 78.

67. Initially it was called the *Jiji Shimpō Kōkoku Toritsugigyo,* and then in 1884 its name was changed to *Kōhōdo,* to separate its public identification from the *Jiji.* Ibid., p. 83.

68. Osaka Honsha, *Asahi Shimbun Hanbai,* p. 44.

69. These calculations are based on the annual totals for newspaper circulation reported to the prefectural government, and reproduced in Hijikata, "Miyako Shimbun shi" (Part 4): 65.

70. Lee, *The Origins of the Popular Press,* pp. 120–129.

71. *Mainichi,* p. 344.

72. These figures are calculated by taking the total number of copies published in the year, as reported to the Tokyo prefectural office, and dividing by the 300 publication days common in the press of the day.

73. The slowest was the oldest and most venerable of the *ōshimbun,* the *Tokyo Nichi Nichi,* whose editor, Fukuchi Genichirō, resisted the changes in format and the incorporation of novels. The newspaper maintained its dignity by something of a compromise, choosing such novels as Disraeli's *Contarini Fleming,* which it serialized in translation in 1887; a novel by a British Prime Minister apparently was seen as upholding the paper's emphasis on its elite position. Takagi, *Shimbun shōsetsu,* p. 110.

74. In the following year it renamed its Osaka newspaper the *Osaka Asahi Shimbun.*

75. Total annual circulation went from 28,543,000 copies in 1884 to 55,647,000 in 1889. Hijikata, "Miyako Shimbun Shi" (Part 4): 65.

76. NSHS, pp. 515–517.

77. The *San'yō Shimbun* in Okayama bought a Marinoni press from the *Osaka Asahi* in 1907, for example; the *Kitaguni Shimbun* in Kanazawa acquired a Marinoni in 1912. For the provincial newspapers, the threshold at which the investment in the Marinoni became imperative was ten thousand copies. It was not until after the Russo-Japanese War that the provincial newspapers began to surpass that level.

78. The next advance over the Marinoni came with the *Asahi's* purchase in 1922 of a high-speed American Hoe press with three times the speed of the Marinoni. NSHS, p. 517.

79. Anthony Smith, *Goodbye Gutenberg: The Newspaper Revolution of the 1980s* (Oxford: Oxford University Press, 1980), p. 80.

80. "Matrices" are the type cases that keep the type in a prearranged order so as to facilitate the task of the typesetter. Type matrices for alphabetic scripts are much simpler than those for a written language with several thousand characters.

81. NSHS, pp. 546–547.

82. This is not to assert that the removal of the technological constraints should be considered a *cause* of the "new journalism," only an important facilitating condition. To my knowledge, none of the standard accounts of the "new journalism" have tried to establish a technologically deterministic argument for its emergence.

83. The *Osaka Asahi* increased its size from four to six pages in 1893, from six to eight pages in 1896, and from eight to ten pages in 1899.

84. *Mainichi,* p. 28.

85. Hijikata, "Miyako Shimbun shi" (Part 7): 19.

86. These covered the following anniversaries: the 1,000th issue (May

19, 1878); the 1,500th issue (January 18, 1880); the 2,000th issue (September 20, 1881); the tenth anniversary of the founding (November 2, 1884); the 3,000th issue (January 18, 1885); the 5,000th issue (May 15, 1891); the twentieth anniversary (June 1, 1893); the 8,000th issue (October 15, 1899); the 9,000th issue (July 12, 1902); the thirtieth anniversary (November 3, 1903); the 10,000th issue (April 8, 1905); the move to new premises (March 13, 1909); and the 12,000th issue (September 25, 1910). *Yomiuri Shiryō*, p. 155.

87. *Mainichi*, p. 360.

88. Yamamoto Fumio, *Nihon no Masu-Komyūnikē-shon shi* (Tokyo: Tokai Daigaku Shuppankai, 1970), p. 53.

89. Ibid., p. 89.

90. *Mainichi*, p. 344.

91. *San'yō Shimbun*, p. 41.

92. *Mainichi*, p. 545.

93. Perhaps the most controversial kind of popularity contest was the *Osaka Mainichi's* 1902 popularity contest for the local candidates for the national Diet, in advance of the elections. Ibid., p. 354.

94. Tokyo hyakunenshi henshū iinkai, *Tokyo hyakunen shi 3* (Tokyo: Tokyo-to, 1973), p. 1,370.

95. Hijikata, "Miyako Shimbun shi" Part 9: 62.

96. *Mainichi*, p. 545.

97. *Yomiuri*, p. 230.

98. *Mainichi*, p. 546.

99. Osaka Honsha, *Asahi Shimbun Hanbai*, p. 216.

100. Ibid., pp. 31–32.

101. Zen Nihon Shimbun Remmei, *Shimbun Taikan*, p. 175.

102. Ibid., p. 172.

103. *Mainichi*, pp. 60–61.

104. These data are given by Yamamoto, *Nihon no masu komyūnike-shon shi* (Tokyo: 1974), p. 70.

105. Zen Nihon Shimbun Remmei, *Shimbun Taikan*, p. 180.

106. *Mainichi*, p. 26.

107. Zen Nihon Shimbun Remmei, *Shimbun Taikan*, p. 180.

108. Ibid., pp. 152–153.

109. Ibid., p. 181.

110. Hijikata, "Miyako Shimbun shi" (Part 12): 115.

111. *Mainichi*, p. 353.

112. Ibid., p. 361.

113. Osaka Honsha, *Asahi Shimbun Hanbai*, pp. 128–129.

114. Zen Nihon Shimbun Remmei, *Shimbun Taikan*, p. 177.

115. NSHS, 658–659.

116. Zen Nihon Shimbun Remmei, *Shimbun Taikan,* p. 180.

117. Ibid.

118. *Mainichi,* pp. 338–339.

119. *Asahi Shimbun Hanbai hyakunen shi,* p. 103.

120. *Mainichi,* p. 357.

121. Lee, *The Origins of the Popular Press,* p. 87.

122. *Mainichi,* p. 352.

123. Takagi, *Shimbun shōsetsu,* pp. 70–71.

124. *Yomiuri,* p. 223.

125. Ikeda Kazuyuki, "Sanmen kiji no naka kara" in Nakanowatari, *Masukomi kindai shi,* p. 83.

126. Peter Figdor, "Newspapers and Their Regulation in Early Meiji Japan 1868–1883," *Papers on Japan* vol. 6 (Cambridge: East Asian Research Center, Harvard University, 1972); Altman, "Shimbunshi"; James L. Huffman, *Politics of the Meiji Press: The Life of Fukuchi Gen'ichiro* (Honolulu: University Press of Hawaii, 1980); John D. Pearson, *Tokutomi Soho 1863–1957: A Journalist for Modern Japan* (Princeton: Princeton University Press, 1980).

127. Albert A. Altman, "The Press," in *Japan in Transition,* pp. 240–241.

128. F. C. Jones, *Extraterritoriality in Japan: And the Diplomatic Relations Resulting in Its Abolition* (New York: AMS press, 1970), p. 109.

129. T. Philip Terry, *Terry's Japanese Empire* (Boston: Houghton Mifflin, 1914), p. clvii.

130. Carol Gluck, *Japan's Modern Myths: Ideology in the Late Meiji Period* (Princeton: Princeton University Press, 1985), p. 71.

Conclusion

1. Henry Dyer, *Dai Nippon: A Study in National Evolution* (London: Blackie and Sons, 1904), pp. 425–426.

2. Dietrich Rueschemeyer has coined the term "the Schumpeter Principle" for "the assertion that the persistence of social structures, types, and attitudes once they are formed provides an explanation of different social and cultural patterns." "Theoretical Generalization and Historical Particularity in the Corporate Sociology of Reinhard Bendix," in *Vision and Method in Historical Sociology,* ed. Theda Skocpol (Cambridge: Cambridge University Press, 1984).

3. Dyer, *Dai Nippon,* p. 2.

4. Ibid., p. 11.

5. Ronald P. Dore, "More about Late Development," *Journal of Japanese Studies* 5–1 (Winter 1979): 150.

6. Ronald P. Dore, "Late Development," in his *British Factory Japanese Factory* (Berkeley: University of California Press, 1973); Robert E. Cole, "The Late-Developer Hypothesis: An Evaluation of Its Relevance for Japanese Employment Practices," *Journal of Japanese Studies* 4–2 (1978); and Dore, "More about Late Development."

7. Cole, ibid., p. 263.

8. For example, Marion J. Levy, Jr., in *Modernization and the Structure of Societies* (Princeton: Princeton University Press, 1966); C. Kerr, J. T. Dunlop, F. Harbison, and C. A. Myers, *Industrialism and Industrial Man* (New York: Oxford University Press, 1964); D. J. Hickson, C. J. McMillan, C. R. Hinings, and J. Schwitter, "The Culture-Free Context of Organization Structure: A Tri-National Comparison" *Sociology* 8–1 (1974): 59–80.

9. This has been elaborated at length in Alexander Gerschenkron, *Economic Backwardness in Historical Perspective* (Cambridge, Mass.: Harvard University Press, 1962).

10. Dore, *British Factory Japanese Factory*, pp. 414–415.

11. Ibid.

12. Ibid., pp. 410–411.

13. Dore, "More about Late Development," p. 150.

14. Ronald Dore makes this argument specifically in terms of the measures taken to counteract unions in the West, and the adoption of preemptive measures in Japan.

15. Cole, "The Late-Developer Hypothesis," p. 260.

16. Andrew Gordon, *The Evolution of Labor Relations in Japan: Heavy Industry 1853–1955* (Cambridge, Mass.: Harvard University Press, 1985), p. 5.

17. Robert Herndon Fife, Jr., *The German Empire between Two Wars: A Study of the Political and Social Development of the Nation between 1871 and 1914* (New York: Macmillan, 1916), pp. 286–291.

18. Oura Kanetake, "The Police," in *Fifty Years of New Japan,* ed. Okuma Shigenobu (London: Smith Elder and Co., 1910), vol. 1, p. 281.

19. Ibid., p. 281.

20. John W. Meyer and Brian Rowan, "Institutionalized Organizations: Formal Structure as Myth and Ceremony," *American Journal of Sociology* 83–2 (1977): 345.

21. Howard Aldrich, *Organizations and Environments* (Englewood Cliffs: Prentice-Hall, 1979); Michael T. Hannan and John Freeman, "The Population Ecology of Organizations," *American Journal of Sociology* 82–5 (1977): 929–964.

22. Bill McKelvey and Howard Aldrich, "Populations, Natural Selection, and Applied Organizational Science," *Administrative Science Quarterly* 28 (1983): 111.

23. The data available for the Meiji period do not allow a rigorous testing of the population ecology model against others. One reason is the difficulty of mapping the population of organizations, which is not identical with the number of newspapers. Especially in the 1880s, newspaper firms that had their newspaper closed down resumed publication under a different title. Outside the major metropolitan centers, publishing enterprises often launched three or four newspapers before finally succeeding. In such cases the number of newspaper titles is considerably greater than the number of organizations. And the problem of adjusting for multiple lines of business occurs even for the analysis of the Meiji newspaper: a publishing firm that carries out other publishing activities may continue to support a newspaper when a firm whose only publishing activity was the newspaper would have folded.

24. William Evan, "The Organization-Set," in *Approaches to Organizational Design*, ed. James D. Thompson (Pittsburgh, Pittsburgh University Press, 1966); Meyer and Rowan, "Institutionalized Organizations"; Paul J. DiMaggio and Walter W. Powell, "The Iron Cage Revisited: Institutional Isomorphism and Collective Rationality in Organizational Fields," *American Sociological Review* 48 (1983): 147–160.

25. DiMaggio and Powell, "The Iron Cage Revisited," pp. 150–153.

26. We see this process underway today, with the rediscovery of Deming's quality control theories and the claims that many aspects of Japanese management actually originated in the United States. See for example, Leonard Nadler, "What Japan Learned from the U.S.—That We Forgot to Remember," *California Management Review* 26–4 (1984): 46–61.

Index